A Critical Introduction to *Don Quixote*

PETER LANG
New York • Bern • Frankfurt • Berlin
Brussels • Vienna • Oxford • Warsaw

L.A. Murillo

A Critical Introduction to *Don Quixote*

PETER LANG
New York • Bern • Frankfurt • Berlin
Brussels • Vienna • Oxford • Warsaw

Library of Congress Cataloging-in-Publication Data
Names: Murillo, L.A. (Louis Andrew), author.
Title: A critical introduction to *Don Quixote* / L.A. Murillo.
Description: New York: Peter Lang, 1988.
Includes bibliographical references.
Identifiers: LCCN 87029315 | ISBN 978-0-8204-0516-2 (hardback: alk. paper)
ISBN 978-0-8204-7093-1 (paperback: alk. paper)
Subjects: LCSH: Cervantes Saavedra, Miguel de, 1547–1616. *Don Quixote*.
Classification: LCC PQ6352 .M87 | DDC 863/.3
LC record available at https://lccn.loc.gov/87029315

Bibliographic information published by **Die Deutsche Nationalbibliothek**.
Die Deutsche Nationalbibliothek lists this publication in the "Deutsche
Nationalbibliografie"; detailed bibliographic data are available
on the Internet at http://dnb.d-nb.de/.

© 1988, 1990, 2003, 2017 Peter Lang Publishing, Inc., New York
29 Broadway, 18th floor, New York, NY 10006
www.peterlang.com

All rights reserved.
Reprint or reproduction, even partially, in all forms such as microfilm,
xerography, microfiche, microcard, and offset strictly prohibited.

Contents

Preface ix

I
THE EXEMPLARY STORY

1. Introductory 1
2. Chivalric Romance 7
3. Chivalric Books and Ballads 13
4. *Part One*. The Title 16
5. Going Mad   Ch 1 19
6. A Literary Madness   Chs 2–7 28
7. Parody 34
8. The Autonomous Character   Chs 8–10 41
9. Pastoral Interlude   Chs 11–14 46
10. The Love Adventure   Chs 15–17 50
11. Male Chastity 53
12. Comic Movement 55
13. The War Adventure   Ch 18 58
14. The Ineffectual Hero   Chs 19–21 64
15. The Gratuitous Act   Ch 22 69
16. The Penitent Knight   Chs 23–27 75

II
THE QUIXOTIC FICTION

1. Fiction-within-fiction 83
2. Cardenio-Dorotea   Chs 27–28 89
3. Turning Point   Ch 29 92
4. Sancho's Trip to El Toboso: Triangle   Chs 30–31 96
5. The Inn: Castle, Stage, Palace   Chs 32–47 100
6. *Novel of the Curious Impertinent*   Chs 33–35 103
7. Fernando and Dorotea 107

v

8. The Captain Ruy Pérez and Zoraida 111
9. The Captive's Tale   Chs 39–41 113
10. Mambrino's Helmet: Hoax as Adventure   Chs 42–46 123
11. Return to Village   Chs 47–52 128
12. *Part Two*: Third Sally   Chs 1–8 132
13. Dulcinea Enchanted   Chs 9–11 136
14. The Structure of Illusion 144
15. Knight of the Mirrors   Chs 12–15 146
16. Knight of the Green Coat   Ch 16 150
17. Knight of the Lions   Ch 17 155
18. Camacho's Wedding   Chs 18–21 158
19. The Cave Adventure: Prototype   Chs 22–23 162
20. Illusion Shattered and the Three Phases of *Part Two* 173

III
THE MYTHICAL DON QUIXOTE

1. The Ducal Castle: Fiction and Society   Chs 30–57 177
2. How Dulcinea is to be Disenchanted 184
3. Comic Movement 186
4. Countess Trifaldi 188
5. Clavileño 192
6. Governor Sancho of Barataria 198
7. Altisidora 207
8. Doña Rodríguez 211
9. Interlace 215
10. Sancho and Ricote 220
11. Departure 223
12. "The Knight of Faith"   Chs 58–60 226
13. Barcelona: The Summer of Myth   Chs 60–65 233
14. Roque Guinart and Don Antonio 236
15. Ricote and Ana Félix 244
16. Knight of the White Moon 247
17. The Winter of History   Chs 66–73 252
18. Return to Palace 253
19. Return to Village 255
20. "The Christ of Fiction": Sanity and Death   Ch 74 256

Charts

I	Correspondences	22
II	Narratives, Part I	86
III	Parts I & II compared	147
IV	Interlace	217
V	Pairs of lovers, Part II	246
NOTES AND REFERENCES		263

ERRATA

Page 270, additional note for page 263: Jean Canavaggio's new biography, *Cervantes*, Paris: Editions Mazarine, 1986, is available in Spanish (translation by M. Armino), Madrid: Espasa Calpe, 1986, and English, (translation by J.R. Jones), New York: W.W. Norton, 1990.

Preface

This study has been twenty years in the making. Conceived about 1966, as a companion volume to my edition (Castalia, 1978), planned and outlined in detail by 1973, the first chapters were not set down until about 1976. And then it has turned out rather different from what I had envisioned. My original intention was to provide and explain the critical ideas a reader needed to enter the 'structure' of Cervantes' fictional creation. Proceeding through 'exemplary story' and 'Quixotic fiction' to 'the mythical Don Quixote', I would provide a single, unified analysis and interpretative 'reading'. About two-thirds of the way into it, for lack of interest, or misgivings about what seemed an overly general approach, I all-but-dropped the project. The way had disclosed so many individual themes and questions demanding a separate study, like the background sources of the cave episode or the structure of the puppet play. For some years I ignored my project, preferring to pursue the isolated questions because they were more challenging. Then I saw Vladimir Nabokov's *Lectures on Don Quixote* (published in 1983), and, while much intrigued and fascinated by this notorious attempt by the future author of *Lolita* to do literary criticism without engaging in critical ideas, convinced that a study of the kind I had begun was needed more than ever, I gained a new impetus and finished it, despite an illness, in the Fall of 1984.

From today's vantage point I believe I can discern a double value to my efforts. One is that my approach does reveal and recover the greatness of Cervantes' achievement in Part II against his own very great originality in Part I. The other relates to a question of the first magnitude: why Cervantes, as literary creator, should have become, even before his story reaches its climax in the ducal episodes, obsessed with the novel idea of penitential mortification as the comical trial of purification leading to a cure for his mock-mythical protagonist. The answer of course lies beyond the bounds of my study, somewhere in the starry universality of art.

Berkeley.

Miguel de Cervantes Saavedra

Don Quixote is the comical masterpiece whose success in 1605 established Cervantes as Spain's leading author of prose fiction. He was then past middle age . . ., having lived in poverty and obscurity for many years. He had weathered, and failed at, two or three careers: soldiering in his youth and ending ingloriously in Algiers as captive of Turkish pirates; a government post as roving commissary and tax-collector, ending in bankruptcy and jail; and a literary career (as a playwright, he expected) of some promise, begun with his pastoral romance *Galatea* twenty years before.

While at work on the continuation of *Don Quixote* (Part II, 1615), he completed and published his 'short' or *Exemplary Novels* and his dramatic works and the poem *Journey to Parnassus*. He died (April 22, 1616, in Madrid) without completing his last and most ambitious work, the modern Byzantine romance *Persiles and Sigismunda* (1617), confident of his powers and fame.

No authenticated portrait or likeness of Cervantes is known to exist.

I

THE EXEMPLARY STORY

1. Introductory

Don Quixote is a story about a self transformation. While retaining certain features of age-old mythological 'tales of metamorphosis,' it is itself a marvellous transformation of such narratives into a story of great psychological and moral complexity. It is also one of the great comical stories of all time. The hero, emaciated and middle-aged, is an hidalgo[1] of La Mancha who, driven by madness, has self-styled himself into a knight-errant. That a middle-aged member of a decaying social class should take up a career as knight, when the age of chivalry is long past, is a situation only a little less comical than the many he brings about as his transformation unfolds. Most readers think of Cervantes' book as a comical treatment or comical 'history' of chivalry. Relatively few are prepared to find that the book reads like a comical history of chivalry because it is also told as the clinical history of a singular abnormality. *Don Quixote* is not only about madness, it is about a literary madness, and for this reason it is important to see the relation sustained within its covers between the literary subject of a transformation and the moral and psychological dimensions of the hero's madness, because together they determine the unique fictional nature of the story.

Not the least of the many surprises it contains is the way Cervantes tells it. Although he tells it as a progression of connected events, realistically depicted, and divided into chapters and episodes, the story is not so much told by a narrator as it is unfolded from within. That is, the illusion it produces is not so much that it is told, but that the story unfolds from within according to the dynamic of its inner secret. The controlling principle behind all this is a conception of life and of the resources of fiction that is constantly pressing to their limits the assumptions by which we distinguish between life and art. I propose to call that controlling principle Cervantes' exemplary idea.

Cervantes himself used the term *exemplary* to describe his shorter *novelas*, published in 1613. By calling them exemplary he did not of course mean that they were moralistic in the sense that they presumed to teach a moral doctrine or to provide examples of moral rectitude, but that they were, individually, the incarnation of a moral idea. That is, as narratives executed with deliberate art they were governed by a moral conception of human behavior. By design they aspired to be psychologically true, and they could not be moral or exemplary unless they were. Like all great artists, Cervantes did not think that truth lay in depicting perfect or even normal or realistic behavior. A more profound (and entertaining) way was the depiction of abnormal passions and deeds. In the story of an hidalgo with an inordinate passion for books of knight-errantry he found an ideal opportunity. The exemplary idea that Cervantes worked out in *Don Quixote* is that a character may be inspired by a heroic and passionate literary mode to undertake a complete transformation of himself into a personification of that mode. The abnormity of his madness resides in the attempt to make real an idea of himself that however powerful psychologically and however attractive morally, is true or valid only in the imagination. There it may exist as an illusion, or as a 'fiction.' In actual life it runs counter to reality and reason, and is doomed. It can survive only in the realm of the imaginary 'real.' And to survive even there it must be dislodged from the mind that gave it birth. For its moral tone and premises Cervantes' exemplary idea is totally serious. Why, then, is his book comical? For the contrasts (imposed by the same exemplary idea) between the hidalgo's heroic aspirations and the reality of his psychological state and social position. And for the 'fictional' nature of his mad endeavor.

Once affected by his madness, the hidalgo who calls himself "Don Quixote" abandons his home and goes out into the countryside in search of adventures. He is, in so many words, a severe case of social and psychological alienation. He makes three such sallies or outings. In the course of each he attempts to perform feats similar to those he read about in books of chivalry. Although the opening passages of the story are written in the style of Cervantes' *Exemplary Novels*, the entire book is a merger of this style with a parody of the style of the books Don Quixote imitates, so that in fact the style of the book literally unfolds with the story of his transformation from a real to a 'fictional' character. The story begins and unfolds as the 'fictional' transformation of the hero from an obscure hidalgo into a 'renowned' knight-errant, and ends when, on returning to his home for the third and last time, he regains his sanity and dies. The sundered 'fictional' personality that is Don Quixote is reunited with his true self, an hidalgo of a village in La Mancha. Since his transformation is also the course, in the clinical sense, that his madness takes, we anticipate that the climax and close of the story will be the resolution of his madness according to the moral and psychological dictates of Cervantes' exemplary idea.

From the beginning the illusion of the hidalgo that he is a knight-errant like Amadís de Gaula is the 'fiction' of his deranged self that will unfold with sweeping movements within the framework of an exemplary story.[2] From the beginning Cervantes' story is an elaborate generation of a 'fictitious' character. As such it may claim a special status. It is not only a superior work of imagination but about the very process by which fictions arise from life, illustrate, transform, embody and ennoble it. A work that would self-consciously seek to illustrate this would need likewise to be on purpose comical.

If I were asked to say briefly and simply what purpose I thought Cervantes had in writing *Don Quixote*, I would reply, without hesitation, that his purpose was to tell a magnificent story. It was as a teller of stories that he undoubtedly prided himself. He did not see himself as the satirist of his age or of chivalry, nor as the novelist we know today. He saw himself as a consummate master of storytelling. He was aware that he had absorbed a thousand age-old themes and techniques of storytelling in the process of discovering his own. Critics and scholars have given great importance to the statements he makes in the Prologue (1605) to *Don Quixote* and elsewhere in the book about his purpose "to destroy the authority and influence that books of chivalry have in the world," "to arouse men's scorn for the false and absurd stories of knight-errantry," by holding them up to ridicule. My opinion is that they can be taken as statements of his aim, and not necessarily of his explicit purpose. His story is so vast, so complex that no statement of this kind can represent his overall literary purpose. Perhaps at certain moments Cervantes believed that they expressed his uncompromising aim. Yet it is not unlikely that they were in fact a pretext. As the purpose behind what he attempted and accomplished in creating the characters of Don Quixote and Sancho, the large cast of secondary characters, and in devising the vast edifice of adventurous fiction that fills his book, these extirpating statements about an already blighted literature cannot be taken at face value. Cervantes may have believed on occasions that the ridicule and discredit of chivalric stories explained his purpose, but these statements no more explain the motivating force behind the creation of *Don Quixote* than they do the reason for its success. Moreover, the moral intentions behind the depiction of an hidalgo gone mad from reading books of chivalry are far more significant than the satirical intentions to hold those books up to ridicule. And it is apparent that Cervantes took over positively many features of those books to construct his own kind of chivalric story. Finally, one may consider that, as an avowed aim, those negative intentions toward chivalric books have proven incidental to what Cervantes established permanently in the art of story telling.

In certain quarters today the most praiseful remark one can make about *Don Quixote* is to call it the *prototypal novel*, and even the *novel of novels*.[3] The remark reflects the high place Cervantes holds in literary history as well as a mass of opinion accumulated in scores of books, articles and essays written in support of what amounts to a canon of modern criticism. Cervantes may indeed be the master novelist of all time, and if he is, it is because he is the supreme story teller. In the mind of many the self-conscious way in which Cervantes mounts one level of story on another, or the several levels of fantasy and fiction on a representation of life that is utterly devoid of either, has become a distinguishing feature of the novel as form or structure. Another is of course the process by which characters evolve and acquire unsuspected qualities and significance. I assume that all this and more is now axiomatic and I will not elaborate on the book's prototypal dimensions nor attempt to reduce its proportions of life and fiction to any presumed structure, or theory, of the novel.[4] My purpose will be to provide as complete an insight into and analysis of the literary nature of *Don Quixote* as is possible within the limits of a small book. Moreover, in order to appreciate the importance of his masterpiece for modern literature one must first make an effort to see it as Cervantes' fiction. He did not and would not have thought to call it a *novela*, for this term in his day applied only to the shorter prose narrative (the Italian *novella*). He was aware that, though it shared important elements with his *Exemplary Novels*, *Don Quixote* was an audacious and innovative blend of diverse literary materials and techniques. It was a 'character' story that assumed comically the proportions of a burlesque epic and a chivalric 'history.' It was mock-history of chivalry and psychological *novela*, with an assortment of other 'tales' and stories, all woven into one astounding, comical revelation of a 'strange case.'

How may one describe the essentials of a book so self-consciously a combination of themes and modes? *Don Quixote* is, first of all, a comical story, and as we shall see the very origin of its comicness lies in its brazen meshing of two narrative extremes. We may enumerate the others in the following way: (2) the story of a self transformation. The knight Quixote is the transformed personality of an obscure hidalgo. Behind Cervantes' elaborate apparatus we can discern the outlines of stories about exotic, magical transformations (humans, imaginary beings, animals) that in the hands of earlier story tellers evolved from *metamorphoses* or tales of mythological transformations. What Cervantes accomplished for modern literature was not only the complete elaboration of this subject in moral and psychological terms, penetrating into abnormality and clinical psychology, but its isolation or 'discovery' as a prototypal motif of fiction.

(3) the story of the regeneration and rejuvenescence of a middle-aged hidalgo.

(4) the love story of his devotion to Dulcinea, his lady. It does not matter that we have to invert the knight-lady relationship into the platonic passion that a fifty-year old bachelor has for an adolescent villager, whom he imagines to be the 'Princess Dulcinea.' As in a chivalric love story, Don Quixote fulfills his vows of fidelity, chastity, service and honor, to the lady of his heart and soul. In this respect Cervantes clearly outstripped all his predecessors in chivalric romance, for love triumphs in the absence of a real object. Dulcinea is a 'fiction'; or, rather, she is the image of regeneration. In his madness Quixote recasts his life and image of himself into that of a virile, young knight; it is his passion for his young love that rejuvenates his soul and body. But if Dulcinea is ephemeral, 'fictional,' Sancho, whose fleshy weight will absorb her immateriality, is physically all-too apparent alongside Quixote.

(5) a story of male companionship: through the thick and thin of adventures master and squire become an inseparable pair, mutually dependent, acting one upon the other, the ties that bind their contrasting personalities made inextricable with each incident. Their psycho-physio partnership becomes a comical symbiosis of the male soul in action.

(6) a realistic story about life, social beliefs, character and manners, in the Spain of Cervantes' time. In search of adventure, the hero and

squire come into contact with individuals embodying the motley stratification of Spanish society: peasants, farmers, soldiers, Moriscos, workers; merchants, priests, jurists; middle, upper and aristocratic classes. Even minor personages are drawn in their picturesque or amusing idiosyncrasies. Cervantes had an immense curiosity about his fellow countrymen along with keen powers of observation that enabled him to give depth to multitudinous details in his interpretation of Spanish society. Yet, however all-absorbing his picture of it, however realistically precise, the life he depicts is drawn to and caught up by the attraction of the hero and his illusion, so that to a large extent the realistic portrayal of Spanish society appears under the aspect of Quixote's chivalric idealism, the characters of the established social order now reacting against it, or jokingly sharing it and embellishing it. Thus the realistic depiction of Spanish life is compromised, if not deformed, by the fantasies of Quixote's illusion.
(7) a chivalric story: it imitates, through parody, the epical, heroic, or romantic elements of chivalric literature (prose or verse). In his madness the hero imagines that his encounter with everyday reality constitutes an adventurous test or trial of his honor and prowess, but in fact of his illusion. Cervantes incorporated into his book two great structural themes of chivalric romance: the quest (Part I) and the abduction of a maiden and her rescue (Part II) and resolved them in Quixote's illusory triumph and eventual disillusionment. As a quest story his book brings together the themes of the hero's elect status, his venturing forth; isolation through test and trials; submission to, and idolatry for his lady—in an illicit, passionate and secret love; and recasts them into an account of the hero's moral purification, in the search for an illusory 'fictional' identity and fame.
(8) the fiction-within-fiction: the hero's madness bears within it the force to generate the fiction of his enterprise in the real world, to give rise to the pseudo-reality of his chivalric personality. By degrees it will impose itself in the mind of other characters, beginning with Sancho's who, in the governorship of the island he expects to receive as reward for his services, has a vested interest in it, despite doubts about the sanity of his master. The story of the enlargement of Quixote's madness into a mythical figuration of him is the process by which deceptions and hoaxes are artfully perpetrated and staged in the form of a chivalric adventure, designed by their perpetrators to humor him, or to effect a cure, or to entertain themselves. Yet Quixote, inspired by madness, may be said to invent genuine fictions because

he believes them to be real, while his mockers invent 'sham' fictions of lesser or greater quixotic proportions, depending on their likeness to the hero's image of himself. This world of illusion maintained by interlocking fictions we shall call 'the Quixotic fiction.'

When we pay tribute to Cervantes as the creator of our modern novel, we should recognize that his achievement is also the brilliant transposition of the chivalric quest of Arthurian romance and the epic form onto the quest-journey of a comical hero, who, in a modern, realistic world attains as a final goal the inner illusion of authentic being. Quixote's three outings trace the outlines of the going forth and return of the hero in adventurous and heroic tales of exploration and discovery; in terms of Cervantes' exemplary story they run their course past mock triumph to self-fulfilment and eventual disillusion. As the sustained fiction of his book the hero brings about his transformation into a renowned, mythical Don Quixote, but on return to the village, to reality and sanity, he recovers his true self, in the person of the hidalgo Alonso Quixano, who then dies. Hence, as the story of a voyage to eventual self-discovery the hero at its close is elevated into the higher awareness of disenchantment that is the voyage completed. In the process he has undergone rejuvenation from within, and from without the social reality and historical time of his existence are brought to a carnivalesque consummation, for in the regeneration of the self is borne the regeneration of the historical time and the social reality that it embodies. Thus the exemplary story has been enlarged by the creative Quixotic fiction onto the grandiose scale of epic narrative, its center occupied by the hero's mythical identity. *Don Quixote* is not just the parodic inversion of chivalric romance that terminates its long evolution with a joyful bang; it is the transposition and distillation of its essence into a magnificent elixir of fiction, at once an exemplary story, a fascinating portrait of Spain in her hour of greatness, a paradigm of literary enterprise, and, from beginning to end, a celebration of life in the comic spirit.

2. Chivalric Romance

A chivalric story is a very special kind of fiction. The critic and reader of English have the advantage that in this language the term *romance* designates a large body of imaginative literature, mostly prose, that stretches like a vast sea from classical antiquity to the present. Chivalric stories belong to this large corpus.[5] English critical usage (unlike Spanish) permits a distinction between *romance* and *novel* (more precisely, the modern novel), although a novel may, like any other prose fiction, contain various features of *romance*. While *romance* and *novel* designate two different kinds of prose fiction, the terms are not mutually exclusive in all cases. *Don Quixote* is precisely a prototypal work that combines both novel and romance in a most cunning and astounding manner. In the Spain of Cervantes chivalric stories were called *"libros de caballerías"*—books of chivalry, and were considered a kind or genre set apart. They were assumed to be 'histories' (stories) of adventures; their contents were essentially marvellous and legendary, yet accepted as vaguely historical in the modern sense. Though Cervantes could not have conceived the term, these books were *romance* for what they narrated as for their form, that is, for the way the story was told. Undoubtedly it was their best features as romance that attracted him, as it was their worst that repelled him.

A great deal has been written about these books as the final, degenerate expression of medieval chivalric romance.[6] Their popularity in sixteenth-century Spain, however, represents only the last phase of a great narrative mode. When Cervantes mimics the style or ridicules the excesses of chivalric stories he has uppermost in mind these late *prose* versions. In its beginnings, in the second half of the twelfth century, chivalric romance is a narrative composed in verse (octosyllabic couplets). The great poetry of the later Middle Ages (1000–1500) was successively the epic, the romance, and the love lyric. Of these the romance or *roman* (in Old French) was perhaps the most innovative, and certainly the most influential for the art of narrative. The verse romance was itself a combination of motifs and devices adapted from the medieval epic, from Classical and Celtic myths, stories and legends, and from folk tales. Its creators did not think of themselves as inventors of a new form but as reciters or tellers of stories handed down by tradition.

Because it was a story with a venerable past, the romance or *roman* might be told very much as if it were about real or historical persons and events, like King Arthur and his court, but in fact it was about legendary, mysterious or fictitious characters and marvellous and even supernatural happenings. That is to say that its materials were the store of exotic traditions handed down by generations of story tellers in oral or written form. The single most important body of these materials were the folk and hero-tales and legends of Celtic origin, known as the 'matter of Britain' or Arthurian legends.[7] It is this storied material that provides the enchanted world, between myth and legend, in which the heroes of medieval romance seek adventures: a world of monsters, giants, dwarfs, of sudden transformations and vanishings, of mysterious castles, enchanted weapons, fays, temptresses, abducted maidens (or princesses as Quixote supposes). By the twelfth century the Arthurian tales had become in many cases the popularized and traditional versions of a much earlier Celtic mythology. The mythical origins of the knight-heroes of romance account for what is perhaps the most decisive quality of chivalric romance: the hero-knight enjoys a special status between the world of ordinary mortals and a supernatural world of semidivine and magical potentates.

Unlike the warrior-heroes of the Old French epics who fight for a common cause as Christians against infidels, the knight-heroes became the subjects of stories woven around their individual feats and personalities and their personal quest for fame and superiority. Since in most cases they derived from semi-gods of Celtic (or Germanic) mythology, like Lancelot or Gawain, their enterprise was told as the search for personal adventure. Their trials and feats acquire a purely personal value, and for this reason may appear to a later age like ours or Cervantes' arbitrary or even purposeless. But it is exactly this apparently arbitrary, fortuitous, and unpredictable nature of their adventures and solitary quests that constitutes much of the tension, the interest and wonder of their stories. Thus the materials that constituted the chivalric romances—stories derived from myths, legends, folktales—very much determined the way they were presented to an audience. The creators of medieval romance like Chrétien de Troyes, who composed his narratives in the period 1160–1190, employed great skill in organizing their materials into the form of stories that in the very way the narrator told them preserved the marvellous and almost enigmatic nature of their content.[8]

But even as they refashioned the traditional materials they did so with an interest and concern for what was genuinely new or contemporary for their period and society, the courtly and no longer strictly feudal society of Northern France. It is this element that makes their stories *chivalric* romance. In the earlier epics which reflect both the feudal hierarchy of loyalties among Christian kings, lords, and knights, as well as the crusading spirit of combat against a fanatical enemy, the knight-warriors wage war against heathens with little regard for rules or respect for the human dignity of their adversaries. In the verse romance the adversary confronted by the hero-knight is more often than not another Christian knight and the combat between them is, ideally, one between equals in sense of honor and the rules or conditions of combat. That is to say that the hero-knights of romance treat their adversaries and equals (as well as superiors and inferiors) according to an elevated idea of Christian honorableness and respect for the dignity of all, excepting the cruel, cowardly or ignoble. It is usual to refer to this idea as the chivalric code of honor and Christian service. With it is closely linked the idea of 'courtesy,' to be discussed below. Like the epic, the romance is essentially a story about conflict, but whereas the epic concentrates on the conflict between warring nations and beliefs, and puts less importance on the conflict within the individual soul of a knight, like Roland at Roncesvalles, the romance concentrates on the inner conflict of the knight-hero, as he strives to live up to an exalted sense of honor and knightly allegiances. For the poets or romancers of the generation of Chrétien de Troyes the hero's inner conflict was above all sentimental—that is to say a conflict between love and knightly obligations. For them as for its subsequent evolution down to Don Quixote's imitation, the chivalric story is centered in the passionate conception of the hero in love.

The love interest is of course the other element that distinguishes the verse romance of the twelfth and thirteenth centuries from the epic, and reflects the tastes and manners of the courtly society for which it was intended, no doubt a society in which the preferences of women played an important part. 'Courtly love' is a term applied to a large group of lyrics, themes and doctrines that expressed a new concept of love and the relationship between lovers that emerged in the South of France just before and in the same period the poets of romance in the North were composing their works. 'Courtly love' is a 'modern,' that is, a sincere and personal expression of the feelings of heterosexual love: attraction, pleasure or torment, on the part of the male lover directed to a lady, who because of her sex and beauty is conceived as a being of nearly divine attributes. The earliest expression of this feeling is the work of Provençal poets of the twelfth century, its profoundest, Dante's love for Beatrice in the *Divine Comedy*. The lyrics of the Provençal poets are erotic, delicate and vehement, and much of their vehemence is a kind of compensation for the inequality, real or imagined, between the poet and the lady he addresses. She is in many cases an older, married woman of elevated or aristocratic rank. Their relationship, then, once she concedes to it, is adulterous, illicit. Since 'courtly love' is in one important respect (the socio-economic) an expression of real sentiments and relations, it is evidence that in an age when marriages were arranged according to family interests the true sentiments of love for women as for men were a matter outside of marriage. While it follows that 'courtly love' involves an adulterous (or at least secretive) relationship, even more important, for the literary depiction of it, is that it must be an intensely passionate relationship. This passionate nature of love is then assumed to be superior to almost all social barriers, family and feudal allegiances and even honor. Here, then, the nature of the conflict for the hero of romance. He is conceived by the romance storytellers to be an ideal lover because he is capable of passionate feelings that conflict with his sense of personal worth and his loyalties as a knight to others, to his king or lord, or his family's honor. The two great love stories of medieval romance, Tristan and Isolde and Lancelot and Guinevere, are stories of passionate adultery.

But the knight is also a lover according to rules of 'courtesy,' the proper manner in which the true lover approaches the lady and renders loyal service to her, submitting his mind and heart to her will. The submission of the male lover no doubt reflects the high status of women among medieval nobility and even their status in sexual relationships, but also their influence on the refinement of manners in courtly society, where their tastes in the expression of feeling were likely to predominate. The hero-knight engaged in adventures of the heart as of the sword, which test his ability to surmount the trial of the conflicting loyalties of love and honor, is a conception that draws on both sentimental and heroic attributes to produce what we may properly call a *romantic* figure of manhood. The knight's submission to his lady, if carried to extremes, becomes a form of idolatry, the case of Lancelot for Guinevere and Quixote for Dulcinea. But it is also the way to a spiritualization of erotic passion, and to the theme that through submission and trial the knight-lover becomes worthy of the lady he serves. The importance of Chrétien de Troyes in the emergence of the chivalric romance resides in that he more skillfully than others combined into one narrative pattern the motifs and characters of Arthurian tales with the doctrines of 'courtly love,' which had penetrated into Northern France from Provence in his generation.

It was this fusion which produced for all time the picture of King Arthur's court as a model of chivalric manners: honor in combat, courtesy and 'service' in love, the hero-knight the devoted, loyal 'vassal' of his lady. So powerful was the fascination and charm of the Arthurian legend in this form that it attracted to it, in a further blending, the legends of the Carolingian heroes. But this later stage is the work of the Italians, Pulci, Boiardo, and Ariosto, of whom we shall have more to say, because their refinements included the comic and ironical treatment of love and chivalric honor.

In the next phase of Arthurian romance there appeared the first prose versions. By the first third of the thirteenth century an anonymous author had written or compiled a group of works of great length known as the *prose Lancelot* or the *Vulgate cycle*.[9] It is not difficult to distinguish the prose versions of Arthurian stories from their form in verse. The verse narratives, though written, were meant to be recited or told before an audience, and their form—the organized order of disclosures, episodes, and motifs—was pressed to this end. In this way the recital of the story preserved much of its imaginative (what we would call its fictional) nature. The story sounded vaguely like history, but there was no need to think of it as such. At any rate, it was not a chronicle of real events, but a conscious ordering of legendary or fabulous ones. The prose versions, on the other hand, were composed in other intricate ways that insured that they could be fully understood or enjoyed only by reading them, and in most cases by isolated readers. Moreover, they were composed in vast cycles so that they read almost like chronicles or biographies. As one might expect, the prose versions of many of the French romances were in due course translated into medieval Castilian and became very popular in Spain.

In the next two hundred years, 1300–1500, chivalric romance developed in both verse and prose, but whereas in verse-form it preserved and enhanced its qualities as poetic fiction and even as fantasy, despite a tendency toward comic treatment, as in the Italian poems, in prose it became vulnerable to the kind of modification that impaired its viability as fiction. It was made to pose as pseudo-history, that is, as a more or less 'truthful' representation of a past age, and to assume the realistic and even behaviorist approach of a pseudo-history. These tendencies in prose and verse are represented in the three major works Cervantes knew well and on which he based much of his conception of literary chivalry: Ariosto's poem *Orlando furioso* (1532) the masterpiece of the Renaissance epic-romance, and *Amadís de Gaula* (1508) and *Tirante el blanco* (original in Catalan, composed 1460–90, published in Castilian in 1511), the masterpieces among Spanish *"libros de caballerías."*

3. Chivalric Books and Ballads

While Cervantes knows that an extensive chivalric literature exists in other European languages, what he thinks of and calls *"libros de caballerías"* are Spanish products (originals, and/or translations from French and/or Italian). We will not need to go into an extended discussion of what these books were like because any reader of *Don Quixote* can find out for himself: no one has given a more vivid idea of them than Cervantes. Some critics and scholars will disagree with this statement, but in reply I would say that it is now up to them to furnish a better idea of what those books contain.[10] Not directly, but sideways, *Don Quixote* is all about those books. One can, for instance, reconstruct from what Quixote describes or imagines, or from the hoaxes and narratives of others, a rather accurate idea of what goes on in a book of chivalry. Of course the big difference is that those books are serious and, except for Quixote's illusion about them, his adventures in Cervantes' book recreate a highly comical version of chivalry.

The truth is that Cervantes had an ambiguous attitude toward those books and toward the whole idea of literary chivalry. He disparaged the naive attempt of their authors to depict the adventures they wrote about as a representation of life. He objected to their ill-conceived attempts to create and sustain an imaginary world or to portray credibly hero-knights of flesh and bone. Yet Cervantes clearly endorsed the whole aim and idea of a chivalric story: to give pleasure, to entertain, to give release to an inspired imagination. In a sense, then, his purpose in *Don Quixote* was to recreate their best qualities as fiction in a new form, one acceptable to 'critical' reason and even to an orthodox morality. His instinct told him books of chivalry were inauthentic as pseudo-history or pseudo-biography; that their authors had failed to take on and command the resources of prose and all that they rendered possible or impossible for a chivalric romance written for modern times.

Take the question of authorship in *Don Quixote* as it is revealed to readers on the one hand and how, on the other, it is made overtly to control the flow of narrative. Don Quixote knows that a book of chivalric exploits is authored by a sage historian, because this is the convention in the Spanish books of chivalry, at least in those that attract him most. That fictitious author is part of the whole chivalric fabric, yet the one most exposed to the reader's disbelief. According to the formula, the hero's life and exploits have taken place in a remote past; so unique and marvellous were they, so great the fame won by the hero in that time, that deservedly an account of them was preserved as a historical record. This vaguely known document is the 'original,' preserved in some exotic language like ancient Greek, Latin, or Arabic, and comes from the pen of a 'sage historian' that is, a historian with magical powers of omniscience. Obviously he possesses all the powers of knowledge and observation necessary to write a complete account of the hero's exploits and love affairs down to the last minute detail. His 'original,' fortuitously uncovered by the Spanish author and translated and perhaps even interpreted by him, is what we read: a kind of miracle of literary archaeology. This Spanish version is all the more authentic for its fidelity to the exotic and archaic nature of the 'original.' While using this device the Spanish authors assumed that their works gained credibility as both history and fiction. They took it up with the seriousness of a historian. Of course it is that very seriousness which limits their narratives and makes them tiring. Cervantes, on the other hand, makes the authorship of Quixote's adventures a matter of pure fiction, as we shall see. His appeal to the reader's credibility is on an entirely different plane, the plane established by his exemplary idea. All of which permits him to use the device not just as one more fictional pretension to historical 'truth,' but even to serve himself by his own self-conscious control of it.

Cervantes' attitude toward the prose chivalric books and his statements about them are, after all, a smokescreen. Quixote goes mad from reading them, but once mad he is inspired, not by the prose books, but by the poetry, the verse of chivalry.[11] The inspiration for his name, his horse's, and Dulcinea's, come to him from poetry, and while his poetic inspiration combines with themes and affairs taken from prose books, so that the combination is hardly perceptible, only the prose books are blamed for his madness, and singled out for censure and ridicule. What Cervantes as narrator does not tell us is that, besides the prose books, Quixote knows well the versions of chivalric legend available in verse to him and to all Spaniards in the sixteenth century: Ariosto's *Orlando furioso*, the literary or 'learned' Renaissance epics, and the popular Spanish chivalric ballads. Cervantes has slyly laid hold of the themes and resources of chivalric poetry, moulded them and subverted them into his story with the same comical irony he applies to the prose narratives, without drawing any distinctions. How account for this inconsistency? He was acquainted with the whole body of chivalric writings—legends, poems, stories, available to him in Spain; in addition to the prose romances: the poems of Pulci, Boiardo, and Ariosto, and imitations of them in Spanish; the Spanish heroic poems that also reflect chivalric customs, like the 'learned' epics about Charles V; and the ballads of a Spanish popular tradition that had re-made the legends of Arthurian and Carolingian heroes into Spanish poetry. While this entire corpus looms over Quixote's adventures and Cervantes draws on the familiarity of his readers with all of it for his effects, he draws attention to the Spanish prose books because as prose they are his only competition.

The scrutiny of Quixote's library in chapter 6 reveals that, in addition to many prose romances, he owned copies of pastoral romances, of learned epics like *La Araucana* and *El Monserrate*, and romantic poems imitating Ariosto (like *Angelica's Tears*), and some lyric poetry. His collection reflects some reading habits of a village hidalgo around 1592. Conspicuously missing are ballads and Ariosto's *Orlando furioso*.[12] I say conspicuously because later on Quixote shows a great familiarity with ballads and Ariosto's poem. These ballads belong to the body of popular poetry called *El Romancero*. The word *'romance'* in Spanish means 'ballad.' They are traditional poetry in many cases sprung from the remains of medieval Castilian epics, composed and elaborated anonymously (by poets called *juglares*). They flourished in the fifteenth and sixteenth centuries. Although many of them treat of chivalry and epic themes, one group in particular is designated 'chivalric' because they are versions of the legends about the Carolingian and Arthurian knights. A number of Quixote's adventures are based on incidents taken from ballads, i.e., the ballad of Lanzarote (I.2), the ballads of Durandarte (II.23) and Don Gaiferos and Melisendra (II.26). One of the enigmas of Cervantes' book, for scholars, is that while quoting them Cervantes never speaks of (or refers to) ballads in any printed form. Which leaves one to think that for him and Quixote the chivalric ballads were traditional, that is, oral poetry. They had been collected and published in printed collections since 1550. Neither Quixote nor anyone else in the story speaks of printed ballads—when so many printed books of different kinds are mentioned. The characters seem to know ballads by oral tradition and recite them from memory.[13]

Quixote goes mad from 'reading prose.' This is the prosaic fact in Cervantes' book. The same result, according to its physiopathology, could not have been produced by chivalric poetry, yet this poetry is what 'inspires' Quixote's madness. There are at least two reasons why Cervantes cannot acknowledge the chivalric poems in the same terms as the prose books. The most obvious is that the Italian poems, above all *Orlando furioso*, while refined and aristocratic works, were for all their fantasy an ironical and comical picture of chivalry. The very idea of Orlando crazed by love is comical. The other is that the Spanish ballads also provided a picture of knights in love and combat that was popularizing and with a tendency to realism that often bordered on the comical. The best example of this is the ballad of Lanzarote, and Cervantes took many details for his story from this single ballad.[14] Since Quixote reduces the aristocratic fantasy of Ariosto's poem to his own prosaic poetry, and contrariwise elevates to this level the popular themes of the ballads, Cervantes could not acknowledge explicitly precedents for a comical and ironical treatment of chivalry in verse used as allied materials in an assault on the prose romances, which were vulnerable for their defects as narratives in prose.

4. Part One. The Title
El Ingenioso Hidalgo Don Quixote de la Mancha[15]

It is a combination of the kind of title Cervantes gave to some of his *Exemplary Novels* and the parody of the typical title of a romance of chivalry, like *Amadís of Gaul*, or even *Lancelot of the Lake* (Old French, *Lancelot del Lac*, Spanish, *Lanzarote del Lago*). The coupling of *hidalgo* and *don* is particularly satirical. A separate treatise could be written on each of the title's four (or five) components; we shall point out briefly only the essentials of each, poetic, linguistic or stylistic.

The first half—*El Ingenioso Hidalgo*—is very similar to other titles devised by Cervantes for his *novelas*: *El Celoso Extremeño* (*The Jealous Extremaduran*), *El Licenciado Vidriera* (*The Glass Licentiate*) and *El Curioso*

Impertinente (*The Curious Impertinent*). In each case the typifying adjective describes the principal moral-psychological characteristic of the protagonist. On *Ingenioso* as descriptive of Quixote's idiosyncracy see pp. 20–25 below. *Hidalgo* refers to his social standing, and in 1600 it was absurdly comical and pretentious for an hidalgo who was no more than an hidalgo to claim the honorific title *don* designating the social rank and wealth of a knight (*caballero*), see p. 31.

The use of *don or doña* (from Latin *domĭnus, domĭna*), a title of respect and used with the first name, is not too common in the romances of chivalry Quixote imitates, but it had been quite general in the social usage of medieval Spain for persons of high social standing. That Cervantes' hidalgo uses it with the name he devises for himself, indicates that he considers Quixote to be a first or Christian name. Thus he "hits on" a name that was already, without modification, a military term for a piece of defensive armour covering the thigh: *quixote* (from Latin *cŏxa*, 'thigh,' Old French *cuissart* or *cuissot*; Catalan, *cuixot*, English, *cuisse*). 'Quixote' was also a Spanish surname.

But since the hidalgo was "eight days" in devising his name, one assumes that he put it together from various elements, so that it would contain and express a certain conceit or 'meaning,' similar to the name for his horse, Rocinante. Hence we may assume that he took the radical *Qui-xo* from his surname. In the book's opening passage we are given three different or possible versions of his surname: *Quijada, Quesada, Quejana*. In chapter 5 the neighbor who finds and takes him home calls him "Señor Quijana . . .", ". . . el honrado hidalgo del señor *Quijana*", and we might have accepted this as definitive evidence that his surname is *Quijana*, but for the declaration at the close of the story that he is "Alonso Quijano the Good." So the name *Quixote* has been "made up" by adding the ending *-óte* to the radical *Qui-xa*, producing an inspired but grotesque approximation to *Lanzarote*, the Castilian form of Lancelot's name. The hidalgo has had in mind the ballad of Lanzarote which he recalls in chapter 2, reciting the opening verses and inserting *Don-Qui-xó-te* for the quadrisyllable *Lan-za-ró-te*. Popular tradition had given Lanzarote a *rocín* or *rocino* (hack) for a horse, and the hidalgo owns a *rocín*. Of all allusions, similarities or coincidences contained in the name *Quixote*, Lanzarote of the ballad is by far the most important. The others are: the augmentative suffix in Castilian *-ote*, which denotes "clumsy, large, awkward," hence from *libro* (book), *librote* (large, clumsy volume); from *gigante* (giant), *gigantote* (clumsy, ridiculous giant); the similarity to the name of a comical character in the prose romance *Primaleón and Polendos* (1534), "the hidalgo Camilote"; and the comical and ridiculous rhymes with certain nouns ending in *-óte*: *alborote, escote, estricote, pipote, azote, cogote,* all of which appear in the octosyllabic verses Quixote composes in chapter 26 of Part I. The hidalgo is of course oblivious to the comical effect of these rhymes and coincidences; he perceives only their possibilities as poetic conceit and resemblance to, and onomatopoeia with *Lanzarote,* the hero who undoubtedly inspires his linguistic creation.

Quixote insists on placing *don* before his name on every occasion. But, in general, most knights depicted in Spanish chivalric romances did not use it, nor are they generally called '*don*.' The hidalgo insists on it so that his name will ring with the quadrisyllabic dignity of 'Lanzarote,' and '*Don* Belianís.' And he adds "de la Mancha" so as to proclaim as his 'lineage' his land of origin:

> ... acordándose que el valeroso Amadís no sólo se había contentado con llamarse Amadís a secas, sino que añadió el nombre de su reino y patria, por hacerla famosa, y se llamó Amadís de Gaula, así quiso, como buen caballero, añadir al suyo el nombre de la suya y llamarse *don Quijote de la Mancha,* con que, a su parecer, declaraba muy al vivo su linaje y patria. ... I. 1, 77

> ... remembering that the valiant Amadís had not been content to call himself simply Amadís, but added thereto the name of his kingdom and native country, in order to make it more illustrious, calling himself Amadís of Gaul, so he, like a good knight, also added the name of his province, and called himself *Don Quixote de la Mancha,* with which, he thought, he proclaimed very clearly his lineage and native land. ...

We have only to recall the exotic lands that disclose the origins of family and place of chivalric heroes like Don Belianís de Grecia or Florismarte de Hircania, to recognize the satirical parody of a knight from La Mancha, a region of New Castile undistinguished in the eyes of contemporary Spaniards, except for its many Moriscos, and a most unlikely setting for chivalric adventures.

The first half of the title *El Ingenioso Hidalgo,* then, alludes to the exemplary story about an "ingenioso" hidalgo, while the second *Don Quixote de la Mancha* alludes to the parodic depiction of his adventures according to the style of a 'history' of chivalric feats.

The complete title combines and counterpoints the idea of an objective, realistic narrative about the character and the idea of a parodic narrative in the style of a chivalric romance about him, but yet according to his illusion of himself, the illusion indicated in the name he has chosen for himself. The objective narrative refers to him as "*ingenioso hidalgo*"; he—the character—calls himself "*Don Quixote de la Mancha.*" The very title, therefore, has already disclosed a relationship between two poles of fiction. The first contains and unfolds the other; but, conversely, is also encompassed by the literary illusion of the second. The title points to their merger in the structure of the Quixotic fiction.[16]

5. Going Mad   Ch 1

From the start the story is focused on the peculiar character of the hidalgo. The opening passage describes him as a man answering to a certain social and literary type and then insinuates the psychological traits of his idiosyncrasy. The social type is the impoverished hidalgo of a village, his spare, isolated existence appeased by the memory of military glory of his ancestry. The social type of '*hidalgo de aldea*" had been detailed, even idealized, as early as 1539 by the writer Antonio de Guevara who wrote of his dull but happy idleness in the country, fondness for the hunt, his frugal foods, dress, lodgings. Closer to Cervantes' time, we find the popular attitude toward his honorable poverty expressed in disparaging proverbs: "*Hidalgo de aldea, la pobreza allá le lleva*" (Village hidalgo, it's poverty has him there), "*El hidalgo, antes roto que remendado*" (The hidalgo, better tattered than mended), "*El hijo del hidalgo, un pie calzado y otro descalzo*" (The hidalgo's son, one foot shod and the other bare). True to the type, our hidalgo prominently displays some old arms belonging to ancestors, he owns a hack and a greyhound, his diet is frugal and his dress simple, by necessity. He is unmarried, lives with two females, a young niece and an older housekeeper. His age is nearly fifty, his 'complexion' is darkish; his build is wry, lean, bony; his face gaunt-featured; he is an early riser and a lover of the hunt. In his moments of leisure he reads books of knight-errantry, with so much delight that . . .

As a character the hidalgo is 'interesting' only for his peculiarity. His qualities as a fictional subject have had to be expressed as an antithesis to a heroic character: he possesses no superior natural gifts, no admirable qualities; nothing about his past or present is distinctive: he has only social and psychological traits common to many men. Among them is a passion for reading chivalric books. In order to satisfy it, buying all of them he could, he has sold many hectares of his tilled lands. An excess and idiosyncrasy that, comically, casts the first outlines of an individual.

One point to keep in mind about these disclosures turns on that activity pursued by both the hidalgo and Cervantes' readers: the act of reading, the discriminate, yet total immersion in a story. The hidalgo will take on the attributes of an 'interesting' individual precisely as he unfolds as the subject of a transformation brought on by that very activity in which the reader is about to immerse himself. From the onset the hidalgo's uniqueness is inseparable in the reader's mind from the 'fictional' nature of his character as Don Quixote. The analogy is clear: within the pages of a book of fiction a subject as ordinary as the common reader may acquire a storied uniqueness.

The occasion for the hidalgo's transformation was reading, but the 'cause' that brings it about lies deep in his character, in what readers of Cervantes' time would have recognized as his 'temperament' or 'humor,' from the adjective *ingenioso* in the title, and from the initial disclosure about his physiognomy: "he was of sturdy complexion, lean-bodied (dry of flesh), gaunt-faced . . ." *Ingenioso* is the key word. Long before Cervantes it had been associated with the man of 'choleric temperament,' descriptive of one of his mental attributes. In the fifteenth century the Archpriest of Talavera, expounding the four humors—sanguine, choleric, phlegmatic, melancholic—described the qualities of choleric men: "They are hot and dry, hence fire, which is hot and dry, is their corresponding element; they are quick to anger, extremely haughty, clever with words, and daring; they have great courage, are nimble-bodied, very wise, subtle and *ingeniosos* (i.e., ingenious, sharp-witted, resourceful, imaginative); they are lovers of justice, but not always good at executing it."

The 'choleric man' is of course one of the four types propounded by the ancient doctrines of the four humors and the four temperaments. In 1605 a reader could assume that, as indicated by his complexion (*"era de complexión recia"*) and physiognomy, the hidalgo had a 'temperament,' determined by the prevalent humor (choler) of his organism that would explain his behavior, much as a reader of Joyce today assumes that Leopold and Molly Bloom have a subconscious.

According to these doctrines—current in the Middle Ages and the Renaissance—the physical features of an individual are determined by the interaction or mixture of four fluids or humors (from Latin

The Exemplary Story

humor, 'fluid,' 'moisture') in the body: blood, choler or yellow bile, phlegm, and melancholy or black bile. Thus his physiognomy and physical constitution are indicative of his 'complexion' or 'temperament,' or what we would call his psychological type. Cervantes' contemporaries would have understood the description *"era de complexión recia, seco de carnes, enjuto de rostro, gran madrugador y amigo de la caza"* [he was of sturdy complexion, lean-bodied, thin-faced, an early riser and a lover of the chase] as an allusion to the temperament and psychological traits of the hidalgo. The following composite description has been drawn from the various instances throughout the book in which details are supplied as to what he looks like. All of them have been incorporated into the traditional image of Don Quixote propagated subsequently by Cervantes' illustrators and Quixotic iconography. The hidalgo is

> *alto de talla, largo de miembros, flaco pero recio, seco de carnes, huesudo y musculoso, rostro estirado y enjuto, el color moreno y amarillo, la nariz aguileña, lacio el cabello que antes fue negro y ahora entrecano, abundante vellosidad, venas abultadas, voz ronca, y en conjunto feo y mal entallado.*

> tall and thin, lean and lanky, bony and muscular, long-faced, gaunt, dark and yellowish skin, an aquiline nose, straight hair formerly black now streaked with grey, abundant hair on his body, veins prominent, his voice hoarse: he is altogether unbeautiful, unattractive.

This description fits the type known to have a "dry and hot" temperament and a choleric humor, according to the ancient theories.[17] But in the design of cause and effect that brings on the hidalgo's alienation and abnormality it is the interaction of his choleric humor with melancholy that proves decisive. This will be best seen in our reply to these two questions: Why did the hidalgo devote himself so completely to reading books of knight-errantry? Why, as a result of this, did he lose his sanity? The fictional design traces the cause and effect of a clinical case.

The humoral theories were the principal medical, physiological and psychological doctrines of Cervantes' time, and they continued to be influential until very recently.[18] Their origins go back to the medical and philosophical ideas of ancient Greek thinkers. As they had evolved down to Cervantes' day, they provided a complete explanation of human characterology (psychology) evolved from a pathological physiology. From a theory about four humors or fluids in the body that determined the state of health or illness in an individual, they had developed into a doctrine about the different 'temperaments,' the psychological types determined by each one of the four humors.

These doctrines taught that the body and mind are closely related and mutually influential. The body's organs are conditioned by a combination or mixture of the humors, all of which determines in a given individual not only his physical appearance and character but also the state of his health. This mixture or balance of the humors would account for all differences between individuals as to physiology and psychology and their health or illness. The ideal man or woman would have the four humors in ideal proportions, in which blood—the humor that is 'hot and moist'—would predominate. A disbalance of the humors would bring on an abnormal condition and disease. From their earliest versions in classical times these doctrines had worked out on many levels a systematic connection between the body's 'microcosmos' and the 'macrocosmos' of the physical universe. The four humors were related to the four elements, fire, earth, air and water; to the four seasons of the year and to the four planets, and so on. Choler and the choleric temperament were in ascendancy in the season of summer, melancholy (black bile) in winter. Choler and the choleric temperament corresponded to youth, melancholy to old age. The following chart illustrates some of these correspondences.

CHART I

humor or fluid	temperament	primary qualities	element	age	season	planet
blood	sanguine	hot and moist	air	adolescence	Spring	Jupiter
phlegm	phlegmatic	cold and moist	water	middle age	Autumn	Moon
choler or yellow bile	choleric	hot and dry	fire	youth	Summer	Mars
melancholy or black bile	melancholic	cold and dry	earth	old age	Winter	Saturn

The predominant humor determines the individual's appearance and behavior, but the balance or mixture of the humors determines the qualities or traits of his temperament, for this is the meaning of the term. Now the hidalgo's physical appearance—tall, lean, muscular, bony, wry faced—indicates that he is of 'hot and dry' temperament, that is, the predominant humor in his organism is choler or yellow bile. As such he would suffer, constitutionally, from a deficiency of phlegm (water). A disbalance of acute 'hot and dry' is precarious for him. But in Quixote's body choler and melancholy prevail in their combination or interplay, so that he is both choleric (hot and dry) and melancholic (cold and dry). As such he is susceptible to choleric periods, rage, passion, exultation, which then give way to periods of depression. This interplay of choleric and melancholic periods is the decisive unfolding of his personality in the story. Individuals of 'hot and dry' or choleric temperament are quick to anger, proud, revengeful, bold, with a natural tendency to develop 'enthusiasms,' 'passions,' or manias. Here, then, is the clinical source of the hidalgo's idiosyncrasy. His liking for chivalric books is carried to the extremes of passion or mania because it is driven by and satisfies a profound craving of his personality. His subsequent behavior on the road indicates that those long periods spent reading chivalric books were symptomatic of a prepsychotic inclination.

According to these doctrines pathological conditions are due mainly to humoral abnormalities, or a disbalance in the condition of the humors. Having taken up the reading of chivalric books, the hidalgo pursued it with the intensity of a 'hot and dry' passion of his choleric humor. Didn't the content of those books also appeal to and satisfy the other, the melancholic, depressive side of his humor? To be sure. It was his temperament which led him to develop a passion for reading. And when, by reading to excess through days and nights, with the consequent lack of sleep, he exacerbated his humoral deficiency, his brain was affected; it "dried up." From his niece we get this description of the hidalgo going mad after two whole days and nights of reading:

> arrojaba el libro de las manos, y ponía mano a la espada, y andaba a cuchilladas con las paredes, y cuando estaba muy cansado decía que había muerto a cuatro gigantes como cuatro torres, y el sudor que sudaba del cansancio decía que era sangre de las feridas que había recibido en la batalla, y bebíase luego un gran jarro de agua fría, y quedaba sano y sosegado. . . . I. 5, 107

> he would cast the book from his hands, and would draw his sword and slash at the walls, and when he was very tired he would say that he had killed four giants as big as towers, and the sweat that he had sweated from exhaustion he said was blood from wounds he got in battle, and then he drank a great jugful of cold water, and became calm. . . .

The copious amounts of water relieved the extreme 'dryness' of his body, the humoral deficiency now seriously affecting his wits.

Once the passion set in it became all-consuming so that he neglected his sport—hunting, and even his household affairs:

> . . . se enfrascó tanto en su letura, que se le pasaban las noches leyendo de claro en claro, y los días de turbio en turbio; y así, del poco dormir y del mucho leer se le secó el celebro, de manera que vino a perder el juicio. I. 1, 73

> . . . he so immersed himself in his books, that he spent the nights reading from twilight till daybreak and the days from dawn to dark, and thus from little sleep and much reading, his brain dried up, so that he lost the use of his reason.

Cervantes' sentence has of course a satirical, comical ring to it, as if from so incidental a cause as excessive reading, through days and nights, the loss of sanity is a wholly disproportionate result, but that is exactly the gist of the 'clinical' detail he is describing. From the severe lack of sleep there resulted the physiological loss of moisture in the brain; due to 'hot and dry' passion the brain was unable to rehumidify itself for lack of phlegm. From the cerebral physiological disbalance there followed the psychological disbalance that gives rise to a pathological condition. The loss of moisture in the brain was the clinical 'cause'; the 'effect,' the loss of reason (*juicio*), that is, the loss of the ponderative or rational faculties. Having lost contact with reality, and in the absence of any force to inhibit the process, there set in a lesion and hypertrophy of his imaginative faculty.

Now, according to the same theories, the man of choleric humor, as one given easily to passions or manias, posesses a strong imagination, so much so that, as we noted, the word *ingenioso* was readily applied to him. The manner in which this term now becomes applicable to the hidalgo is apparent in what followed:

> Llenósele la fantasía de todo aquello que leía en los libros, así de encantamentos como de pendencias, batallas, desafíos, heridas, requiebros, amores, tormentas y disparates imposibles; y asentósele de tal modo en la imaginación que era verdad toda aquella máquina de aquellas sonadas soñadas invenciones que leía, que para él no había otra historia más cierta en el mundo. I. 1, 73

> His imagination became filled with a host of fancies he had read in his books: as much enchantments as quarrels, battles, challenges, wounds, courtships, loves, torments, and many other absurdities; and so firmly did his imagination conceive that all this stuff was true that no history in the world seemed more authentic to him.

In the choice of *ingenioso* Cervantes intended an allusion to a prepsychotic inclination in his hero as well as to the psychotic excess that subsequently brought on his transformation. This disclosure makes clear, moreover, that while Quixote's misconception about chivalric books is due to an unbridled imagination no longer subject to the restraints of prudence and reason, its dynamic surges from deep within his character. The fictions of chivalric books are assumed by him to be true-to-life, historically true, because they contain his own life as their possible moral truth. Deep within the sedate middle-aged hidalgo suffers from a personality disorder centered in an imaginative idea of himself. Now, of all the traits one attributed to men of 'hot and dry' temperament none stands out more than their capacity in mind and imagination to engender and deal with 'subtle and refined concepts.' According to the Renaissance theorists, they were rich in intelligence and imagination.

The theorist who most likely suggested the adjective *ingenioso* to Cervantes, and most likely influenced his design, was Juan Huarte de San Juan (1526?–1588) whose sensational *Examen de Ingenios* (*Examination of Men's Wits*, first published in 1575, numerous editions to 1604) was known to all educated Spaniards.[19] It was most likely from Huarte's doctrines on psychopathology that Cervantes learned that a prolonged lack of sleep would dehydrate (dry and harden) the brain, that prolonged sleep would restore its moisture, otherwise a psychical disorder would set in that would affect the imaginative faculty by way of an injury, or lesion, giving rise to an abnormality, the delirium of a monomania. From Huarte's theory of humors also Cervantes could have devised the psycho-physiological complex of a choleric-melancholic, endowed with intelligence and a fertile imagination, and predisposed to extremes of mania, which in Huarte's words is "a hot and dry cerebral disbalance." From acquaintance with Huarte's typological psychology Cervantes could have formed the idea for a story whose hero is motivated by causes lying deep in the recesses of character, where physiology and psychology interact, and issue in moral actions, and from here conceive an entire development for a story based on psycho-moral characterization rather than on 'imitation of life and manners' or plot. It is even probable that Huarte could have suggested that a humoral abnormality such as Quixote's would release an imaginative and intellectual potential that might not have surfaced otherwise.

Huarte's theories, however, could have suggested only a scheme for the unfolding of a psychotic personality typified as *ingenioso*, for there is marked divergence between Huarte's rather deterministic teachings and Cervantes' conception of his hero's 'gratuitous acts.' Our clinical case is, after all, only a description of what happens in the story as Cervantes tells it, not why it happens. The *why* is rooted in the will or soul of the hidalgo, in his deepest desires, illusions, dreams. He does not will to go mad, but his desire to become a knight-errant is entirely gratuitous, autonomous. There is no compulsive 'reason' for it, no clinical, deterministic 'cause.' Huarte's doctrines may have suggested the 'clinical' idea of a choleric-melancholic, constitutionally pre-psychotic and predisposed to imaginative visions and conceits, but that, having lost his sanity, this *ingenioso* in the delirium that ensues should undertake the life and actions of knight-errant according to his whim and illusion, and in the face of a hostile reality, is a situation of character that only Cervantes could have hit on.

The clinical basis to the story and character of the hidalgo is surely one of the factors that make *Don Quixote* a fiction of such lifelike proportions as to impress its fusion of psychology to imagination as thoroughly 'modern.' After each of his three sallies, on returning home, Quixote is put to bed by the female members of his household, and allowed to sleep for long periods. They give him cool, comforting fluids and foods. These details suggest that Cervantes and his readers of 1605 recognized the most obvious symptoms of a humoral disorder and the treatment prescribed for it by theorists and doctors. The symptomatology of Quixote's syndrome, to use our modern terms, will call for long periods of sleep and prolonged rest, in order to restore the moisture to his brain, 're-humidify it,' which is not too easy, because of the dry heat of the Manchegan summer and because the hidalgo also suffers from a constitutional insomnia. In terms of modern clinical diagnosis, Quixote is alienated from his real person or self by reason of his insanity. In his life as a sedate hidalgo he was constitutionally neurotic and prepsychotic, which explains his mania for reading escapist literature. Once he loses his mind and is on the road, his delirium unfolds into a full-scale recreation of scenes from chivalric fictions; that is, his behavior and sense experience are interpreted by his deranged imagination.

The psycho-somatic nature of his adventures has been variously analyzed and interpreted by modern clinical specialists.[20] One set of opinions has established that Quixote shows the classical symptoms of paranoia, characterized by delusions of grandeur, egolatry, and persecution, and organized into a coherent, internally consistent delusional system. The attack on the windmills, for instance, develops from an initial sighting—giants, with the deranged imagination in control and interpreting all sense experience and egolatrous claims to be the knight elected to exterminating them; and, after the charge at the sails and severe physical punishment, the claim that the elect knight is the object of persecution by envious and hostile enchanters.

Yet another opinion holds that his delirium takes the form of hallucinations. Seeing giants where there are windmills is a false perception of reality. The sight of ominous objects with sails is indeed an external stimulus (not always present in hallucinations), but, according to this opinion, Quixote does not charge at the physical object of the stimulus—windmills, he charges at the objects conceived by his imagination—giants. The arguments for interpreting Quixote's adventures as primarily hallucinatory are, however, much more complicated, as we shall see.

A further opinion holds that Quixote manifests the symptoms of a delirium of imagination (not to be confused with the delirium of paranoia or hallucination).[21] His deranged mind does not respond primarily to the visual stimulus of windmills, we are told, but to their *'transformation'* into giants. His imagination imposes on objects a storied, fictionalized or fabled 'meaning,' here the chivalric image of giants, with himself at the center opposing the evil adversary. He is similar to the clinical patient who does not 'invent' what he sees (he does in fact perceive objects) but does 'invent' the idealized image and story he imposes on reality, with himself of course the subject and protagonist of the story. The technical term for this type of delirium is *mythomania* and *mythomaniac*.

But the most interesting symptom of Quixote's case is the consistency and 'logic' of his delirium; under the spell of his imaginative fabrications, they have the internal consistency of elaborate and highly systemized delusions. As in classical cases of paranoia, his entire personality is affected. To the amazement of his hearers, he will defend his chivalric enterprise and fantastic expectations with the apparent conviction of reason and logic. So forcibly that he seems insane only with respect to his fixation. But this is a surface impression, because in fact the hidalgo's entire personality and character are deeply and radically affected. His delirium is only the most obvious evidence that his mind and personality have assumed an illuminated and exalted state, that his madness consists of a total transformation of his self, in fulfilment of latent possibilities. It is this change that explains both the mad consistency of his defense of chivalry and the apparent sane consistency of his discourse on other subjects.

6. A Literary Madness   Chs 2–7

Don Quixote's madness can be explained only partly in pathological or even psychological terms because it is uniquely a *literary* madness. And here I am not referring to its direct 'cause,' the exorbitant reading of escapist books. It is a literary madness for the reason that the hidalgo conceives himself to be, while mad, a literary figure, the knight-errant whose personality, actions and feelings occupy the center of a magnificent and heroic world. To himself those wrathful outbursts express the inner trials of an exalted, passionate soul and elect conscience. This concept of the heroic personage is only a slightly distorted version of actions committed out of intense feeling and the inner suffering they accompany, whether conceived as fury, rage, wrath, or delirium. To be the literary heroic figure is to live unceasingly on the level of a superior awareness of one's obligations in a world that reflects, in its marvellous and magical operations, the elect nature of that passionate conscience. Unlike the epic hero of pagan or Christian poetry, the knight-errant of romance undergoes the tests and trials of heroic exertion as an individual more meaningfully related to the magical, preternatural world of his elect status than to the world of social relations in which he is depicted. It is this unique isolation of the literary figure of the knight that forms the key to Quixote's madness.

The uniqueness of this literary madness is moreover derived from its antecedents, the passionate or 'mad' behavior of epic and romantic heroes, their fury or wrath as depicted by poets. In the epic tradition the wrath of Achilles or the fury of Hercules are conceived to be on a level of human conduct so unique and so elevated as to exclude any comparison with norms. So great is their poetic power that these figures banish any thought that would subject their passionate behavior to the laws of ordinary men, and much less to clinical exposé. Yet in a sense it is precisely the abnormity, the magnificient excess of their behavior that poets elevate and depict as heroic. A novelist, approaching the same behavior, would probe and analyze.

The Exemplary Story

The major literary antecedents of Quixote's madness are to be found in the depiction of fury and wrath in heroic poetry and romance. The wrath of Achilles, the fury of Hercules, or the romantic madness and depression of chivalric heroes: the furious jealousy of Orlando, the love madness of Lancelot, Yvain, Tristan, and Amadís. These are major antecedents, not because they coincide (they do not) at any number of points with Cervantes' design, but because they approximate its center: Quixote's image of himself. Is it necessary to say that, according to that image, Quixote is heroic, not insane? By comparison the more direct antecedents are minor and anecdotal. I refer to the antecedents, possible or probable, of a character who goes mad as a result of reading certain books. But here we are outside the heroic tradition, as we are outside Quixote's illusion.

For centuries Cervantes' comical effects have provoked the reaction that Quixote's literary insanity is but a vehicle for ridiculing either a literary mode or the social conventions of chivalry depicted in that mode. I do not say this has been an entirely wrong reaction, on the contrary. But those comical effects have concealed much that is not only interesting and revealing of social and psychological details in the character of his hidalgo, but, more seriously, how the comical elements adhere to the moral conception of Don Quixote. It is this adherence of the comical elements to the psychological depiction of a moral idea that makes an exemplary story. Since the moral idea underlies the literary transformation of an hidalgo into knight, we shall need to get a better look at Quixote's condition as an *hidalgo*.

The exemplary story gets underway disclosing how, as an effect of having lost his sanity, the *ingenioso* hidalgo undertakes the complete rehabilitation of his life and character in the exercise of knight-errantry as depicted in the books he read. His enterprise is thus a psychological aberration demanding the social alienation of his person: from this angle what he attempts is an abnormity, and not only at variance with the social reality in which he thinks and acts, but also a sundering of the psychical forces and moral potential of a mature man. But that very sundering brings on a release of an imaginative faculty, at once poetic and moral, capable of devising and sustaining all the ingredients of story and attributes of person and character of himself as a knight, that is, capable not only of devising the circumstances or situation in which he will assert his role and identity as a knight, but likewise of responding to them, as a full experience of the senses and with the consciousness that he does so as heroic exertion.

The image of himself as "Don Quixote" is a potential of character in the idle and obscure hidalgo. Though alienated from his true self and from social reality, his madness issues in 'creative' psychical projection because it precipitates his transformation and rise to a status of conduct consecrated by tradition as manly excellence. Here lie both the splendour and the misery of his illusion. His heroic fixation can only confirm his radical isolation. But isolated and, as it were, protected by his madness, he can devise and carry out actions that confirm his role as hero in complete conviction as to their worth. And, moreover, this isolation confirms his unique status as an elect being. All of this, for the reader of 1605 who could guess its implications, or for modern readers, is comical because it describes an *hidalgo's* rehabilitation. What then is the background of the social group or class of which Quixote is first a type and subsequently its most notorious if not illustrious member? Our reply must keep in mind just what the role of hidalgos had been throughout Spain's Middle Ages, and how their lot had fared since the end of the Reconquest (to 1500), in the years of the world empire of Charles V and Philip II.

In the Middle Ages the *hidalgo* is not so much a social grouping as a socio-political and militaristic concept of nobility. The Castilian hidalgo incarnates the qualities of Christian nobility and sense of honor. He descends from distinguished, i.e., wealthy and powerful parentage; hence his 'nobility' (his lineage) is uncontaminated by non-Christian (i.e., Semitic) blood. His active enterprises are noble: war and hunting. When he is not fighting or hunting he enjoys idleness, leisure (*ociosidad*), for it is an outward sign of his nobility that he does no manual labor; in fact and by royal decree he is disgraced and loses his status as hidalgo if he engages in manual labor. As a Christian warrior his sense of worth, dignity and inner being are dominated by the idea of honor.

The hidalgos arose as a warrior caste in the historical and military process called the Reconquest. Theirs were precisely the families whose leaders and sons provided the impetus and strength that carried it out. The incentive for war and its political aims came from the Crown, but since the war against Muslim forces was not only one of conquering territory and populations, but also redistributing land and recolonizing it, the kings of Castile offered as incentives to the more energetic of their nobility the opportunity that military expansion offered for personal enrichment and aggrandizement. The wealth, privileges, and power of the hidalgos came into being with the southward military expansion of Castile, and it is toward its close that they emerge as a social class, comprising the *lower* nobility. Although all of the nobility of Castile had the status of 'hidalgos,' by 1500 the term described more precisely this third and lowest level; above the hidalgos (who were of course the most numerous) were ranked the knights (*caballeros*) distinguished for their superior wealth and power, and the grandees, the (few) most powerful and wealthy Dukes and Counts.

The hidalgo families, therefore, acquire the characteristics of a social group or class in sixteenth-century Spain when those historical conditions that fostered them begin to fade. With military expansion no longer a possibility on the peninsula, their more vigorous and ambitious sons found few opportunities at home and answered the call to military careers in the imperial armies of Charles V, on the continent or in wars of conquest in the New World. For the rest the glories of a military past and illustrious ancestors must compensate for the reduced social and economic circumstances that their privileges provided. By 1530 the hidalgo was visibly the Spaniard of nobility who depended (not on enterprise, but) on inherited wealth (principally land ownership) for his income, and instituted privileges such as tax exemptions and the reputation of purity of blood to maintain his standing. The most vulnerable and hard put to maintain their status and honor were the impoverished hidalgo families living in isolated villages, and preserving the memory of military exploits of ancestors. Two versions of the life of these village hidalgos appear in the literature of the period, the famished hidalgo in *Lazarillo of Tormes* (ca. 1535) and the idealized type described by Antonio de Guevara.

By 1600 the hidalgo families formed a segment of the formative Spanish middle class that included some professionals, lawyers, government bureaucrats, doctors, merchants. As a social grouping with pretensions of nobility, the hidalgos were now precariously close to losing their prestige, not only for the pitiable poverty of many families, or the very remoteness of their military past, but for the little credence given to their claims of blood purity. For the other side of the truth is that this hidalgo class was the social class into which large numbers of Jewish converts, known as 'new Christians' or *conversos*, both before and after the expulsion of Jews in 1492, had been assimilated.[22] The aspersions cast on the hidalgos by Spanish society in general (for their shaky pretense of '*hidalguía*' and old-Christian purity of blood) are reflected in the figure of the hidalgo and his conspicuous lack of prestige in Lope de Vega's plays. No element of his book is more revealing of Cervantes' audacity than his attempt to 'rehabilitate' a member of a social group so lacking in prestige, lustre, and interest to his contemporaries.

Now the essence of Don Quixote as *'hidalgo de aldea'* is that he is a social nonconformist, and in the very sensitive questions of honor and purity of blood. Quixote will express in words and deeds a fine concept of honor, but will never maintain that the honorableness of his deeds or person rests on the traditional concept of blood purity. Nowhere does he claim to have in his veins an 'old Christian's purity of blood.' It is left to Sancho to boast that he, a peasant, descends on 'all four sides' of parentage from 'old-Christian' stock, thus echoing the social myth, dear to Lope de Vega, that true purity of Christian blood was to be found in the Castilian peasantry, not in Castilian nobility.

Going mad for the hidalgo, and assuming the name and identity of a knight, involved a social nonconformity that was as comical as the physio-psychological 'cause' issuing from his humoral temperament. Yet the depiction of a character from both sides, social and psychological, raised the narrative to a moral idea, for the challenge to both Quixote and his author. With the character's motivation drawn on social and psychological lines, the narrative of a literary madness centers on the illusions generated by a personal will. The hidalgo has informed his new role and identity as an act of will. He 'wills' to be Don Quixote. It is this moral idea that unfolds with and within Quixote's literary madness, shapes his transformation and insures his autonomy.

But what ideas, what concept of manly honor and purpose motivate the hidalgo? They are above all literary, or poetic, but this is not their most important feature in the book. It is their relation to the inner springs of motive and desire, conscience and will, that matter most.

> En efeto, rematado ya su juicio, vino a dar en el más estraño pensamiento que jamás dio loco en el mundo, y fue que le pareció convenible y necesario, así para el aumento de su honra como para el servicio de su república, hacerse caballero andante, y irse por todo el mundo con sus armas y caballo a buscar las aventuras y a ejercitarse en todo aquello que él había leído que los caballeros andantes se ejercitaban, deshaciendo todo género de agravio, y poniéndose en ocasiones y peligros donde, acabándolos, cobrase eterno nombre y fama. I. 1, 74–5
>
> Finally, having lost his wits completely, he fell into the strangest fancy that ever

The Exemplary Story

entered a madman's brain, which was that he believed it was necessary, both for the increase of his honor and for service of the state, that he should become a knight-errant, roaming through the world with his horse and armour in quest of adventures and practicing all that had been performed by the knights-errant of whom he had read, redressing all manner of wrongs, and exposing himself to chances and dangers, by the overcoming of which he might win eternal renown and fame.

These phrases disclose the first of the 'ingenious' conceits that arise from and sustain his illusion. He has two social goals, one personal, the other altruistic. The personal one, "for the increase of his honor" is couched in terms of an hidalgo's obligation. The conceit is centered in the idea of knights-errant in quest of adventures, for this is the literary concept imposed on a social one. Knights, as depicted in books, are single instruments of justice who, beyond this, pursue for themselves the one and only reward equal to and worthy of their efforts, "eternal renown and fame." Now, of course honor and fame are both the purpose and end of a noble Christian life as conceived by medieval society and its literature, but the hidalgo has in mind the literary and heroic ideal of 'honor and fame,' its consecration by and in literature. Here, then, its 'ingenious' nature, sprung from personal will, desire, and illusion.

Missing from this initial declaration of his purpose is the temporal element that will shape it into the elaborate 'revival' of chivalry in a 'detestable' modern age. This temporal element is from the start a projection into a future time, and Quixote expresses it as such in the invocation that follows his greeting to the sun in chapter 2.

—Dichosa edad y siglo dichoso aquel adonde saldrán a luz las famosas hazañas mías, dignas de entallarse en bronce, esculpirse en mármoles y pintarse en tablas para memoria en lo futuro. I. 2, 80

—Oh, happy the age and fortunate the time, wherein my famous feats shall be revealed, feats worthy to be graven in brass, sculptured in marble, and painted on wood, for future instruction and memory.

In chapter 9 the personal narrator restates with mock praise Quixote's purpose and goals already achieved and reported on in literary 'historical' documents:

el primero que en nuestra edad y en estos tan calamitosos tiempos se puso al trabajo y ejercicio de las andantes armas, y al desfacer agravios, socorrer viudas, amparar doncellas. . . . I. 9, 141 [the first who in our age and in these such calamitous times took up the toils and exercise of knight errantry, to redress wrongs, aid widows, protect maidens. . . .]

The several parts fall into place in Quixote's discourse on the Golden Age, where, on drawing contrasts between the pastoral felicity of the Golden Age and the "present detestable times," in which female virtue is no longer safe, he will affirm that knighthood was instituted to stay the course of progressively greater evil, to protect the virtue of damsels, and to aid and defend the weak and helpless. Only much later, at the beginning of Part II, will Quixote express his conceit in the explicit terms of a revival of chivalry. "¿Qué se platica del asumpto que he tomado de resucitar y volver al mundo la ya olvidada orden caballeresca?" II. 2, 55 [What do they say about my enterprise to revive and restore to the world the forgotten order of chivalry?] Its intricacy lies, of course, in the equivocal imposition of a poetic temporal element (the mythical four ages) on a socio-historical condition. The decayed moral order of the present (a social condition) calls for the revival of knighthood (a fictional way of life). This is pure delusion in the clinical sense and pure illusion in the literary sense. But note how both its delusory and illusory aspects are lifted as it were to a moral justification. Quixote means to be a moral instrument in these "detestable times." Does it matter that his intentions are sprung from a picture of time and justice that is largely literary, if these intentions are moral and pure and aspire to do good in the social world and establish right over wrong? Does their literary inspiration disqualify them from the good and the right? This conceit contains from the start the suggestion of a redemptive role for knighthood, or that Quixote's literary madness will be bound only by the fiction of his fame.

7. Parody

A sector of critical opinion holds that parody is Cervantes' primary technique in *Don Quixote*. While it is a technique by which he introduces and reduces to comical incident many ingredients of a chivalric story, on large and small scale, parody remains throughout a secondary technique and a subordinate style. Cervantes' primary technique and style are those of his own exemplary narrative. What the reader discovers in the initial chapters are the style and technique of the exemplary novelist. They introduce the hidalgo, describe his condition, and particularize his madness. Throughout the story they delineate and unfold his characteristics. They account for, control, and sustain the unity of the story across its series of episodic adventures. In chapter 9 they expand easily to incorporate the parody of a chivalric romance composed by a sage historian. The exemplary purpose, style, and technique are primary and major; in relation to them parody, however rife, is a means, subordinate and contained.

The first six chapters of *Don Quixote*, taken separately, would constitute the most comical of Cervantes' exemplary novels. And it is through the comical that such a technique as parody intrudes, or is introduced, into a story with an exemplary aim. In a purely technical sense parody consists of the exaggerated, hence comical, imitation of an original, and may imply both criticism and censure. The mechanics of parody in *Don Quixote* reveal Cervantes as a master of storytelling. While drawing the hidalgo according to the truth of his story—its social, psychological and moral basis—he reveals the source and motives of his madness, and having established its reality, it follows by natural design that it is the hidalgo who imitates, who 'parodies' chivalry, its style and imagery; all cause, motive, and design for imitating the style and action of a chivalric romance originate in Quixote's illusion, not in the exemplary narrator. To understand this is to grasp the first rule of Cervantes' technique and a secret of his humor.

But Quixote's independence from his narrator is only the most radical in the story, for all of Cervantes' characters are themselves. They possess a mind and a will of their own, with whims, fears, desires. What in Quixote is crucial—the imitation of chivalry—according to the exemplary design of life, is in others whimsical, incidental, or malicious. The first six chapters may not have been written to form a prelude to the rest of Part I, but in result they serve as one. They mark the early stages of Quixote's madness.

Once possessed by the idea, the hidalgo devises the procedures by which he becomes, or makes himself into a 'knight'. Assuming both a logic and order to what he devises, and that it all unfolds within his conceit, what inner movement of his illusion do they obey? First, the steps he takes shows that he begins with the most material considerations and proceeds to the spiritual: from his armor to his lady. Second, he is inspired, not by the prosaic—prose—content of books of chivalry, but by the poetic essence of the chivalric ideal in war and love as expressed in the language of poetry—verse.

The material considerations are about the arms he will bear. From the remains of armor and weapons of his ancestors he improvises an outfit for himself; the pasteboard visor is a detail no reader forgets. Then his mount. The hack in his stable—unnamed up to now—becomes "Rocinante," a name devised to express variously what he has been, *rocín*, and what he is transformed into, the steed of a famous knight. He spent four days in devising this name, for it has not only an 'etymological' meaning, but also a poetical one; as an imaginative conceit it is a conscious imitation of the names for horses in *Orlando furioso* and in the tradition of names for legendary horses. The singularity of this escapes most everyone. It is neither the practice nor the inspiration of authors of Spanish chivalric books to give a name to the knight's horse, no matter how famous the knight. The horses simply go unnamed, whatever their strength, speed, or color. The hidalgo has ignored the prose of chivalric books to find inspiration in the poetry of Ariosto. The next step is to devise a name for himself, *Don Quixote de la Mancha*. We have already indicated its source and inspiration. The poetic tradition Quixote follows is the story of Lancelot in popular Spanish ballads. Lastly, he invents the name for his lady, or, better said, he invents the lady, for Aldonza Lorenzo is only the pretext for the insubstantial image of Dulcinea.

Anyone acquainted with chivalric books, and reflecting on this process by which a name for this or that brings into material existence a 'knight,' knows none of this ever happens in any of those books. No knight ever named himself after this fashion, or his lady or his horse, though many acquire or have bestowed on them any number of titles or surnames. It amazes that Quixote should think it was necessary to give a name to his horse which was surely not indispensable. But it should also amaze that it does not occur to him to give his sword a name. He does have one; he uses it to test the pasteboard beaver. By long and glorious epic tradition, knights bore a sword with a name that described its famed qualities, '*Durendal*' (Roland), '*Tizón*' (the Cid), '*Balisarda*,' (Ruggiero). Why then does Quixote not feel compelled to give his sword a name? By what subliminal process did the hidalgo suppress the idea? For what reason did Cervantes eliminate it?[23]

From the 'genesis' of names the story goes on to disclose, in Quixote's opening monologues, the emergence of a chivalric personality. The hidalgo ventures forth alone, unseen by anyone, one hot morning in July. The excessive heat exacerbates his clinical condition. His madness is literary, and so his delirium expresses itself conceitedly and rhapsodically in monologues that dramatize his illusion, comical fixation and isolation. "—¡Oh princesa Dulcinea, señora deste cautivo corazón! . . . . Plégaos, señora, de membraros deste vuestro sujeto corazón. . . ." [O Princess Dulcinea! Lady of this captive heart! I pray thee, sweet lady, deign to remember thee of this poor subjected heart. . .] The subject of an exemplary portrayal 'parodies' the style of a chivalric narrative. Hereafter the narrative has only to simulate his conceit, or deranged thinking, to achieve this effect: "Casi todo aquel día caminó sin acontecerle cosa que de contar fuese, de lo cual se desesperaba, porque quisiera topar luego luego con quien hacer experiencia del valor de su fuerte brazo." I. 2, 81 [He traveled almost the whole of that day without meeting anything of note, which reduced him to despair, for he was eager to encounter someone on whom he could try the strength of his doughty arm.] But while his ravings trace the outlines of a literary figure of himself, from his will and imagination there issues a feasibly moral picture of chivalry, and one in which he can assert his entire personality. Hence the link between our story and the life and purpose of chivalry as depicted in romance is Quixote's fantasy, his illusion. This is the nuclear core of parody. That is to say, it is the only element in the story that bears a direct connection to literary models, because any other element is only an indirect comparison, or a comical exemplary coincidence.

Now while Cervantes will make the parody of chivalry most explicit through Quixote's fantasy, the entire personality of his character is involved, for this is both the purpose and the process of the exemplary story. The scene of arrival at the inn in chapter 2 is nothing like a knight's arrival at a castle, except in Quixote's imagination (and in the illusion Cervantes can maintain in the reader's mind). All cause, motive, or design for parody of chivalry originates in Quixote's illusion and emanates from it. To see this in all its comical implications can only increase one's delight in Cervantes' story. The scenes at the inn comprise the first test of Quixote's madness, and its effect on others. From this point forward the technique of parody undergoes the first of many elaborations. As the story unfolds, his fantasy will impose on the personality of others something of his inner resolve and rather most of his picture of chivalry, as the combined effect of his ability to articulate, in seemingly rational and artistic speech, a chivalric style and the strong impress of his choleric temperament. As a result, either in order to humor and appease the madman who is dangerous for his erratic and arrogant behavior, or because of his genuinely courteous and considerate manner and the appeal of his fanciful fixation, others (the innkeeper and the two women at the inn) and according to their whim and personality become infected by his illusion and play and perform a 'parody' of chivalry along with him. The nearly farcical scenes of his meal, the vigil of arms and the dubbing in the stable, are comical realism and approximate a parody of chivalry where they simulate Quixote's illusion and thus satisfy it. The force of his illusion, through the force of his personality, has the power to impose the 'fiction' of the arrival of a knight at a castle, his reception, and dubbing. The narrator unfolds an exemplary if farcical story, the characters, infected by Quixote's madness, perform the parody of a dubbing scene.[24]

On the surface it appears that Quixote's imagination is the dominant factor. He must 'imagine' a knightly scene before he can assert and enact his role as knight. The inn is a castle, the stable a chapel, and so on. Yet his delusion is such that all his surroundings—persons and things—are caught up in the total representation of chivalry he attempts to enact—picaresque innkeeper, 'damsels,' carriers; but they are caught up in the total expression of his personality; his ingeniousness, his emotional vehemence, and will. He is like the conscience, the maddened conscience, of chivalry at the center of its ludicrous representation. None of this resembles even remotely anything in the originals, for obvious reasons. Quixote is not a knight in any real sense. The laws of chivalry as well as the laws of any sane country would forbid it. Only in the mind of a madman could the scene in the stable constitute a dubbing ceremony. Quixote is a knight only in his delusion and in the 'fiction' sustained by an exemplary technician.

Our pleasure from a sustained resemblance and imitation of chivalric action and scenes stems from the exemplary depiction of Quixote's madness. We see the fiction of himself as knight isolated in his mind and ridiculous behavior, in his conscious 'creative' imitation, but also in what he is unaware as imitation or parody because it is his whole self, himself as the character of an exemplary story that is involved. We note that he follows scrupulously the authority of his written models. He must be dubbed knight before he can undertake any adventures. But it is his emotional vehemence—rage, arrogant and impassioned boldness, that strikes the psychological and hence comically truthful resemblance between the hidalgo and literary knights.

Now, we know that Quixote's motives (his psychological motives) proceed from his madness, but his character has a psycho-physiological motivation that he shows in his wrathful outbursts, his pride and arrogance; they are due to and express his choleric temperament. It is Cervantes' supreme conceit that his choler, as psychological and verisimilar motivation, should 'coincide' in his depiction with the wrathful nature of so many literary knights, when provoked to strike and kill, or with their passionate being.

In most chivalric stories the rage and fighting spirit of knights needs only a slight provocation to combat, to bring down on an opponent the full might of a wrathful blow. The 'psychology' of this motivation is that there is very little or none, or very little or none is needed to produce the desired effect on readers. Amadís of Gaul is aroused to frenzy in combat by his *"gran saña,"* his great wrath. The knights act and react not automatically as some suppose, but in accord with their heroic depiction. Quixote is unaware of how the choleric outbursts of his "hot and dry" temperament, provoked and exacerbated by delirium, instill with a comic likeness to chivalric adventures his attacks on the carriers while keeping vigil over his arms, or his attack on Juan Haldudo, or his defiant challenge of the travellers to Murcia. The reason is that he is living passionately his adventure, and without the exemplary depiction of his character and his temperament we could not have his parody of chivalry.

The exemplary story and technique describe the hidalgo and depict his actions; they provide the reason or 'cause' of his madness and indicate his motives, moral and psychological. Since they provide the motives behind his imitation of chivalry they likewise provide the psychological and moral motivation that explains his 'parody.' The exemplary story will unfold with Quixote's imitation of chivalry, but its aims cannot be defined as parody, for it aims at much more. It aims to bring forth what was not depicted in 'heroic' chivalric books, the complete and verisimilar psychology of the hero-knight.

Two other considerations will illustrate further the nature of Quixote's madness and its depiction. The first is one of characterological verisimilitude. How likely, one asks, that a man approaching the age of fifty would have the physical capacity to undertake and withstand the violent actions and horrible punishment that Quixote does and takes? Here, too, Cervantes' readers in 1605 had a clue in the psycho-physiological theories of humors we discussed above. One of the characteristics of men of "hot and dry" temperament is that, due to their durable constitution, they are able to preserve their youthful physical strength and resistance well beyond the limit for others. Quixote's illusion is that his violent exertions correspond to the exploits of men depicted in stories in the vigor of their manhood, Amadís or Lancelot in their adolescence and youth. Young knights, however, have not only prowess in battle, but also the zeal and sexual ardor, and attraction, of men in their prime. In his madness Quixote is comically rejuvenated because he places himself in the body and spirit of an aggressive, amorous, and virile young man. Dulcinea, of course, is no older than the adolescent lady of ardent love poetry. The figure of Quixote, the middle-aged bachelor rejuvenated in the love for an ideal girl, is another Cervantean anticipation of Joyce.

The second consideration deals with the subject of books as the 'cause' of madness. Chapter 6 portrays the curate and barber holding a scrutiny of Quixote's books and consigning most of them to the fire. The culprits are declared guilty more for esthetic than for moral reasons, perhaps because no good moral effect could come from books judged to be so bad esthetically. In the hope that, by removal of the cause, the hidalgo will return to his senses when he cannot have books of knight-errantry to read, and curate and barber, with the niece and housekeeper as accomplices and serving as the 'secular arm' of the inquisitorial team, conspire to get rid of the condemned ones, and wall up and close the room where he kept them. They convince Quixote that an enchanter, out of malice, has carried them off room and all. Their little plot doesn't work. Their supposition was ill-founded, and the reader who supposes that Quixote's madness is all about 'reading' books will not do any better.

Dozens of illustrators have depicted Don Quixote reading, now quietly, now excitedly, in his study, and all contrary to the story. Many of Cervantes' imitators have committed the same error. It is the hidalgo still sane who reads. Once mad and become Don Quixote, the character never again takes up a book of knight-errantry, is never again shown reading nor does he show any interest to do so. This is not an idle detail in the story, but a fundamental one, intrinsic to Cervantes' exemplary design. The objection will not hold, that, since his books are destroyed or taken away, he has none in which to read; if his madness were a passion for reading them and not actively living them, he would have found a way to buy others. The point is that reading them, while the indispensable condition to madness, is not what his madness is about, or what Cervantes' story is about.

Whether by observation or intuition, Cervantes knew what scientific diagnosis of the insane could tell us: the insane do not read.

Reading, after all, is a highly rational act. However imaginative or emotive, or however we may be tempted to think of it after Borges and others as 'magical,' the operation of following letters with sense is so thoroughly rational no unbalanced mind can perform it in this way. I believe in some cases the deranged may be seen *to seem* to read, and to comprehend what they read, but they cannot sustain the mental process demanded. While on the road in search of adventures Quixote has in mind vividly the scenes and circumstances of the books that have driven him mad, but he does not recall them with literal precision. Rather, he 'recreates' adventures while enacting his role as knight. In his calmer moods he has the verbal and imaginative facility to recall precise details, but this is not the same as reading. Time and again he finds it difficult to pay close attention to the rational discourse of others. When he interrupts Cardenio's story in chapter 24 he reveals that he has not been the rational listener. He is conspicuously absent while the curate reads the revealing story of a pathological obsession, "The Curious Impertinent," to the company at the inn (I. 33-36). And when, in the opening scene of Part II, he learns of the publication of the adventures of Part I in a book, he shows no inclination to inform himself about it by reading it. No, reading in books of chivalry is not central to his madness. The verisimilar idea that a madman could not perform the rational act of literal and moral apprehension that we identify with reading is, however, second to the other: Quixote's madness begins when action replaces reading, when the Quixotic 'deed' replaces the 'letter.' His story is about what certain books can instill or inspire, their potential in terms of personal and 'real' life.

8. The Autonomous Character   Chs 8-10

Of the various scenes in the opening portions of the story none are more vivid than the two when Quixote, impelled to attack insolent travellers and monstrous giants, is brought down ignominiously, his bones and armor rattling. In each case his reaction to the baleful turn of events, different in detail, is consistent in that the physical punishment he suffers confirms his image and fixed illusion as hero-knight. The ability to survive and overcome reverses depends on the force of illusion and power of madness to perpetuate itself, seeking those points of contact between a hostile reality and the reaction and endurance of his imagined, noble and persecuted knight.

The windmill adventure is the very first Quixote attempts in the company of Sancho. It is probably the single most famous incident in the entire book, depicted by many artists and become proverbial in several languages. Yet it is one of the very briefest. One can discern three moments in it, sighting, charge, and aftermath, but it is over in a flash. Quixote sights the objects and declares they are giants and that this flight will make them rich. "What giants?" Sancho asks. Then, heedless to warnings and attributing Sancho's shouts to fear, he spurs Rocinante to a charge. We can assume the hidalgo had known and seen windmills on the plain of Montiel all of his life; now he sees and charges at giants. His error, simply put, is one of sight perception. Sancho at his side even explains to him how the sails may deceptively appear as arms. A slight wind rises, at the moment he charges, and the sails begin to move (all of which heightens the illusion that they are monstrous). But a greater error is involved also, the moral one of man defiant and haughty executor of divine will: or, putting them together, the flaw of human pride on the scale of heroic exertion—excess of pride and hopeless (if not senseless) overreach. But of course the comicness of the scene rests on the entirely 'gratuitous' nature of the attack. His madness, raised to a pitch by the 'ingenious' conceit of a single knight challenging a host of giants, is reinforced by a display of choler. His motive and the scene do not even approximate what goes on in a chivalric story, which is why we laugh. But without Quixote's autonomy, and the author's withdrawal, the elements of story would not fall together comically.

At the moment of attack the physical circumstances of the scene—wind, movement—have 'coincided' with the error of perception brought on by his diseased imagination and his fiery will. Quixote's delusion is that giants threaten ominously. Cervantes produces the fictional illusion that all details of the scene—the physical reality and the personal will and motives of characters—exist independently of the narrator's control and viewpoint. Quixote's madness compels him to impose the scene and sense of a chivalric adventure on a dull, seemingly inert reality of La Mancha. The illusion Cervantes maintains is that nothing in that reality, or in the scene and events that ensue, has been or could be preconceived by the author.

The complete autonomy with which Quixote asserts his identity as knight is dependent on the illusion of craft that Cervantes can sustain. The same elements of story that build up the charge and attack are present in the aftermath. Laid out flat by the violent blow of the sail and his fall, to Sancho's "I told you so" he replies with a reflection worthy of a beaten but never defeated soldier: "success in affairs of war is highly unpredictable" and then "a vile enchanter has transformed the giants, depriving me of victory.' The delusion of grandeur is wrapped ingeniously around a delusion of persecution. Already we see that Quixote's madness establishes a more vivid connection between himself and the magical operations of the preternatural world of chivalric stories than the prosaic reality of the landscape and villages of La Mancha, where windmills are common for grinding grain. The connection and its mechanism is 'transformation,' the very procedure that in chivalric romance survived from its origins in primitive mythology. The insertion of this entirely 'fictional' element—transformation—as the antithesis to an everyday reality is both the surprise and consequence of Quixote's autonomy in mind and action. Quixote, then, will act and rationalize according to the release of an imaginative and emotional vehemence dominated by his madness; the author, exemplary in this respect also, has withdrawn from any claim to motivate his character.

But Quixote as autonomous character is only one half of a narrative unfolding that separates and distances him from the all-seeing, all-knowing author. And although one half, still the better or riper. Contemporary criticism has had much more to say about the authorial devices employed or hit upon by Cervantes than about the autonomy of Quixote. So much so that one suspects the cart has been put ahead of the horse. Cervantes' authorial devices would not amount to a fraction of what some critics think if their result were not the fictional autonomy of his characters. Up to now we have followed an account both comical and exemplary with few and stray indications to suppose that it was in some way related to the style of a chronicle or history of chivalric feats. Now the exemplary account will unfold to reveal the basis for our suppositions.

On the afternoon following the windmill episode Quixote and Sancho arrive at the crossroads known as Puerto Lápice (the Pass of Lápice), where his combat with the Biscayan takes place. The exemplary author tells it in such a way (ironical) that what we look on is a real but comical combat between two cholerics, and bordering on murderous rage. Their rage and exertion are real, and should have decided the battle. But here the parody has shifted to envelope the two mounts. The Biscayan is riding on a 'hired mule,' from the local 'rent-a-mule' no doubt, and the least dependable mount on which to fight with sword and shield. This of course Quixote cannot perceive; his own imitation is on the lofty level of heroic and passionate exertion. In chivalric stories a mighty combat between two knights equal or nearly equal in strength and fighting skill is often decided by the footing, turn, or even temper of the horse of one of them.

When the battle between Quixote and the Biscayan is at its height, the author suddenly breaks off the account, declaring that he possesses no more of the story, thus confessing that it is not 'original' with him. When (in the following chapter) he completes the description of the battle, he does so as a *second* author who is retelling Quixote's adventures from a translated version of an original in Arabic. The reader who has kept in mind Cervantes' Prologue to Part I will recognize the personal tone and use of the first person in this second author's revelations. He will also understand better why, in the Prologue, he called himself not "father" but "stepfather" to his character. But of course Cervantes is striving to create one more illusion, that the Arabic historian Cide Hamete Benengeli he now introduces is the 'creator' and perhaps 'father' of Don Quixote, since he is his 'first' author and historian of his exploits. We should approach the whole device and technique of multiple authorships as one more element of Cervantes' invention, of his originality in storytelling. Of course the feature that most interests modern readers is the 'self-conscious' dimension of the whole. This feature provides not only a subtle flexibility, an ambiguity and a complex authorial verisimilitude to an exemplary story already underway, but is also a further advance toward the separation of character and authors. For what has the author to be 'self-conscious' about, if not his sustained illusion of an autonomous world and its characters? Even its animals. For the 'hired mule' whose fear and panic 'decides' the combat between Quixote and the Basque has of course also acted 'autonomously.' It was no preconception, no predetermination, on the part of the authors that this beast should 'decide' the incident, nor that in doing so should show any resemblance to those animals whose acts and whims decide combats in chivalric stories.

It is important to observe that the "historian" of Quixote's exploits, Cide Hamete Benengeli, has come into the story directly from the mind of the mad hidalgo. He literally calls him into existence in those invocations of chapter 2. For this reason, initially, the so-called "history" must be seen as inscribed within the exemplary story, though the unfolding of Part Two (1615) will describe the inverse. The great novelty of Cervantes' story is that, in order to disclose and account for the hidalgo's transformation, it reveals almost nothing about the first fifty years of his life and even justifies this exclusion in the name of truth. But of course the whole life span of the hidalgo is not what Cide Hamete knows or writes about. Cide Hamete, whether we think of him as a pseudo-historian, pseudo-author, or 'fictitious' author, is the historian of Quixote's chivalric deeds and of his rise to fame; he could not have existed prior to Don Quixote's chivalric identity, or better put, prior to his madness. He comes into existence, so to speak, out of that madness and identity. He is really a prolongation of the parody of chivalry and of chivalric styles of narrative initiated by the hidalgo in chapter 2. As such he betrays his "ingenious" origins variously.

History of Don Quixote de la Mancha, written by Cide Hamete Benengeli, Arabic historian. In chapter 9 we learn its title and author, an Arabic historian with some claim to the exotic nature of other chroniclers of chivalric deeds (Xarton for *Lepolemo*, Fristón for *Don Belianís de Grecia*); but he is also 'modern,' that is to say, a contemporary of La Mancha. One can presume that his Arabic is not too pure or classical. An "Arabic historian" knowledgeable about La Mancha in Cervantes' time is just as likely to be a Morisco, as is the boy who does the translation of the original into Castilian. In chapter 16 we are given the mocking detail that Cide Hamete knows a great deal about the carrier in the inn, and is said to be a relative of his. We surmise that like the carrier—an occupation monopolized by Moriscos—Cid Hamete is also Morisco, and his exoticism of the same kind as Dulcinea's.

This then is another point about which the narrator of the whole may be 'self-conscious,' for he is reporting on a document (the original Arabic version) suspect for its lack of Arabic purity or genuineness, and also decidedly 'fictitious' for its naive reporting of Quixote's feats. The only narrator who uses 'I,' who speaks or writes directly in the first person, is the second author, who may also be thought of as responsible for the exemplary story. All of Cide Hamete's comments are reported or cited: he never speaks directly to the reader as does the second author.

9. Pastoral Interlude   Chs 11-14

Of the various threads that sustain Cervantes' exemplary idea across scenes and episodes the most important is the unfolding of Quixote's madness and humor in occasioned outbursts of choler and imaginative conceits, the rise and fall of his psychosomatic states. Closely tied to this are other aspects of his character: the release and expression of exalted feeling, not only arrogance and pride but also sympathy and compassion. His imaginative capacity to sustain both a picture of himself as hero of action and feeling and the social and physical surroundings that accompany him is another thread. All these are closely related to the course of cause and effect in adventures that while linking one episode to the next unfold the psycho-moral characterization of Quixote and, to a lesser extent, of Sancho and others.

After each of the hidalgo's violent expenditures of choler there follows a period of relative calm. His most violent outbursts occur early in the story. They lessen gradually. As the periods of calm become more extended the hidalgo begins to show increasing signs of a depression that becomes eventually an acute melancholy. His choleric outbursts have reached a new pitch of intensity in the fight with the Basque, and, whether because of the rather serious cut on his ear or because a feeling of triumph has momentarily satisfied his thrust for adventure, after leaving the scene at Lápice, there follows a period of calm that lasts for two days. At this point in the story Cervantes introduces a pastoral interlude.

The goatherds Quixote and Sancho meet that night are an intrinsic part of the life and landscape of La Mancha. They represent its social reality and are no intrusion in the story. The same cannot be said about the 'feigned' shepherds and shepherdesses who live in the countryside among the goatherds. They are more 'literary' and belong in several respects to the pastoral conventions of sixteenth-century literature. But as he moves among goatherds and shepherds Quixote can feel that he moves in a social world in harmony with his chivalric fixation. This pastoral world appeals to his imaginative perception of reality, and he make no effort to transfigure or disfigure it. He does interpret it in terms of his 'profession,' in his discourse on the Golden Age. There are several reasons why Quixote can feel a kinship between the chivalric and the pastoral. As he sees them they are both versions of idealistic fiction as well as of idealized reality.

While one employs and justifies violence to subdue violence and evil, the other aspires to a harmonious peace with nature. But Quixote has the ingenuity to construe that what they have in common is a passionate conception of erotic love. For this reason it is important to recall that the appearance of shepherds and goatherds, and other rural and pastoral figures, were common in chivalric romance from its earliest period in the Middle Ages.

Hence Quixote's declamations in his discourse on the Golden Age express his poetic conception of the fusion of the two life styles. But while the discourse reveals an inner turbulence gathered to a calm, it also reveals a certain passivity. In the social grouping of goatherds and shepherds there is no provocation to rash or mad acts; his intervention in the pastoral incident that unfolds will be minimal. Yet the significance of the episode is that Cervantes has brought his character face-to-face with a complex social reality so drawn that Quixote can note and share in its emotional—erotic—vehemence, but can hardly intervene to redress or solve it. The period of calm is an interlude for the fact that Quixote, passive but interested, can observe and share feelings.

It is apparent that Cervantes' main interest in the episode was to put his character in touch with men and women of feeling and sensitivity. Of course the most feeling and sensitive are lovers. But in this case the lover is dead. Chrysostom has committed suicide out of his all-but-pathological despair over Marcela's rejection of him. In an almost secret way Chrysostom is both a parallel and a contrast to Quixote. Both are from the same social class. But Chrysostom's family had wealth and provided him with an education so attuned to his spirit that he turned poet and sage, and then, attracted fatally by Marcela's beauty, to a 'literary' life style. He is not a shepherd for a livelihood, but out of a passionate anxiety. In his case the force of erotic love was of such vehemence that, struck by Marcela's coldness, it drew him to the egocentric, suicidal act. But more, his passionate courting, poetry, and death have been eminently 'literary.'

As a pastoral romance and fable the Chrysostom-Marcela episode is a tragic case of an unrequited love.[25] Marcela, however, did not take up the care of sheep for any sexual or erotic motive. Rather the reverse: she finds in the solitude of fields and hills the indispensable state for the preservation of her freedom and chastity. She is a woman 'liberated' from both family and Church (she could have found a place in a convent) in that she neither needs nor wants the care of either for the fulfilment of her womanhood. Hence feeling and knowing no erotic needs or motives, she can express none: I mean she expresses her ideal and desires in pastoral living in purely intellectual and dialectical terms, in contrast to Chrysostom, who expresses his love and despair in poetry with hopeless male erotic vehemence. As a case of 'unrequited love' they are enveloped in a bucolic or pastoral 'illusion' sustained by a literary tradition. Yet beneath their literary appearance is the reality of their social class and personal psychology. Chrysostom belongs to the class of hidalgos; he is financially 'independent' and has not yet chosen a vocation, except to be a shepherd in the hope of claiming Marcela's love. Her father was even wealthier than Chrysostom's, but of the "rich farmer" class ("ricos labradores"); her social standing is the same as Dorotea's. Marcela then does not have the class status of Chrysostom, but she is wealthier. How much did Cervantes mean to suggest in these details of an unequal relationship in spite of appearances, beauty, wealth, youth? Though far apart emotionally and sentimentally, the two are equals in sensitivity and intelligence. It was sex and the erotic that drove a cleavage between them.

The illusion of pastoral romance barely conceals the facts of their social reality. Like other Cervantine heroines, Marcela, for her beauty and attraction, may be supposed to have reached the age of late adolescence. She may be as young as sixteen and no more than nineteen. But Chrysostom was a mature man of thirty or more, nearly middle-aged. An older man was attracted to and courted desperately a girl who could have felt no erotic interest in him.

What I am stressing is that neither Marcela nor Chrysostom can be understood simply as pastoral figures, and their attitude toward love and sex in only one dimension. In terms of the extremes of their arbitrary acts they border on the abnormal and pathological. Nothing revealed about or by Marcela excludes the possiblity that her brave and ideal concept of chastity and freedom are not the rationalization of a frigid woman, incapable of sexual feelings; a deviant of sorts content to have 'friendships' with male friends in the socially unconventional setting of pastoral life. The delicate and sensitive abnormity of Marcela's position (but abnormity no less), indicates her parallel to Quixote's madness, to his social alienation and extreme individualism.

The entire episode, moreover, takes place, or has taken place, on the fringes of socially acceptable behavior and religious orthodoxy, and this is its other parallel to Quixote's adventures. The reasons for Chrysostom's suicide, as well as the act itself and his decision to be buried in a wild place, have placed his remains and his soul beyond the authority and sacraments of the Church. His burial is carried out according to his instructions as a pagan ceremony. He was learned in astrology, as Quixote says. All we know about him we learn indirectly from others and from his poems, but what we know suggests that his poetic and intellectual gifts tended toward the profane and secular, and once attracted to Marcela, became outright pagan. His poetry shows no evidence of belief in or feeling for Christian forgiveness or redemption. He carried to an almost pathological insistence, in the face of her rejection of any erotic or sentimental entreaty, his desire to 'eternalize' Marcela in his verse. His personal despair was thorough, not only emotional or erotic but moral and philosophical. One may wonder whether it was not already anxiety and despair of middle age that drove him to surrender so vehemently to the love for a young girl. Unlike Quixote, who is mad, Chrysostom was driven by love, will and imagination to possess a feminine ideal in a beautiful woman of flesh and bone, of mind and body. His suffering, as expressed in his last poem (where he says he will hang himself), was material and spiritual, sexual and lyrical. He attempted to live and love according to and for a purely personal ideal, and killed himself for it. Marcela's ideal of purity and freedom is equally personal, secular or profane, and unorthodox; but as a woman she feels no dependence on males, for sexual or social desires or needs. After her proud defense she disappears; Quixote attempts to follow her, supposing she needs him to defend her right. He cannot recognize that Marcela is the woman and damsel who refutes his notion of defenseless feminine virtue, his idea on erotic love stated in the discourse on the Golden Age.

As pastoral romance or novelistic pastoral the interlude remains an explicitly serious fiction within the exemplary story. Cervantes gives to his pastoral characters all the solemnity of tradition, and the outcome of their story bears the significance of the tragic erotic. He has placed his hidalgo as listener and observer in a social reality that is complex and real. In the interacting of lives that is Chrysostom's and Marcela's story we have a picture of contemporary life drawn to a scale nearly as large as the hidalgo's. And as a picture of contemporary life in at least one respect on a higher plane. In their story the erotic is treated seriously and its outcome is tragic. Within the episode, when Quixote's illusion dominates the erotic and sexual in

50   *The Exemplary Story*

chivalry the treatment becomes comical. In the conversation with Vivaldo on the way to the burial Quixote was pressed to justify his profession, and the center of his defense was of course his love and service to Dulcinea. His reply convinced everyone he was mad. Yet no sane author or poet could have given a more exact justification of chivalric romance; his defense of it is comical in that chivalry as illusion fulfills itself entirely in literary terms, in images, incantations, and adventures. And Dulcinea is preeminently the image of ideal womanhood.

Immediately following the serious treatment of erotic love Cervantes gives us its comical version. He begins by reducing the sexual to the level of animal attraction.

10. The Love Adventure   Chs 15-17

After a futile search for Marcela, Quixote and Sancho come to a pleasant meadow of fresh grass with a stream nearby; here they decide to pass the sultry hours of the afternoon; they have come upon the *'locus amoenus'* 'the pleasant place,' of their own bucolic incident. These pleasant natural surroundings excite and incite the senses. From not too far away there comes to the nostrils of Rocinante the scent and attraction of mares. And since Sancho, unawares that so underfed a horse was oversexed, didn't trouble to tie him, Rocinante took off to join the mares. They (like Marcela) are not interested in sex at this hour and reject him with kicks and bites, break his girths, and leave him stripped of his saddle, and "naked" ("en pelote"). Their owners, some carriers, wrathful rustics from Yanguas, rush to defend their mares and beat Rocinante to the ground with sticks. At this point Quixote and Sancho rush to aid their beast and are in turn thoroughly thwacked by the carriers, and are left stretched out alongside the animal.

The severe drubbing they take is comical action that frames the scene's exemplary sense. A sexual instinct in his beast has resulted in a severe beating for the hidalgo and his squire. We are now in the element of sensation and instincts, of physical contact, violence and pain, of the flesh, glands, senses and organs of the body.

While prostrate, and between moans, Quixote promises to provide Sancho with the cure-all, the balsam of Fierabrás. This as been the first beating Sancho has suffered on this trip and his shock is tremendous. Quixote and Rocinante are so badly bruised they cannot travel together. With his master slung over Dapple's back, Sancho leads them to an inn where they expect to have their sore bodies treated. There the sensations running through Quixote's body will be intensified by the touch of female hands. The innkeeper's wife, his daughter and Maritornes apply plasters. The contact, the intimacy, the touch of female hands on his hurt ribs, arouse, if not instincts, fantasies in the hidalgo. He begins to imagine the love adventure. Having arrived at a castle and been greeted as a wounded knight and touched by woman's hands, his erotic fantasy traces the outlines of the adventure adequate to his condition: a bed-ridden knight accosted by a love-smitten princess.

The situation Quixote imagines recalls the narrative in Book I of *Amadís of Gaul*, and resembles incidents recounted in others. In *Amadís*, Helisena (the pious, chaste daughter of King Garínter) and King Perión, a guest in her father's castle, are drawn to each other irresistibly by an overwhelming passion. She reveals her secret to Darioleta, her damsel, who then, by discreet cunning, overcomes all obstacles and arranges to bring her mistress by a hidden entry and in the silence of night to his chamber and bed, where their secret marriage is consummated (and Amadís conceived). Quixote fantasizes that the innkeeper's daughter is the princess overcome by his attraction, and lying on his make-shift bed in the loft, conceives the 'literary' situation of an illicit, irrepressible passion aroused in the female by a manly, though chaste (and sexually passive) knight. Once again an overt parody of chivalric romance occurs in Quixote's 'ingenious' conceit, now empowered by the full force of a body wracked by pain and delirium. While the chivalric and romantic elements are enveloped in Quixote's parody, the exemplary story gives us the hilarious 'love adventure' as sensory experience.

When Maritornes approaches his bed, Quixote's mind and senses are already heightened by imaginative conceit; in his imagination he sees (and feels, smells, touches) a divine-like female; yet like a psychopath he forcibly restrains her at his bed. The original of this situation in chivalric romance would depict a sensuous woman with an overpowering aura of seductive sensuality, all the more alluring for the forbidden, secret and illicit nature of the encounter. As an exemplary re-creation of it we have sexual adventure as a sensory experience, with due attention to all the senses involved in close contact of two bodies. Quixote's senses are aroused to experience what his fervid imagination releases as image and sensation, while we have only the repellant picture of Maritornes before us. The comical erotic resides in the discrepancy between what Quixote parodies and what he and we have before us as evidence of the senses. As a 'literary' product the adventure is all the more ludicrous for the fact that its erotic motives as conceived by Quixote are secret and illicit, for in this way they correspond to his notion of what he must repress in the very act of expressing it.

Maritornes is on her way to the carrier's bed. The coarse carnality, the promiscuity of her sexual habits with guests at the inn have no bearing on Quixote's purely 'imaginative' sensations. He verily feels silk, perceives pearls, golden tresses, perfumes, scented breath; he cannot be undeceived. But he has needed the closeness of a feminine body to imagine it all. Hence the question, does he really feel an erotic impulse, is the love adventure real or imagined for him? Too often a reader here gets distracted by what he perceives to be the object of satire: the idealistic conception of amorous passion. Hence he often fails to note that Quixote's 'conceit,' entirely consistent within its literary suggestions, is an 'autonomous parody' entirely incidental to what goes on in the inn, or to the contents of the books he imitates. Cervantes emphasizes the nauseous presence of Maritornes as seductress, not because he is satirizing a literary convention, but because he means to outdo all rivals in the representation of the erotic as physical sensation, from the ethereal odors a woman's body emanates to a man's reactions in the secretion of glands. To this end we have Quixote bruised and battered, but physically alive on his make-shift bed.

Tentóle luego la camisa y, aunque ella era de harpillera, a él le pareció ser de finísimo y delgado cendal. Traía en las muñecas unas cuentas de vidrio; pero a él le dieron vislumbres de preciosas perlas orientales. Los cabellos, que en alguna manera tiraban a crines, él los marcó por hebras de lucidísimo oro de Arabia, cuyo resplandor al del mesmo sol escurecía. Y el aliento, que, sin duda alguna, olía a ensalada fiambre y trasnochada, a él le pareció que arrojaba de su boca un olor suave y aromático. I. 16, 203

Then he felt her shift and, though it was of sackcloth, to him it seemed of the finest, most delicate satin. She was wearing on her wrists some glass beads; he fancied they were rare oriental pearls. Her hair, which was almost as coarse as a horse's mane, he took to be strands of the most glistening gold of Arabia, whose splendour eclipsed the very sun. And her breath, no doubt reeking of last night's stale salad, seemed to him to shed a sweet and aromatic fragrance.

11. Male Chastity

The occasion, moreover, serves to set off one of the book's major sexual themes. If Quixote imagines a scene where he plays the passive role, the wounded knight accosted by the aggressive female, this is because the occasion fits into the larger and complex image of himself in love. We have noted that, although he conceives for himself the role of enamored knight, his madness provides for the expression of it exclusively in terms of loyalty, submission, and service to Dulcinea; an idolatry so extreme as to eliminate any idea of sexual gratification. His madness imposes certain taboos: he may not (is not worthy to) approach Dulcinea directly, hence he circumvents any idea of going directly to El Toboso; he may address her only in a certain way and for a certain purpose. Above all, he is pledged to her on behalf of a lofty concept of manhood—chastity. This is curiously quixotic, of course, original with him, nonexistent in the books he imitates:

> y, teniendo toda esta quimera, que él se había fabricado, por firme y valedera, se comenzó a acuitar y a pensar en el peligroso trance en que su honestidad se había de ver, y propuso en su corazón de no cometer alevosía a su señora Dulcinea del Toboso, aunque la mesma reina Ginebra con su dama Quintañona se le pusieran delante. I. 16, 202-3

> and taking all this chimera which he had fabricated for the sober truth, he began to feel anxious as he reflected on the perils to which his honor and chastity were exposed, and he resolved in his heart to commit no treason against his lady Dulcinea del Toboso, even though Queen Guinevere herself and her lady Quintañona should appear before him.

In the representation of the erotic as sensory experience Cervantes has carried out more than one inversion of traditional elements. But surely the most comical is the inversion of the roles of aggressive and passive partner, of female modesty and male chastity. In *Amadís*, as in literature in general, not male but female modesty and chastity is the moral question and poetic theme. But in Arthurian romance, where love and sexual attraction may ignite passion with the power of a magical spell, the chaste and pious woman once aroused to sexual ardor (like Helisena) may take the initiative, and then her own modesty is the major obstacle she must overcome to approach the man of her choice. Quixote thinks he will be threatened by the woman beside his bed because, in his conceit, he is irresistible, and has aroused the princess to an act that endangers his 'chaste' loyalty to Dulcinea.

Now the typical knight (but not Amadís) in this situation would willingly oblige the enamored princess. But even while doing so the typical knight is in a position of condescending, of relative weakness, for in erotic matters, so to speak, he is not in his own element. This is the gist of Quixote's apt, even elegant phrasing. In this feminine element his will and power are subject to forces beyond his control, to instinct, to sensation, to sentiment. In affairs of the heart the knight is not his own master; he is submissive, passive. There was then an implied weakness in the depiction of warriors in sexual and amorous scenes, particularly in bed, as the story of Lancelot bears out. It is this possibility that Cervantes exploits, by a total inversion.

In the medieval tradition, with its monachal and sacerdotal emphasis and bias, male chastity is potentially a most serious question. For many medieval authors the subject is solemn and moral, even tragic. Woman is an unclean and sinful creature; or, if chaste and saintly, an angelic purifier; chastity is linked to ascetic and penitential practices and beliefs. It is above all, and on all occasions, serious.

Nowhere does Cervantes reveal with more success his modernity than in Quixote's comical inversion. For the supreme way to make sex and chastity comical is to make male chastity an object of wit. Cervantes' witty conceit is to depict Quixote as the "chastest knight that ever was in La Mancha." What Cervantes intuited as comical was the supposition inherent in the whole idea that a man's chastity could be threatened by a woman. A man might be tricked, seduced, or bewitched by a woman, but he cannot be 'forced' by her. Nature herself has designed the threat the other way. Quixote, the middle-aged abstainer, laid out like a convalescent, conceives that the presence of a sensuous woman at his bedside is a threat to his chastity, not because he lacks moral strength to resist temptation and seduction but because she can 'force' him, having been aroused to bewitch and intoxicate. But of course his 'conceit' is a smoke screen, concealing a psychological depth that is also comical. How far 'down' do we need to go to perceive that Quixote's pleadings to the vision of divine beauty (Maritornes) are an unconscious admission of inadequacy?

Cervantes' scene is the indispensable antecedent to Fielding's scenes, in which the virtue (virginity) of young boys is threatened by the predatory wiles and charms of older women; but Fielding has at least made a motion toward naturalizing the situation. The Englishman's wit in this matter is the equal of Cervantes' because Quixote will always appear grotesque in his own fantasies. If we feel that in this scene Quixote appears too ridiculous, perhaps the reason is that here Cervantes' wit and exemplary story are both author and master to Quixote's parody.

12. Comic Movement

Nothing is more misleading about the episode in the inn than the farcical surface—the fistcuffs in the dark, beatings and vomits—in this comedy of eros, or erotic adventure gone amok. The surface is nearly pure farce, but just beneath the surface and extending to great depth, there is Cervantes' exemplary depicition and aim.[26] Or better still, its direction. For the thrust of Cervantes' story at this point is one and the same with movement that swings from the ethereal images of Quixote's fantasy to the sweaty organism that is Sancho's body. The structural notion is that of movement, physical and eventually organic, from body to body, but toward one body in particular. It can be described as a kind of law that determines that adventure as sensory experience will gravitate, from its origins in the erotic images of Quixote and his sensations, toward the corpulent, watery weight of Sancho, and with dire accuracy toward the digestive organs, incorporating as well flesh, glands, and entrails. Quixote's imagination is set free, but the sense of adventure swings to Sancho's body, as if to declare that erotic feeling gravitates from the heart to the digestive organs. This schema of patho-biology is generated where sex and magic interact, from the mind to the heart to the digestive tract.

In this episode Cervantes devised the comic principle that was to sustain his story of contrasts to a triumph of inventive storytelling in Part Two: given that the adventure of chivalry is born of Don Quixote's fantasy, once released it will inevitably swing to and toward Sancho's body, as if drawn by the gravitational pull of the mass and weight of his rotundity; the sense of an adventure is drawn into orbit around that fleshiness, so that the reader is unable to separate the idea of chivalric adventure, nor Quixote to extricate his fantasy from the presence of Sancho's body, with its wants and urges, protective defenses, thirsts and unrelenting hunger, indeed its very physiological functions, from ingestion to evacuation.

Bearing in mind that we are tracing a structural procedure as well as a technique, it is worth our while to follow this movement in some detail. When Quixote restrains Maritornes, and utters into her ear his pleadings, the carrier suspects a trick or treachery to deprive his lusts, and creeps toward the bed, and, when he sees Maritornes struggling to free herself, he gives Quixote a terrific blow on the jaws, then jumps on him and tramples his sore ribs. The bed breaks with a crash. This wakes the innkeeper, who calls out to Maritornes, who, when she hears his steps approaching, looks for a place to hide. She jumps into precisely Sancho's bed. Why there? Was there no other place to hide?

Sancho awakens and begins to beat off what he thinks is a nightmare. She hits back and they scuffle. The carrier then comes over to help her, while the innkeeper comes over to beat her. All the action is now on Sancho's bed. When the noise of the tremendous scuffle awakens and draws the officer of the Holy Brotherhood, Quixote is lying in a swoon on his bed, so that the officer takes him for dead and calls out an alarm. This stops the brawl; the officer lets go Quixote's beard and goes out to find a light.

Quixote awakens and calls out piteously to Sancho, who replies in a grievious tone. Quixote's so-called erotic adventure has led to another severe beating for both, but of course Sancho cannot fathom this. At this point Quixote interjects the idea of a magical enchantment to explain the pain and outcome: the hand of a monstrous giant has pounded him mercilessly. Sancho complains he too was mauled. Quixote will now make the magical balsam that will cure them. Every suggestion of an 'adventure' originates in Quixote's mind, but eventually, by direction of comical movement, finds its center of gravity in Sancho's fleshiness.

The 'magical' balsam, in Quixote's mind, will restore the body's health and vigor; it is a 'cure' for scuffs, blows, drubbings and whacks. When Quixote drinks down a good portion of it, in the presence of Sancho, the innkeeper and the officer, its effect on his stomach (predictable for the ingredients mixed in it: oil, wine, salt and rosemary) is a violent vomiting that cleans out his inards, then a heavy sweat, which puts him to sleep for several hours. On waking, he is convinced the balsam has worked according to its magical

The Exemplary Story 57

properties. Sancho is amazed by his cure, and calls it a miracle; he begs for and swallows the remainder.

> Es, pues, el caso que el estómago del pobre Sancho no debía de ser tan delicado como el de su amo, y así, primero que vomitase, le dieron tantas ansias y bascas, con tantos trasudores y desmayos, que él pensó bien y verdaderamente que era llegada su última hora; y viéndose tan afligido y congojado, maldecía el bálsamo y al ladrón que se lo había dado. . . .
> En esto hizo su operación el brebaje, y comenzó el pobre escudero a desaguarse por entrambas canales, con tanta priesa, que la estera de enea, sobre quien se había vuelto a echar, ni la manta de anjeo con que se cubría, fueron más de provecho. Sudaba y trasudaba con tales parasismos y accidentes, que no solamenta él, sino todos pensaron que se le acababa la vida. Duróle esta borrasca y mala andanza casi dos horas, al cabo de las cuales no quedó como su amo, sino tan molido y quebrantado, que no se podía tener. I. 19, 211

> Sancho's poor stomach was not so delicate as his master's, and so before he could vomit he was racked by so many bouts of writhes and pangs, so many sweats and swoons, that he thought that surely his last hour had come; and in his agony and dismay he cursed the balsam and the scoundrel who he given it to him. . . .
> At this point the beverage began to work, and the poor squire began to discharge at both ends, so swiftly and violently that neither the rush mat on which he had thrown himself nor the coarse blanket with which he covered himself were of any use to him. He sweated and sweated in such a paroxysm of strains and stresses that not only himself but all present thought he was on the point of dying. This hurricane of misery lasted almost two hours, and at the end of which time he found himself not cured like his master but so shaken and shattered that he could not stand.

In the first instance of movement, from Quixote's erotic fantasy to Sancho's body, there were blows, cuffs, and whacks. The second instance adds magic to sex, with a disastrous outcome for Sancho; for, by the law of comic movement that determines cause and effect, the test of adventure is ultimately applied to Sancho's physiology, as if to reduce the adventure to the most senseful of corporality. In the love adventure the themes of love and magic are made to revolve around the biological functions of glands and organs of knight and squire, from the effect of ethereal spells (feminine odors) to the vomit instigated by the ingredients in the balsam (magic reduced to folk chemistry).

From sex to magic to entrails: ultimately Sancho's body with its fleshy sensitivity is the test of adventure, because it produces the most comical effect. Yet Quixote takes this turn of events as magic and enchantments; ". . . todo este mal te viene de no ser armado caballero

... que este licor no debe aprovechar a los que no lo son" [... all this pain comes from your not being a knight ... for this liquor can be of no benefit to any that are not]. This appeals to Sancho's reason in the form of superstition; but his pained and wracked body feels every hurt, and the magic of the balsam is reduced to the crudest biochemical effect in his entrails.

The third instance arises when they leave the inn. Quixote refuses to believe the enchanted castle has been an inn all the time, refuses to pay the innkeeper, and rides out of the courtyard. Sancho's bad luck, when he tries to imitate his master, is to become the plaything of the roguish crowd. His blanketing, his graceful ups and downs, accompanied by shrieks and pleas, seen by Quixote from outside the yard, underscore and recapitulate the comical movement and sense of adventure; these are attached to, and inseparable from, his rounded physiology. Quixote will insist that it was all enchantment, for he was powerless to come to his squire's aid. Sancho is staggered by the price the life of adventure will exact from his ribs, rump and entrails.

Quixote's imagination grasps the full sense of his stay at the inn as a chivalric adventure; indeed his is the only mind capable of making sense of any and all of its details. Sancho can interpret what he saw and felt only in terms of the physical pain and discomfort endured by his squeamish flesh. Cervantes has drawn a series of contrasts between his characters in terms of mind, idiosyncrasy and body; his comic movement provides a superb symbiotic meshing that will sustain his story to the end.

13. The War Adventure   Ch 18

Only the windmill episode has impressed itself on the universal imagination with greater force and permanence than the episode of Quixote's attack on the sheepflocks, which he takes for armies. The two episodes have several features in common; they follow a similar trajectory, from a sighting (visual stimulus, error of perception), to a charge and an outcome, the whole a release and unfolding of delirium. The windmill episode may contain a greater store of possible symbolic allusion, yet as part of the story's unfolding it remains largely schematic, while the sheep episode, perhaps because it gathers so many thematic threads, is the more complete. Indeed, in

The Exemplary Story 59

at least one sense it represents a climax and a turning point. One may even think of it as the prototypal adventure of Part One.

The suddenness with which Cervantes presents us with the full development of his techniques, themes and situations should never cease to amaze. Nearly all the features noted in the earlier episodes are here caught up and made to reveal new possibilities. As the usual preliminary, the dialogue between Quixote and Sancho recapitulates the adventure just concluded: Quixote is ready for action, having regained confidence by the effect of the balsam, which he carries with him in a vial. Sancho's spirits are low; the blanketing has confused for him the whole idea and aims of chivalry. In his exhilaration Quixote extols the spirit of war and the glories of victory. At this instant he sights a large cloud on the plain. The visual stimulus is all-powerful and decisive; it indicates that adventure as sense perception will follow the ascending trajectory of imaginative exaltation to the moment of charge and physical contact. Unlike the adventure of the windmills, it is not over in a flash. On the contrary, it is prolonged while Quixote describes the imagined coming together of two warring hordes and their leaders.

The exemplary technique places the autonomous character before a visual stimulus—the billowing dust clouds. We do not have simply an opposition between appearance (or illusion) and reality, but an opposition between what Quixote's imagination, once aroused, can conceive and depict as a reality (moral, physical) to itself and what the dust clouds signify to the narrator. Quixote's imaginative conceit is centered in a paranoid delusion about himself, which on this particular occasion demands a vivid and full description of knights arrayed for battle, as if the occasion were an epic scene or stage, all preparatory to the moment when he will charge at the enemy and decide the outcome. Before he charges, as the protagonist of the scene he must describe it because he must create it like a poet, an epic poet. Psychologically this might be explained as one of those instances in which a demented subject 'plays' at situations, convinced of his own vivid description of it as senseful and dramatic reality; or as a child's game of wishful day dreaming. But as an exemplary unfolding of mind and character Quixote's description of the armies moves on a much higher plane, on the level of his literary insanity. We know that as an imaginative choleric he can combine imaginative or 'poetic' motivations for war with physical exertions, that he can explode suddenly, at any provocation, real or imagined, into furor of passionate action. Here he explodes not only with the fury of the insane, but with *furor poeticus* of the inspired. Here the exemplary depiction of him gives us a grotesque fusion of warlike fury and poetic, that is, verbal exaltation.

Since what he has before him is a large portion of the Manchegan plain, the scene he describes takes on, in his mind, the vast scale of an epic battle that encompasses continents, nations, and diverse peoples. As the unfolding of a state of mind within an exemplary depiction it is the high point of Quixote's delirium systemized as extravagant poetic conceit; as a comical situation, the reduction of the epic of chivalry to the utterly prosaic and ridiculous. Yet it is poetic, for its 'kernel' is authentic poetry. The hidalgo has the undoubted gift of reducing to its comical essence the great poetic outlines of the chivalric modes he emulates. His imagination contracts time and history and enlarges one human problem—the marriage of Pentapolín's daughter—to the scale of universal, epic conflict. The scene he describes is neither medieval nor ancient, but both, contained by the power of mytho-poetic creation. What is most fascinating and exquisite about his conceit is that, like all mytho-poetic creation, its nucleus is a 'story' or 'myth,' here of course the 'story' or 'myth' of the knight Don Quixote. Now this 'myth,' as a projection of his ego, is one and the same with the systemized delusions of his madness, above all delusion of grandeur. It is the 'myth' of a hero-knight of elect status, whose feats of invincibility have already won for him an ageless renown. By his powerful charismatic presence alone this knight is capable of ensuring victory to whichever side he choses to fight with.

As in the medieval epic a pagan army is arrayed against the army of a Christian king. The cause for war is one of those situations embroidered by Italian poets of the Renaissance, above all Ariosto: the pagan emperor Alifanfarón is enamored of the Christian king Pentapolín's daughter, but refuses to renounce his Islamic faith in order to marry her. Quixote's invention, his 'fiction,' is beyond verisimilitude; it is 'pure' poetry, pure invention. It consists of an enumeration or 'catalogue,' in the style of the great epic poets, and unfolds according to a symmetrical and hierarchical design. In modern terms it can be called an 'artifice.' It will prove instructive to point out just what Quixote describes. He does not describe actual combat, nor machines of war, nor tactics; he enumerates and describes warriors as 'characters,' that is, their peculiar characteristics, physical, emotional or psychological, as typified by their weapons, devices or emblems of heraldry. Thus, while striving to 'typify' each of the leading knights, his conceits strain the very idea they attempt to express. The epico-heroic figures are over-sized and peculiar to a comic degree: "... el otro de los miembros giganteos ... es el nunca medroso Brandabarbarán de Boliche ...'" "Timonel de Carcajona ... viene armado con las armas partidas a cuarteles, azules, verdes, blancas y amarillas, y trae en el escudo un gato de oro en campo leonado con una letra que dice: *Miau*, que es el principio del nombre de su dama, que, según se dice, es la sin par Miulina...." [the other with gigantic limbs ... is the undaunted Brandabarbarán de Boliche ...; Timonel of Carcajona ... comes clad in armor quartered azure, vert, argent and gold, and bears on his shield a cat or on a field gules with a scroll inscribed *Miau*, which is the beginning of his mistress's name, who, so they say, is the peerless Miaulina....] What they add up to is a pictorially idiosyncratic notion of chivalry. As such it is the setting of his 'story' or 'myth.' While a parody of the epic style in chivalric romance, the substance of his enumeration is essentially 'inventive,' fictive. In other words, a genuine fiction of chivalry, and, despite its prose, poetic and mythical. The following outline suggests the order and symmetry of his 'artifice.'

Emperor	Knights	Nations & Provinces
	PAGANS	
Alifanfarón	Laurcalco Micocolembo Brandabarbarán	Pagan army composed of nations recorded in ancient history, legend. Trojans, Numidians, Persians, Parthians, Scythians, etc.
	CHRISTIANS	
Pentapolín	Timonel de Carcajona Pierres Papín Espartafilardo	Christian army composed of soldiers from provinces of Hispanic peninsula; Andalusians, Manchegans, Toledeans, Basques, etc.

His poetic conceits reach their zenith in the epithets and periphrases applied to soldiers from the Hispanic provinces. Of the ten regions of Hispania he alludes to, five are noted according to a principal river; three according to a plain; one, the Basque, according to a metal (iron), and the last according to a mountain range, the Pyrenees. The final periphrase describes inhabitants of the Apennines; moreover their army includes warriors from all the peoples of Europe, without distinction to historical periods, in short, a mythical grouping.

As the two flocks of sheep under the dust clouds have moved toward one another, Quixote's imaginative frenzy, his *furor poeticus*, has moved upward on an ascending line of poetic invention. Yet its climax is beyond image and conceit. Unlike the inspired poet who invents with words and sounds, Quixote has not just been 'inventing' but describing a reality of sensory perception, and which will oblige him to charge at the climactic moment. While declaiming and describing he approaches the sublime height of literary creator. On this level he is on a par with men of inspired genius whom we would admire almost without reservation. What happens in the next few minutes all-but obliterates this picture of him.

When he first sighted the dust cloud and conceived it to be an army on the march, Sancho, receptive to the idea, pointed out another cloud of dust approaching in the opposite direction. At that point Quixote led Sancho to a hilltop, from where he described the approaching armies. Sancho, then, has been caught up with the idea of armies and battle, and hangs on his words, until the clouds having moved into closer range, he perceives with shock that what his master has described as men are sheep. Failing to see any mounted knights or giants, he objects with dismayed protests. His master replies with vehemence: "Do you not hear the neighing of the horses, the blaring of the trumpets and the beating of drums?" He replies: "I hear only the bleating of sheep and rams."

In the exemplary depiction of the scene we have visual and auditory perception; movement, dusts, clashing sounds. Quixote does see forms and perceives sounds; he has not 'transformed' reality. He has invented on the basis of sense perception a reality that exists in his imagination alone, which surely qualifies as a 'mythical' reality. We may call it illusion or delusion, but, as we have already noted, even as illusion or delusion it partakes of genuine poetic creation. While he looks out from atop the hill and declaims his mythical battle, Quixote is inspired, even if mad; when, aroused to even greater frenzy by Sancho's doubts, he charges downhill onto the plain and into the flocks, he is superbly comical.

From the moment Sancho objected—"Señor, encomiendo al diablo hombre, ni gigante, ni caballero . . ." [Master, I'll commend to the devil any man, giant, or knight (I see)], the adventure as sensory experience has begun to swing from Quixote's frenzied imagination to Sancho. While Quixote is charging and killing sheep, Sancho on the hilltop, shouting cries of alarm and protest, provides the negative (and doubly comical) side of all Quixote has described. In his affected descriptions Quixote merely disfigured a literary convention of chivalry; Sancho's dehortations are that disfigurement reduced to comical debris: "Mire que no hay gigante ni caballero alguno, ni gatos, ni armas, ni escudos partidos ni enteros, ni veros azules ni endiablados." [Look, there is not a giant or knight, nor cats, nor arms, nor shield quartered or entire, nor azures true or bedeviled.]

The line of narrative sequence follows comic movement away from Quixote's fantasy to Sancho's body. The adventure as sense perception begins afar off; on perceiving the dust cloud Quixote conceived a battle about to take place in a legendary time and place; his charge was the action that made it real in terms of bodily blows, lance thrusts, and blood; he killed seven sheep. When the shepherds' shouts are to no avail, they pelt him with stones from their slings. A stone socks him in the ribs. His frenzy tells him he has been wounded: immediate recourse to the balsam that makes him invincible. He takes out his vial and swallows as much of the balsam as he can, until another stone knocks it out of his hand. Another blow knocks him from Rocinante to the ground. The shepherds, believing they have killed him, look him over, pick up their dead and move on. In all this furious action and physical assault not once has the narrator mentioned blood. The stones have battered Quixote's mouth and teeth. His mouth, having just ingested the balsam, is the center of interest as Sancho runs down the hillside to aid him, fearing he is dead. This fixation on the mouth, teeth and cavernous buccal cavity is exemplary. To Sancho's protestations about attacking sheep Quixote answers that again his adversary the evil enchanter, envious of his glory, has transformed the armies into sheep: delusion of grandeur and delusion of persecution.

Just after he mentions the magical explanation he asks Sancho to look into his mouth, for he fears he has lost all his teeth. Sancho peers into his open jaws. At this instant the balsam produces its effect.

The adventure, on the level of the physiological, has now swung to the lowest point, the level of biological functions of Sancho's body; Quixote vomits directly into his face. For a second the alarmed squire fears the worse, that his master is throwing up blood, then he recognizes by its color, taste, and odor (again sense perception) the balsam, and sickened by it all, he vomits also, into his master's face and beard. Comical movement swung from Quixote's conceits, to his wounds, to his magical balsam, and from there to the level of organic functions and reactions, from delirium to flesh organs; from Quixote's mouth and stomach to Sancho's, where the war adventure, having been reduced to purely physiological stimulus and reaction, ends. The sense of it was not blood, guts, and glory, only sickening vomit.

Yet the hidalgo's resources of character are never greater than now when, in this moment of squalor and humiliation, he replies to Sancho's new complaints at this miserable turn in their fortunes: "—Sábete, Sancho, que no es un hombre más que otro si no hace más que otro. Todas estas borrascas que nos suceden son señales de que presto ha de serenar el tiempo. . . ." [—I tell you, Sancho, one man is not worth more than another unless he does more than another. All those storms that come upon us are signs that soon the weather will be fair and things will go smoothly. . . .] War as a liberating and uplifting endeavor, the cry of battle, the fabulous and magical in Quixote's fantasy, are reduced by an exemplary art to the muck and stench of vomit. Why, to what end? we ask. Merely for the sake of comical reduction? A satire of chivalry? Or the exposure of war as a materialistic travesty of the ideal?

Many readers of a military and heroic bent have never forgiven the soldier Cervantes for even suggesting the comparison of fighting men to sheep. Perhaps if they reconsidered Quixote's reply (quoted above) they might find in it the suggestion that his author, looking beyond the comical, sought to cast heroism in a new mould.

14. The Ineffectual Hero   Chs. 19-21

The episodes of chapters 19, 20, and 21 carry to their zenith Quixote's exalted imagination and heroic exertion. Yet by degrees Cervantes begins to lay greater emphasis on his motives and intentions, thus less on the travesty of reality that his fantasy will conceive. The nocturnal adventure with the corpse, fulling-hammers, and the winning of Mambrino's helmet on the following morning, unfold as feats of individual courage and daring, incited by visual and auditory stimuli, and carried out in a variation of the pattern established by the exemplary depiction of Quixote's choler and by comical movement. The hidalgo's will and imagination are free (as they will never be again) to soar and elaborate on the mythos of his heroic role. His

The Exemplary Story 65

illusion is either thwarted or fulfilled, but to no great consequence. The three episodes, each a variation of fortuitous cause and effect and sense of adventure, fully depict the disparity between what he conceives the adventure to be and what really takes place, between his intentions which rise from a literary image of the situation and the outcome.

By now we expect the outcome to be pretty much the reverse of what Quixote expects: any attempt to carry out a chivalric adventure in the physical or 'real' sense is doomed to comic failure. The only possibility of success lies this side of material reality, in the adventure as a psychological possibility, or, more crucially, in moral implications. Now the test of adventure will lay less heavily on Quixote's imagination than on his will. As a consequence his adventures will take on social implications that cast his heroic and pathological exertions in a new light.

In the adventure of the corpse Quixote imagines that he has met with one of those adventures in which a wandering knight comes upon a procession bearing a corpse to its place of burial. On questioning the mourners the knight learns that the dead man is a knight slain by treacherous enemies. The wandering knight then assumes the obligation of avenging his death. This literary situation Quixote applies to a scene that is already phantasmal as sense perception (visual, auditory) for its mysterious and hair raising aspect, and moreover, *is* a funeral: there *is* a corpse. In other words, Cervantes' technique here is different, though not entirely new in the story. What Quixote and Sancho perceive is phantasmal: an eerie procession of torches and mounted men in black garments and white surplices, murmuring prayers as they move across the night's landscape. Quixote does not need to disfigure the scene in his imagination in order to fit it within the 'context' of a chivalric adventure. In fact his imagination and senses are overwhelmed; but the shock, horror and surprise quicken his mind to conceive that here (as a full saturation of the senses and challenge to the will) in all its ominous reality there awaits an adventurous encounter with a corpse.

One might with reason suppose that here Cervantes offered so singular a happening in Spanish life as to amount to a kind of distortion. A procession of priests on the Manchegan plain by night, bearing a corpse with pomp, torches and prayers, from a city in the south to burial two hunderd miles to the north, is as strange for its appearance as for its coincidence with Quixote's explanation of it. The deceased has died in Baeza and his remains are being carried to Segovia. A procession of this kind could not have been a usual sight, the case of windmills, sheep, fulling-hammers, and even a chain of galley slaves in La Mancha. However plausible (night has overtaken the procession before it can make its way to an inn where they expected to arrive before dark), as a phenomenon the procession is weird and terrifying, in a land where religious processions were common. "Esta estraña visión, a tales horas y en tal despoblado, bien bastaba para poner miedo en el corazón de Sancho, y aun en el de su amo. . . ." [This strange vision, appearing at such an hour and in such a desolate spot, was quite sufficient to strike terror into Sancho's heart and even into that of his master. . . .] The uncanny scene has convinced many that Cervantes devised this episode from accounts about the removal of the remains of Saint John of the Cross from Úbeda (near Baeza) to Segovia in May, 1593 (two years after his death). They base their assumptions on various similarities, route, place names, etc. Yet the very strangeness of the procession in Cervantes' story would seem to be the significant link. Saint John's remains were taken secretly from Úbeda and by a roundabout way to Segovia. It would seem that by rendering his funeral procession terrifying and then ludicrous Cervantes was making his own allusion to the clandestine way the saint's remains had been carried to Segovia in 1593.

When the torchbearer Quixote accosts and questions refuses to stop and explain, the hidalgo's dignity and pride are affronted, and in a choleric rage he attacks and disperses the entire procession. Rocinante has never moved more boldly than now in an attack on a group of panic-stricken and defenseless priests. But any illusion Quixote has of a military victory is shortlived. He hears from the fallen Alonso López an explanation about the cause of death of the deceased knight that renders his intervention unwarranted and sacrilegious. His good and noble intentions are shown to be meddlesome and nefarious. The outcome has been a nonsensical dispersal of the procession and a broken leg for Alonso López. Here Quixote does not even have recourse to enchanters or magicians to explain his error, which he partly admits. No error of perception was involved, no disfigurement, for a scene of religious and social meaning did appear infernal. What Quixote does not concede was that, given what he saw and could assume the situation to be, his action was wrong or that he had failed in his obligation: "no pude dejar de cumplir con mi obligación acometiéndoos, y os acometiera aunque verdaderamente supiera que érades los mesmos satanases del infierno, que por tales os juzgué y tuve siempre." I. 19, 233 [I could not but fulfill my duty by attacking you, and I should have attacked you though I had known for certain that you were the very devils from Hell, for such I judged you to be.]

Having satisfied their hunger with provisions ransacked from one of the sumpter mules belonging to the priests, hidalgo and squire have moved on in the dark, in search of water, when they hear the noise of a falling torrent and beyond an awesome sound of thuds, with a rasping of irons and chains. The narrator is scrupulously emphatic about an impending adventure in what the senses perceive: "Digo que oyeron que daban unos golpes a compás, con un cierto crujir de hierros y cadenas, que, acompañados del furioso estruendo del agua, que pusieran pavor a cualquier otro corazón que no fuera el de don Quijote." I. 20, 237 [They heard, I say, the sound of regular blows, and a sort of clanking of irons and chains, which, combined with the furious roaring of the water, would have struck terror into any heart less brave than Don Quixote's.]

If sensory perception has provoked in Quixote the expectation of an adventure equal to his courage (and pathological state), for its danger and difficulty, the circumstances as drawn by the exemplary narrator make evident that the sense of adventure is a test of the incentive to prove himself whatever the danger: "la soledad, el sitio, la escuridad, el ruido del agua con el susurro de las hojas, todo causaba horror y espanto, y más cuando vieron que ni los golpes cesaban, ni el viento dormía. . . ." [the loneliness of the place, the darkness, the noise of water and the rustling of leaves, all caused horror and fright, which increased when they realized that neither the blows ceased nor the wind died down. . . .] As a test, the adventure centers on the qualities that illuminate moral and heroic aspirations rather than on execution; on incentive and motive rather than on outcome.

Immediately he judges the 'sense data' to constitute a perilous adventure, Quixote is ready to charge into the unknown and mysterious dark: "don Quijoxte acompañado de su intrépido corazón, saltó sobre Rocinante, y, embrazando su rodela, terció su lanzón y . . ." [Don Quixote, stouthearted as ever, leapt on Rocinante, and bracing his shield, brandished his lance and . . .]. Yet, since the adventure is first conceptual and imaginative and then physical, he must depict it within the enlarged version of his 'mythos' before he can charge. It is his grandest moment in the entire book, for the adventure opens up before him as the potential fulfilment of moral and sensory expectations.

> —Sancho amigo, has de saber que yo nací, por querer del cielo, en esta nuestra edad de hierro, para resucitar en ella la de oro, o la dorada, como suele llamarse. Yo soy aquel para quien están guardados los peligros, las grandes hazañas, los valerosos hechos. Yo soy, digo otra vez, quien ha de resucitar los de la Tabla Redonda, los Doce de Francia y los Nueve de la Fama, y el que ha de poner en olvido los Platires, los Tablantes, Olivantes y Tirantes, los Febos y Belianises, con toda la caterva de los famosos caballeros andantes del pasado tiempo, haciendo en este en que me hallo tales grandezas, estrañezas y fechos de armas, que escurezcan las más claras que ellos ficieron . . . todo esto que yo te pinto son incentivos y despertadores de mi ánimo, que ya hace que el corazón me reviente en el pecho, con el deseo que tiene de acometer esta aventura, por más dificultosa que se muestra. I. 20, 238

> —Friend Sancho, I would have you know that I was born, by the disposition of heaven, in this our age of iron to revive in it that of gold, or the golden age as it is called. I am he for whom are reserved all great perils, mighty feats and valorous deeds. I am he, I say again, who shall revive the deeds of the Round Table, the Twelve Peers of France, and the Nine Worthies, and consign to oblivion the Platirs, Tablantes, Olivantes and Tirants, the Knight of the Sun and the Belianises, and all that herd of famous knights errant of olden times, by performing in this age in which I live such prodigies, wonders, and such feats of arms as shall eclipse the most famous deeds they ever achieved . . . all this I describe to you serves to spur and rouse my courage, and makes my heart to bound within my breast with desire to embark on this adventure, however arduous it may prove . . .

Then, as part of his heroic projection (he will carry out the adventure alone) he instructs Sancho to wait for him at this spot "for three days." The effect is to so arouse Sancho's fear that he will make every effort to dissuade his master from attempting the adventure; pleas, tears and, finally, ingenuity; he hobbles Rocinante so that his master cannot move forward.

As possibility and incentive the adventure has been fulfilled in Quixote's initial outburst. The ascending line of Quixote's imaginative thrust here reaches its climax. From this point the direction is down, and comically, to and around Sancho's bodily presence. And eventually, as we now expect, to the physiological functions of his organism, the digestive and eliminary (the counterpoint to Quixote's exalted imaginative conceptions). The initiative passes to Sancho who has deceived his master in the dark. Despite Quixote's resolve and courage, the adventure becomes Sancho's; he tells a story to keep his master entertained; his physiology determines the night's notable act;

Sancho relieves himself (here comic movement follows bowel movement); and he becomes the object of his master's wrath, when, on discovering the source of the awesome noise, he bursts into laughter, mockery and mimicry of his master.[27]

The fulling-hammer episode is adventure frustrated, and epitomized in Quixote's wrathful outburst against Sancho. Those two thwacks applied to his back bring comic movement to a painful close. When faced with the reality of the fulling-hammers in daylight, as the sources of the terrifying noises, Quixote was unable to conceive or imagine the outcome in any other way. His phantasy was inert or unable to devise enchantments to explain his illusion. "Cuando don Quijote vio lo que era, enmudeció y pasmóse de arriba abajo. Miróle Sancho, y vio que tenía la cabeza inclinada sobre el pecho, con muestras de estar corrido. Miró tambień don Quixote a Sancho y viole que tenía los carrillos hinchados. . . ." I. 20, 248 [When Don Quixote saw what it was, he stood dumbfounded and ashamed. Sancho looked at him, and saw how his head hung low over his breast in confusion. Then Don Quixote looked at Sancho and saw that his cheeks were swollen with laughter. . . .] The deflation of his spirit brought on by the contrast between the night's apparent danger and real terror and the days' prosaic revelation lays low his illusion. Moreover, Sancho's laughter reduces to mockery any possibility of enchantments to explain reality away. The sense of adventure has vanished with daylight; but his incentive and resolve, battered by Sancho's mockery, survives intact; he has 'executed' an act of daring in resolve and intentions alone.

15. The Gratuitous Act   Ch 22

Up to now the story has unfolded on an ascending line of daring and aggressive acts, inspired by Quixote's imagination and driven by outbursts of choler and fanatical will. His autonomy as a character in an exemplary story and as the arbiter of his will to action are one and the same. He and Sancho have been free to travel or roam about the countryside according to their will, needs, or whim. No contingency, no social pressure conspires to limit their freedom. This phase is explicable as an ascending line of adventure because Quixote's daring and his psychosomatic condition are dominated by the choleric side of his temperament. In chapter 22 we sense that his choler is subsiding and, as a consequence, the melancholic side of his temperament will begin to prevail. His outbursts of wrath and excited imagination will become less frequent and less powerful; psychosomatic depression will make him less aggressive, but more sentimental and sensitive to the plight of others. In this state of affairs he will be more restrained and more likely to heed Sancho's protests and entreaties. Following the encounter with the galley slaves his instigation for adventure takes an inward turn, to feeling, to reflection. Cervantes will not depict him again in Part I as the aggressive madman who charges at imagined enemies or attempts to remedy a situation of undistorted social complications.

In the three adventures immediately preceding Quixote is the ineffectual hero because his actions and incentive to heroic action correspond to no real cause or need in physical or social reality. Now on sighting the chain of galley slaves a seemingly veritable 'cause' for his intervention arises. A group of men, manacled and linked in a chain at their throat, crosses his path, in the most cruel and wretched affliction imaginable. Here, as nowhere else in the story, Quixote is presented with a real cause of human suffering and affliction. Only on one other occasion has the narrator drawn a similar scene, the case of child abuse by Juan Haldudo in chapter 4. In both cases his technique follows his theme, the righting of a wrong. In both cases Cervantes' theme is less Quixote's misperception of reality than the ethics of his action.

From the start the situation in chapter 22 is exceptional: a realistic scene fraught with tension and violence is presented to Quixote's and Sancho's senses directly out of social experience and the hidalgo perceives it directly and makes no effort to 'transform' it.

> . . . don Quixote alzó los ojos y vio que por el camino que llevaba venían hasta doce hombres a pie, ensartados como cuentas en una gran cadena de hierro, por los cuellos, y todos con esposas a las manos. Venían ansimismo con ellos dos hombres de a caballo y dos de a pie; los de a caballo, con escopetas de rueda, y los de a pie, con dardos y espadas. I. 22, 265

> . . . Don Quixote raised his eyes and saw on the road he was taking about a dozen men on foot, strung by the neck like beads on a great iron chain, and all manacled. With them were two horsemen and two men on foot; the horsemen had firelocks and the footmen pikes and swords.

Again the instigation to adventure is visual and auditory (the rattling of irons suggests the infernally damned); but for once the reaction it incites is the most powerful of social feelings, compassion at the sight of another's acute suffering. For its implications this adventure is very nearly the most complex incident in the entire story.

Up to now Cervantes has shown comically how Quixote's actions prove ineffectual as 'heroic' because they do not correspond to any cause, reason, or need rooted in a given social reality, but to an illusion of himself. It is the mad illusion of himself that leads to misconceptions of reality and his place in it. Now in this scene Cervantes depicts him confronted with a situation not only as real and challenging as any faced by a genuine literary hero, but as complex as any for which we can perceive a 'cause.' Moreover, Cervantes has interwoven here another literary element (the essence of the nonheroic) that adds a further complication.

In the *pastoral* interlude of Chrysostom and Marcela Cervantes incorporated into Quixote's story various themes and personalities of the idealistic pastoral romance without in the least disturbing or distorting the tone and rhythm of his own exemplary manner. In Quixote's encounter with the galley slaves with equal skill he incorporates themes and personalities from the realistic (or naturalistic) *picaresque* narrative, in many ways the antithesis of both the pastoral and chivalric romances. Probably the most characteristic feature of the picaresque narrative as Cervantes knew it is the convention of an autobiographical form. The *pícaro* or rogue is his own narrator, and his story is built up from a single point of view. That is, the convention of the autobiographical form serves to unfold a purportedly edifying story, of realistic incidents, reflecting a certain environment and to portray or create a character who is the product (in the deterministic sense) of that environment. The two picaresque narratives Cervantes had in mind were *The Life of Lazarillo de Tormes*, mentioned by the galley-slave Ginés de Pasamonte and to which this character compares his own autobiography, and *Guzmán de Alfarache*, not mentioned, but which Cervantes could not possibly have ignored, for it was the most popular work of fiction in Spain in the years 1599–1604.[28] Why Cervantes did not mention this work, but yet alluded to it in various ways, remains an enigma. Both *Lazarillo* and *Guzmán* produced a strong impression on their time, their originality is truly surprising, but whereas the first is a brief and impressionistic account of seven incidents, the second (a prototype of the genre) is a long and exhaustive account of moral failings, disreputable life and petty crimes, among them those for which Guzmán is sentenced to the galleys.

The principal elements of the picaresque narrative that Cervantes introduces or alludes to in this episode are: punishment as galley-slaves, an allusion to *Guzmán de Alfarache* (it is Guzmán, in the work Cervantes does *not* mention, who composed his autobiography while serving out his sentence as galley slave, not Lazarillo); the autobiographical form, alluded to in the twisted, personal statements and deceptive professions of innocence of the men Quixote interrogates; the immoral life of petty crimes and vice and the mentality (as revealed in first-person narrative) of the mature rogue who sees himself as a victim of a corrupt society, of its privileges for the rich and powerful, but who is in fact a deceiver and social parasite, cynical and hypocritical, living by instinct, deception, and cunning rather than work, and attempting to gain social status and wealth at the expense of others. When Quixote questions each prisoner in turn as to "the cause of his misfortune" each in turn replies with a declaration that subtly characterizes the picaresque mentality with its verbalized evasions. In this way Cervantes gives us a chain of picaresque stories and characters framed by his own exemplary manner. Moreover, these characters are contrasted by the idealistic but mad hidalgo, whose inner state is now receptive to what he sees and hears, a picture and account of human misery and distress. Here the adventure as sensory perception has become a compassionate openness to the plight of others; it is an adventure of 'feeling.' Hence it becomes a sharing of afflictions. From this situation Cervantes draws the motives for Quixote's act of liberation.

Thus Cervantes brings face-to-face two mentalities, the chivalric and the picaresque, and with them two modes of art. Quixote (in his madness), presuming to incarnate the spirit of chivalry, sees himself as a noble-minded, generous champion of the oppressed. His presumptuousness, now suggesting *hybris* (heroic pride), is countered by the moral trait that most accurately typifies the mentality of the petty criminals, their verbal deceptions and desultory pleas of innocence, meant to evade any admission of wrong. These two mentalities are poles apart for what they represent of idealism and ignoble self-interest. Cervantes brings them together as a meeting of lives in turmoil and an interaction of two afflictions. It is his secret that neither state of affliction would really correspond to the literary modes that his episode evokes.

The Exemplary Story

The affliction of the galley slaves is physical and desperately real. As they stand enchained before Quixote in their sweat and rags they are a picture of humanity all-but unredeemable for their lack of conscience and pathetic inability to live honestly. Ginés de Pasamonte is the most intelligent, cunning and energetic; also the most violent and dangerous, and the least likely to turn repentant and introspective, least likely to produce the pseudo-moralistic and confessional work Cervantes would judge the picaresque narrative to be. The affliction of Quixote is mental, spiritual, an anxiety of conscience, but of course pathological and unlike any state of suffering or passionate turmoil depicted in books of knight-errantry. The presumptuous hidalgo as knight, the tricky delinquents pathetically taking on the role of innocent victims of a corrupted system of justice: the encounter casts the norms of behavior, thought, and action in stories of knights and rogues respectively into grotesque outlines of social alienation and abnormality.

From the chivalric mentality that Quixote assumes Cervantes will derive the generous and compassionate act of freedom. From the picaresque character and mentality he derives the recipients of that act, who, once freed, ungratefully mock and attack their mad benefactor, and prove to be as wretched as they are unworthy. Through the problematical relations between benefactor and recipient Cervantes points to a Christian standard of conduct by which Quixote's action is right in intention, though, again, wrong in effect.

Men are created by God and by nature to be free, Quixote says, and it is not right that honorable men should be the executioners of others, and he pleads with the guards to release the prisoners. They refuse, mocking him and arousing his anger; he attacks them and in the confusion the prisoners break their chains and leap on the guards who flee. Quixote's act is not done in the cause of justice nor to repair the unjust oppression of royal authority. It is really done out of the spirit of Christian compassion and charity; though couched in terms of his chivalric mission, it is an act of 'feeling,' of *Charitas*. The Christian, following the example of Jesus, and out of love and compassion for the physically afflicted, takes whatever action is necessary to relieve their suffering, unconditionally and immediately. Cervantes depicts Quixote performing a deed of Christian compassion and a gratuitous act, in the sense that it is bestowed by a free spirit on the recipient without regard to his moral merits or social standing. It is also gratuitous in the sense that it is 'unwarranted' because these men have been tried and sentenced for moral offenses. But of course the situation confronted by Quixote is meant to dramatize the moral conflict of the Christian who, as a matter of conscience, must act according to the higher law of Christian love, though his action violate the laws of the established social order.

Thus Quixote's action is a generous and charitable act of liberation of afflicted souls, for the immediate relief of their suffering; it is valid and even heroic in intent, since it pits him against the authority of the king. It is high-minded and disinterested, as the act of freedom bestowed from above on the oppressed without regard to whether they are deserving or not. His action is, then, both necessary and right along one single thread of visionary motives and valor. On either side it is fraught with inconsistencies and contradictions, not the least his egomaniac belief that it glorifies him and his service to Dulcinea. It is then an action problematical in all respects but one: his selfless motives, for with reference to the state of affliction he remedies, they are uncontaminated by self-interest; they are pure.

But however compassionate or reasonable, his action can be achieved only through violence, and once freed the liberated reveal the other side of their desperate nature, their vindictive, cowardly and cruel arrogance, born of fear and cunning. And when Quixote addresses them as heroic liberator and instructs them to show their gratitude by taking themselves and the chain to El Toboso and Dulcinea, it is Ginés de Pasamonte who replies with the insolence that provokes another wrathful attack. Then the prisoners resort to throwing stones at him, at Sancho and their mounts, bring them to the ground and strip them of half their garments. The result of Quixote's intervention has been to set free a group of dangerous men to prey on the unsuspecting inhabitants of the district.

The afflicted and distressed turn out to be ignobly treacherous and vile. Quixote has been genuinely heroic in conscience, in motives, but again ineffectual in result. The sense of adventure has once more followed an ascending curve of exalted intentions only to end in blows, ridicule, and humiliation. From the initial moment, when Quixote solicits from the first prisoner an account of his misfortune, the motives behind his words and deeds unfold toward a heroic, single-handed fight against odds; from the intention everything unfolds as heroic: courage, audacity, conscience.

It is too much to say that Cervantes discovered or invented the 'gratuitous act' (it appears to be a universal subject), the act that in modern fiction acquires its 'meaning' or sense not from the physical reality to which it is applied, but from the mentality and motives of the doer. But he is the first to have defined it powerfully in fiction and depicted its implications in moral, psychological and social terms. Novelists since Cervantes have depicted the effect of the 'gratuitous act' more often than not as senseless or nearly so. Cervantes depicts it here as problematical in human terms and senseless in one narrow social context. The term 'gratuitous' refers to an act that is given freely, without conditions, and not motivated in response to a 'cause,' reason, or need; it is therefore unwarranted or unjustifiable by the norms of social conduct, and hence its effect in fiction will appear to be dubious, problematical or simply meaningless. In novels of twentieth-century existentialism the 'gratuitous act' is often committed out of 'senseless' motives, the killing of an innocent person, for instance, or a person unknown or unrelated in any way to the doer. In these cases the act is committed in a moral vacuum. Cervantes, as exemplary narrator, is at the other extreme; the situation, even before Quixote intervenes, is fraught with moral implications, replete with an ethical sense. The result is that Quixote becomes emblematic of the Christian's spiritual obligation to relieve the physical suffering of fellow humans as an act of Christian or humanitarian love, and his action a 'creative act' in the context of modern interpretations of Saint Paul's doctrines.

16. The Penitent Knight   Chs 23-27

For the first (and only time) Quixote has committed an unlawful act, and in defiance of civil authority. He heeds Sancho's warnings about the Holy Brotherhood coming out to arrest and punish them, and agrees to turn off the main highway and hide in the wilderness of Sierra Morena. They evade the police to avoid facing the consequences of their action and to this extent their freedom is now limited. Their retreat is thus symptomatic of Quixote's weakening resolve and a change in him toward a subtler mood and depression and melancholy. But also their retreat into Sierra Morena indicates how consistently Cervantes avoids exposing his hidalgo and peasant to the realities of urban life, personalities, intrigues, problems; to courts of law, the marketplace, or the threat of the asylum, to any element but the open road and the wild countryside.[29] Had Cervantes followed up the liberation of the galley slaves with similar episodes of the kind in which Quixote would attempt 'radical' or anarchistic solutions to social wrongs in an urban setting, we should have a very different story.

The change in course makes evident that Cervantes moves his story into those situations where Quixote's autonomy will prevail as the means for his characterization. His will and imagination must be free to react to what he perceives intuitively to hold an adventure in store for him: a solitary traveller wearing a glittering headpiece or a gloomy landscape, like the one that now appears as they make their way into the Sierra. Quixote's search for adventure is Cervantes' subject, and now that Quixote's inner turmoil is tempered into a state of sensitive rather than aggressive expectations, it is the overpowering presence of the mountain wilderness that excites his senses. This landscape evokes not one but various literary situations; its impression on him is above all sentimental. We have seen Cervantes develop the idea of adventure as sensory experience, and from there to adventure as 'feeling,' the encounter with the galley slaves. Now the story moves to unfold adventure as the fulfilment of sentimental yearnings.

As we have come to expect, this adventure is both an image and an experience, and it recreates not one but a cluster of literary motifs. As an appeal to and saturation of the senses, it is, above all, a 'fiction.' The image is that of a knight afflicted with love madness because he has been rejected by his lady. The experience is the overpowering sense of guilt and loss for having offended her (whether or not she has cause to be offended), which will impel the knight to commit the most irrational actions, like reverting to a 'wild' or savage state of being, or to perform penitential trials in the almost impossible hope that they will propitiate or soften her anger. What Quixote imagines and feels as adventure will thus be a combination of motifs from chivalric, pastoral and sentimental narratives. From the chivalric he evokes the situation and motif of the knight afflicted with love madness.[30] Like Amadís, Lancelot or Yvain, the knight is so distraught he flees from any human companionship or comfort, reverts to a solitary existence and takes on the attributes of a 'wild man,' living like a savage in a wild forest. From pastoral verse and narrative he will take the distressed lover's lament recited in idyllic surroundings and directed to sylvan deities. From the sentimental novel he recalls the penitent lover in the wilderness, driven to despair by a sense of guilt and sin, and for whom a trial of penance is both sentimental and ascetic purgation.

The instigation or pretext for this 'adventure of sentiment' will appear caused from without, in order to set off the entirely gratuitous motives behind it. The instigation develops in three successive moments. First, the mood suggested to Quixote's sensibilities by the landscape: withdrawal, isolation, solitude, anguish of the heart. Second, when, on going through the bag and bundle left behind by Cardenio, Quixote finds the notebook and letters, and concludes they have been abandoned by a spurned and distraught lover. Then, third: he sees in this wild place the figure of Cardenio leaping like an animal from rock to rock, nearly nude, in rags, his hair and beard wild and unkempt. What he sees is indeed real life, a demented man, but its impact on his feelings is all the greater because it fits within a literary role and subject of a story, a 'fiction.' By the time he and Sancho and the goatherd have met up with Cardenio, Quixote has discerned the outlines of the story of a disdained lover who, in despair, has reverted to a wild state, and out of anguish and devotion to his lady expects to die in this lonely place. Even after he has heard from Cardenio his real life story Quixote will continue to believe in this fictional picture.

Cardenio then serves as the real-life example and instigation for the adventure Quixote has anticipated. The sight of him leaping from rock to rock provides the visual stimulus to adventure. Quixote is reminded of the two famed cases in chivalric literature in which knights became mad and reverted to a wild state and underwent a penance because they were rejected by their lady: Amadís and Orlando. When he next sees Cardenio (Ch 26) he will not recognize him, and even after the scenes in the inn (Ch 36), he will never really understand that the real life 'emotional' problem of the 'wild man' he saw in Sierra Morena has been solved.

But another very important matter has entered Quixote's mind. It has to do with both the 'purpose' of his madness and its possible cure. Quixote understands that the distraught lover's actions border on despair and hopelessness, and may end in suicide or something very much like it, unless a solution or 'cure' can be found. One might suppose that he has in mind to share compassionately the mad lover's affliction—providing solace or comfort, from one who deeply and genuinely understands his grief. This would be a sharing of affliction between equals, unlike the case of his meeting with the galley slaves. But the hint of a possible 'cure' is also in the way of a subliminal disclosure of the need for a 'clinical' cure for his own madness. It is in this way that Cervantes suggests the theme of a spiritual penance, with its medieval, ascetic associations. This is the theme that completes Quixote's picture of himself, and binds the image of disdained lover (Cardenio) and mad knight (himself) into the experience he will undergo as sentimental adventure. Cervantes' depiction of him in Sierra Morena boldly suggests that Quixote is led to imitate the 'mad lover' and 'penitent knight' because he is unconsciously driven to seek a cure for his madness by way of a clinical, penitential purgation.

Because the adventure is sentimental it is introspective, self conscious. Not only is it imitative but the very subject he seeks to imitate is a reflection of his own demented state. Cervantes, then, has reduced the idea of sense experience as adventure to its most essential element, that Quixote should be aware that his madness is literary, and that in imitating the mad knight gone wild and penitent his madness is turning in upon itself, so that the conscious motives that sustain it indicate the half-suppressed wish to be cured, to be restored to reason. There is nothing in all of chivalric or other romantic literature previous to Cervantes that can be compared with Quixote's conscious and involuntarily comical imitation, though many of its features can be found suggested in earlier works. What is original about it is not so much the conceit of a mad man imitating the mad knight, nor its psychological depth, nor the gratuitous nature of his actions and explanations of his motives, but, rather, the complete awareness and control of the character over his actions, and his insight into the meaning of the experience, above all what it signifies as the 'literary' experience of a character drawn in fiction.

Quixote pretends that the cause of his love madness has been a certain displeasure of Dulcinea toward him. In some way he must let her know that this has driven him to madness and despair. So he will compose a letter to her which Sancho will deliver. The story of Amadís' love sickness and penance (as told in Book II of *Amadís de Gaula*) is his model, but Quixote turns around even this situation. It is Oriana in *Amadís de Gaula* who in a letter to Amadís accuses him (unjustly) of unfaithfulness and banishes him from her sight forever. Amadís never replies, in a letter or any other form. He accepts her cruel treatment of him with complete silence and loyalty, and makes no attempt to defend himself against false accusations. So great and passionate is his love for her that her word, whether reproachful or joyful, is like a supreme law. His submission to her will is so complete that he will not disclose to anyone the contents of the letter, nor seek or accept consolation from anyone. He becomes an outcast, he loses his identity and wanders in the wild forest until he is found by a hermit, who giving him the name *Beltenebrós*, takes him to a remote island and there oversees his penance. The knight's penance consists of fasting and prayers, but also he composes sentimental verses. It becomes a spiritual trial or purgation that leads to his eventual recovery, reconciliation and reunion with Oriana.

Amadís, then, in the heroic manner, becomes the victim of his affliction over Oriana's disdain. Quixote is never the victim of his pretended love and affliction, and the reason is clear. His imitation of the 'mad knight' is sane because it is gratuitous and the reflective, conscious act of a subject afflicted with literary madness.

Though he purports to 'imitate' Amadís and Orlando, his actions are really directed toward a saturation if not gratification of the senses. This is why his imitation can be called artistic or esthetic. His motive is to prove his love and loyalty to Dulcinea in a self-inflicted, penitential trial, and thereby win fame as lasting as Amadís's or Orlando's. While his actions have thus a reason and purpose, these are quite obviously literary, that is, legendary and, in essence, poetic. Moreover, if they are not 'contained,' or related together as poetic they would lack the essential quality that sustains them as 'fictional.' Quixote intends that they will be fictional because they are gratuitous in the real sense. Dulcinea has given him no 'cause.' But he invents the cause, just as he has invented her and the story of their relationship. The 'penitent knight' is gratuitous as a conscious action, but beneath Quixote's reasonings, invocations, gestures, we discern the subconscious urge of a demented personality to act out therapeutically his dementia. He decides to take advantage of the isolation and solitude of the Sierra to subject himself to penitential trials. Once Dapple has disappeared (he is stolen), Sancho must ride on Rocinante on his trip to El Toboso to deliver the letter to Dulcinea.[31] This furnishes Quixote with an indispensable circumstance: he will be left completely alone. Withdrawn from all social contacts, he surrenders himself to his penance.

We see that Cervantes has based his episode on three indispensables: on Quixote's notion of a gratuitous 'imitation,' on the separation of master and squire, and on Quixote's isolation for a period of several days. Together they bring off as a representational parody a sensory experience that is penitential in the expressive as well as psychological and religious sense (and hence jointly catharsis and therapy).

Quixote must live and feel his isolation: he must perform his 'role,' but also direct his performance. Hence what he does in detail is more significant than any detail of what he imitates from his models. None of his models would have thought to insist on a witness, as he insists that Sancho actually see him perform crazy pranks. The emotional vehemence of Amadís's trial is expressed in profuse tears, and Quixote speaks of imitating his weeping. But though he sighs deeply and profusely, Quixote does not weep; in this detail he remains sanely 'dry-eyed.' He selects the most appropriate spot, and begins his performance with a series of invocations and laments. Stripping off his outer clothing, he performs somersaults and crazy frolics before the astonished Sancho, who departs convinced that he can report to Dulcinea that her knight is mad. Left to his own, he declaims in a long monologue a rationalization of his imitation of Amadís which ends: ". . . most of the time he spent praying and commending his soul to God. But what shall I do for a rosary . . .?" He improvises one by tying his shirt into knots, and thinks that a confession like Amadís's to the hermit would be a good idea:

> rasgó una gran tira de las faldas de la camisa, que andaban colgando, y diole once ñudos, el uno más gordo que los demás, y esto le sirvió de rosario el tiempo que allí estuvo, donde rezó un millón de avemarías. Y lo que le fatigaba mucho era no hallar por allí otro ermitaño que le confesase y con quien consolarse. I. 26, 319–20

> he tore a great strip from the tails of his shirt, which was hanging down, and made eleven knots in it, one fatter than the rest, and this served him for a rosary all the time he was there, during which time he recited a million Ave Marias. But what worried him a great deal was that there was no hermit to be found thereabouts to hear his confession and administer consolation.

Then he gives himself to composing his lamentations in verses. In this way, by exhibitionist behavior and emotional outpouring he externalizes his inner needs, and expends a great portion of his psychotic turbulence.

When Sancho returns to look for him, with the priest and barber, and Cardenio and Dorotea, the forceful period of Quixote's madness has been played out. The choleric side of his temperament was played out in the series of adventures leading up to the episode with the galley slaves. In Sierra Morena the melancholic side is largely expended. Once persuaded by a ruse to leave the Sierra, Quixote attempts no more individual feats. What he does, says, or thinks, is still centered in his egomania, but with the fading of his imaginative thrust for adventure he is content to let adventures seek him out. Consequently, the course of adventure but not his autonomous control over them is determined by the other characters, who deceive him with a 'fiction' in order to get him home, in the hope that his madness has a cure. There is, therefore, a profound contrast between the decisions and actions he carries out before his period of isolation in the Sierra, and his state of mind, passive and quiescent, following that period. The important decision, for its lasting repercussions, has been to send Sancho as a messenger to Dulcinea at El Toboso. Not only does this decision mean that Quixote attempts to make real his illusion that Aldonza Lorenzo is Dulcinea, but it obliges him to reveal the intimate secret of who she is to Sancho, who can understand it only in a gross, materialistic way.

The episode in Sierra Morena is, then, the turning point in the action and linear development of story in Part One. Up to this point the hidalgo, inspired by madness, has generated the 'fictions' that sustain his sensory experiences as chivalric adventures. From this point forward the incentive to create 'fictions' to sustain the hero's illusion passes to other characters in the story. Dorotea is prompted by the priest and barber to invent and play out the fiction of Princess Micomicona. But Sancho makes up a fiction of his trip to El Toboso and his meeting with Dulcinea. The force of Quixote's madness has planted or provoked in the minds of others the fiction of his knighthood, in the first instance to deceive him.

II

The Quixotic Fiction

1. Fiction-Within-Fiction

We have been dealing with a structure of fiction-within-fiction from the first moments of Quixote's madness. The very title of the book was a hint. We have seen how Quixote's madness not only bears within it a 'nuclear' force capable of engendering and sustaining the fiction of his enterprise and identity, but likewise of setting in motion an entire chain-reaction of proliferating fictions. His self-transformation is not just a 'creative' fiction; rather it represents the 'generic' force itself that gives rise to a series of fictions that by defining themselves in turn define reality. Now we shall see how the flow and unfolding of Cervantes' story introduces a variety and order of secondary plots contained within the exemplary sweep of Quixote's experience in a kind of hierarchy.

Cardenio's story was the first extended narrative told by the protagonist himself and an apparent interruption in the account of Quixote's adventures. It was the image of a demented lover, not the depth and details of his story, that instigated Quixote's penance. With Quixote out of sight, and before the priest and barber, Cardenio tells the remainder of his narrative up to the moment he fled the scene of the wedding forced on Luscinda, his betrothed, by Fernando, his rival. Then the three find Dorotea, the beautiful daughter of a wealthy farmer who has also sought refuge in the Sierra, for she turns out to be the very woman Fernando abandoned in order to marry Luscinda. Her narrative postpones once more Quixote's reappearance. The practice of suspending one action or narrative with the introduction of another is of course very old and a traditional device of storytellers. It is highly developed in some of the finest examples of medieval chivalric romance in prose. The 'interlacing' of various narratives through multiple digressions is carried to extremes with brilliant results in Ariosto's *Orlando Furioso*. And then the classical precedents of developing subordinate narratives with the appearance of secondary characters in various episodes of an epic poem like the *Aeneid* were imitated in Italy and Spain and sanctioned by critics who based their theories on the authority of Aristotle's *Poetics*. Yet, though linked to tradition and to theoretical and literary precedents, Cervantes' inclusion of subordinate narratives is a radical departure for its scale and strategy.[32]

Once Quixote is induced to leave the Sierra by a hoax, he is led by his companions back to the inn, where, after another discussion on chivalric books, and while Quixote sleeps, the priest reads a *novela* called *The Curious Impertinent*. The reading is interrupted by Sancho who says Quixote has killed a giant in the room where he is sleeping. After the conclusion of the *novela*, a group of strangers arrives at the inn. They turn out to be Don Fernando and his companions with Luscinda, whom he has abducted from a convent. In the scene that follows, Dorotea with great presence of mind begs and convinces Fernando to restore her honor by making her his wife and to consent to the marriage of Cardenio and Luscinda. Quixote now reappears, but then another pair of strangers arrives, the captain Ruy Pérez and an exotic Moorish girl, Zoraida. Before an audience seated around the table and after Quixote delivers a discourse on "Arms and Letters," the captain tells the story of his and Zoraida's nearly miraculous escape from Algiers. He tells it as a 'true' and 'historical' personal narrative, but in fact it is a 'tale' for its literary quality. It is Cervantes' most determined effort to provide variety and serious narrative as relief to Quixote's comical adventures. At nightfall yet another group of travelers arrives, a jurist (who turns out to be the captain's brother), his daughter Clara and their servants. An aristocratic youth has followed them from their village, Don Luis, disguised as a mule boy in their entourage because he is in love with Clara and has stolen away from his father's home to follow her. By now the inn is positively bursting with guests and servants. That night Quixote mounted on Rocinante stands guard outside the walls of what he believes to be an enchanted castle and becomes the victim of yet another love adventure played on him as a trick.

The inn becomes definitely overpopulated on the next day when another group of travelers in search of Don Luis and officers of the holy Brotherhood arrive. By now there are four 'serious' subordinate love plots whirling around the comical figures of Quixote and Sancho, much in the manner of stage comedy: mistaken or concealed identities, mix-ups and fortuitous reunions. Their conflicts are happily resolved by the good will of their protagonists while Quixote looks on, for his own effectuality is purely imaginary. The climax comes when the barber from whom Quixote took the basin he called the helmet of Mambrino shows up and demands to have it back. An argument provoked as a hoax on Quixote and this barber, on whether the basin is or is not the helmet of Mambrino, results in a free-for-all in which aristocrats, police officers, barbers and servants get into a fight. The comical scene is presided over by Quixote who attributes the confusion to the work of enchanters. By aligning diverse techniques of both theater and prose narrative in the spirit of a carnival inversion, and as one sustained representation of contemporary life with its human variety, and Quixote at its center (the unified, single action of Aristotelian theory), Cervantes achieves a totality and synthesis of techniques, themes and effects never before seen in prose fiction. The whole is more than a virtuoso performance; in disarming manner it puts comical prose narrative alongside the achievement of the solemn verse epic as a portrait of an entire society. The comical figure of Quixote takes on the mock aura of both epic and chivalric heroes. Another elaborate hoax convinces him to be allowed to be put in a cage as one more adventure and taken back to his village. The whole idea of a hoax played on Quixote and staged according to his illusion as an enchantment is elevated to the category of sophisticated 'fiction-within-fiction'. The homeward journey is the occasion for yet another discussion on chivalric books and the plays of Lope de Vega between the priest and another traveler, the likeable canon from Toledo. When Quixote replies to the canon in defense of chivalric books from his cage the very nature of this 'critical' discussion exposes the self-conscious process by which the hidalgo has been transformed into a hero of fiction, now comparable to Lanzarote and Amadís of Gaul. Yet one more narrative is introduced by the goatherd Eugenio on the final lap of the journey back to the village.

This strategy provides in sequential order a variety of narratives that for their fictional qualities also comprise a hierarchy of levels or 'orders' of fiction. The highest level or order corresponds to the most creative of them, Quixote's chivalric career, which is also the most 'fictional' in the sense that it is the most self-conscious effort on the part of the character and his exemplary narrator. The schematic outline (Chart II) on page 86 shows the sequence to the end of Part I. We include the Chrysostom-Marcela episode. Their story has already

CHART II

Quixote's chivalry:	Dulcinea		Princess Micomicona		Enchanted inn-castle		Quixote enchanted
[1]	[2]	[3]	[4]	[5]	[6]	[7]	[8]
Chrysostom-Marcela	Sancho's tale Lope-Torralba	Cardenio-Luscinda	Dorotea-Fernando	*Novel of the Curious Impertinent* Anselmo Camila Lotario	Tale of the Captive Captain Ruy Pérez Zoraida	Luis-Clara	Goatherd's story Eugenio-Leandra

shown how Cervantes contrasts the lives and anxieties of others with Quixote's feelings and expectations, and how his affective approach to others elicits and brings out their 'storied' presence. The major theme that connects Quixote's chivalry with the subordinate narratives is love, and each narrative is of course a different treatment of relations between lovers as well as a variation on intrigue or conflict. Four are told in part or completely by one of the lovers involved: Cardenio, Dorotea, Ruy Pérez, Eugenio. Of these only Cardenio's and Dorotea's can be said to come to an end in the sense that a solution is found to their love problem. Eugenio's appears to have no solution. Ruy Pérez's is given a partial solution; its 'happy ending' is predicted for the near future when the captain will be reunited with his father and Zoraida baptized and received into the Catholic faith. Now, as fictions, that is, as lives embodied in narrative form and revealed by a narrator, these are not of the same quality or order. In fact they differ considerably. The Cardenio-Luscinda/Dorotea-Fernando complex and Eugenio's may be called 'stories.' The captain's narrative is very clearly a 'tale.' 'Story' and 'tale' are here two different orders of fiction. They differ for various reasons, as we shall see, but primarily for (1) the kind of literary or fictional elements they contain, and (2) for the way those elements are shaped, provided with a unity, and brought foreward to resolution or ending. When we classify them according to the hierarchy of their fictional complexity, the eight narratives fall into six groups, as follows:

1) The exemplary story. Quixote's chivalry and love for Dulcinea takes the form of a parodic chivalric 'history.'
2) Sentimental story. Cardenio's   Dorotea's   Clara-Luis
3) Psychological *novela*. The Curious Impertinent.
4) Pastoral episode. Chrysostom-Marcela. Eugenio's story.
5) Tale *The Captain's Tale.*
6) Folktale Sancho's folktale.

Before continuing it will be necessary to clear up some of my terms from a theoretical viewpoint. I am not of course discussing fictional *modes*, that is, the broad divisions of the entire spectrum of narrative possibilities. Nor am I discussing narrative *genres* per se (i.e., Italian or exemplary *novella*, folktale, tale, pastoral or sentimental romance, etc.). Although it is usual to say that Cervantes incorporated these and other genres into *Don Quixote*, it is not at all an accurate assumption. A *novella*, or a *tale*, or a *pastoral romance* must exist as a separate (i.e., at least *semi*-independent), autonomous work in order to qualify for full status as one. The stories or *novelle* in a collection like the *Decameron* are each separate and each is a representative of its kind or genre. The narratives (*sic*, 'interpolated' narratives) in *Don Quixote* are separate from one another only relatively and represent different kinds. They are subordinate and made to combine with the main action for a purpose beyond their integrity and distinctiveness as 'tale,' 'sentimental story,' or 'pastoral romance.' The artistic purpose that oversees their blending into the narrative of Quixote's adventures has subverted their distinctiveness and imposed on each its own distribution of their elements. For instance, Cardenio's and Dorotea's narratives are parts of one sentimental story which begins with their separate accounts, continues as a series of dramatic scenes with Quixote on the road and then at the inn, where it is brought to a happy outcome, as a prose version of a stage comedy. Cardenio and Dorotea appear as narrators of their own story but are characters contained within the exemplary story told by a further combination of authors. The *Novel of the Curious Impertinent* is read aloud. Even this semi-independent fiction has been inserted with great care. The illiterate who hear it know it as an oral performance or recitation. Its meaning as prose fiction is subordinate to the larger design established by the controlling principle of interrelation of themes, characters and techniques.[33]

Because one cannot rightfully speak of genres of fiction or narrative included ('interpolated') in *Don Quixote*, I use the terms 'levels' and 'orders' of fiction. My use indicates that I believe that what Cervantes does with the materials of fiction is more significant in his book than the fact that his material resembles pre-existent narrative forms or genres, including chivalric romance. His purpose seems to have been to include as much variety as he could, and to order or structure it according to a broad, yet unified concept of story. The exemplary account of Quixote's mock chivalry depicts, consistently, not irrevocable but gratuitous actions. By virtue of its open elasticity it can provide for 'modern' or 'novelistic' solutions of the moral and psychological conflicts associated with other forms of prose narrative. The subordinate fictions are basically variations on the theme of love (desire, passion, lust) and its complications: triangles, crossed lovers, ruined marriages, jealousy, constancy, betrayal, etc. For Cervantes the sentiments aroused or released by love are very nearly the most powerful with which fiction can deal. The conflicts centered on love are a paradigm of all the forces (social, moral and even metaphysical) which weigh down on and shape an individual's happiness or lack of it.

2. Cardenio and Dorotea   Chs 27-28

Narrator-protagonists, they enhance their own stories by telling them; they do not, however, tell them strictly as stories, but as an absorbing account of the anxiety and alienation of their state of conscience. Their importance is emphasized by the vividness of the scene in which they first appear. This first appearance is an image that announces the motifs and quality of their narratives. Cardenio appears as a wild-man and demented lover, driven to furious penitential trial more by a diseased conscience than a crazed mind. Dorotea appears beside a stream, washing her delicate feet, and wearing the outfit of a shepherd boy. The motif is that of the female who assumes a male disguise in order to search for the lover who has abandoned her. These are two separate images and motifs, but combined they recall the chivalric motif of lovers seeking refuge in a wooded wilderness (Tristan and Isolde in the forest of Morrois).[34] They do not, of course, seek one another. Unknown to them, they are both victims of Don Fernando's lustful intrigues. Protagonists of their *sentimental* narratives, of injured affections, their stories will show how love betrayed wreaks havoc in the affective soul, and so alienates the lover from family and social ties, it drives him and her to a despair and anxiety that border on death. The first image we have of each pictures them at the extremes of their isolation and anxiety.

While their narratives are interrelated, fixed on the same chain of events and later become one, they differ significantly because as self-narratives they express as well as incarnate the character who speaks. Cardenio's hesitant and devious manner of coming to the point is indicative of indecision and timidity in his character, of his failure to see himself as a will-less lover who blames others for his weakness. We hear from the goatherd and see for ourselves how furiously this timid lover can act as a release from his self-consuming rage and 'mad' jealousy of Don Fernando. He has fled into the wilderness to escape the consequences of his indecision and fear. Dorotea's narrative, by contrast, is direct, more honestly that of an introspective sentimental heroine and reveals the impulsive as well as the calculating and rationalist qualities that make up her "discretion." She appears as the injured, cast-off woman in distress, yet the fact of her being here in Sierra Morena means that she has the force to defend herself and the presence of mind to seek for herself the remedy of her suffering. Cardenio, a remorseful lack of will; Dorotea, a great presence of mind; they form a pair of opposites that repeats the 'pastoral' situation of Chrysostom and Marcela with a desperate and 'lyrical' male and a dispassionate 'dialectical' female.

The account of each is a retracing of the events that have brought them to the present state of their affliction. Cardenio tells the first part of his story to Quixote, Sancho and the goatherd (Ch 24). In this version of the events that bind these lives irrevocably he appears in his own eyes as the sentimental (victimized) hero who could not have acted otherwise out of love, friendship and honor. It is self-analysis made self-fictionalizing (note the importance of epistolary conventions) for the morbose lack of awareness of the subject of his sentimental excess and moral deficiency. He takes refuge in the defense that Don Fernando's superior rank and the friendship between them obliged him to suppress any resistance to Fernando when he began to show a treacherous interest in Luscinda. His story breaks off at this point, and when he resumes it, before the priest and barber (Ch 27), he is in a calmer mood. Cardenio's misfortune is not that he is the 'disdained lover' that his wild and mad actions before Quixote in chapters 23–24 suggest, but that having witnessed the marriage scene between Fernando and Luscinda he did not leave his hiding place and intervene boldly to redress his outraged honor; he fled the scene as one too introspective and timid to attempt to save his honor and his love. Cardenio lacks the personal resources to live up to the demands of his social position. In his alienated state he condemns himself to repent and regret his indecision. In his remorse he would willingly perish.

On his own Cardenio could not have solved his predicament. Such a solution is dependent on Dorotea's energetic presence of mind. Their encounter (Ch 28) as cast-off lovers is the low point of their flight, but the very disclosure of their separate stories as one, and now brought within the orbit of Quixote's adventures, makes possible a solution. Their separate accounts are both story and an analysis of the events that have brought them to their present isolation, the penitential phase of their depiction. From this present point their accounts are linked dramatically to the course of Quixote's adventures.

When Dorotea consents to play the mock role of Princess Micomicona for the sake of a possible cure for Quixote, her own real life situation is recast into the fantasy terms of his chivalric fiction. The duality of her role thereafter is a conceit elaborated on her 'lost virtue'—her virginity despoiled by Don Fernando to whom she gave herself as wife—and her "kingdom of Micomicón" usurped by an evil giant whom Quixote is to challenge and kill. In mock terms Quixote will restore her kingdom to her (when he kills the giant in his sleep), but in real life it will be her own self-possession, her own reason and emotive pleas that will convince Fernando to accept her as his wife. The beautiful daughter of a rich farmer, brought up in strict seclusion, she is determined to cash in on her sexual attraction and elevate herself socially by marrying an aristocrat, once that attraction has made her the victim of his trickery and seduction. As sentimental stories the two accounts are woven around the 'secret marriage,' the consent of the female to exchange her virginity for the promise of marriage by her lover. Luscinda, we infer, has been Cardenio's bride since before Fernando came on the scene, and in Dorotea's eyes his claim to her is all-compelling, in legal, moral and emotive terms. Accordingly, the solution to the two accounts will rest on Don Fernando's acceptance of the moral obligation to keep his promise to Dorotea, and is forthcoming when the two subjects of this sentimental story move beyond their present affliction to the scenes that will enact its resolution. Thus we see that from the moment they first appear and provide the account of their afflicted state, they move outward from a 'fictional' frame or image toward the 'real life' figures we shall see in the inn. The process is a complete movement from personal isolation and affliction toward reunion with the longed-for or searched-for partner and the re-integration and social accommodation that ensure the happy outcome of the sentimental story. In the process Cardenio is restored to his senses and to Luscinda, but is completely divested of the absorbing fictional interest he started with. Dorotea as Princess Micomicona is invested with a fictional cast, a mock role in Quixote's chivalry. In this way Cardenio the 'real' madman of Sierra Morena whose example induced Quixote to do penance is counterpointed by the mock princess whose ruse will induce him to take the road home. Their lives are thus intertwined as cause and effect with the exemplary course of Quixote's madness.

Don Fernando's actions have inflicted great suffering on himself and on the affections of the other three. The lives of all four are caught up in the contrariness of affections and they constitute a single 'crisis of sentiments' which defines the intrigue of the sentimental story and points the way to its solution. Cardenio's love for Luscinda and Dorotea's honor are at the mercy of Fernando's own wayward affections or his moral resources for recognizing his error. The crisis of outraged and alienated affections can be resolved only by the rational control of desire and passion. The happy outcome to these lives of lovers in turmoil is of course marriage according to their true sentimental affinities, Luscinda to Cardenio and Dorotea to Fernando. Cervantes has shaped their sentimental story according to his own deepest feelings and purposes.

Cardenio's distraught affections have made him incapable of restoring a rational and moral control over them. But Dorotea is determined to find a way to get Fernando back, and once she knows from Cardenio why Luscinda cannot be Fernando's wife, she has the indispensable argument to press her claim on him, with the force of reason as well as morality. In her tearful entreaty in chapter 36 she will state with great passion as well as reason and moral force why Fernando should accept her as his wife, and he will be compelled to recognize that she is right. No circumstance or agent external to reason and moral will (i.e., the miraculous, marvellous or magical) may intervene to make the solution possible. The only circumstances allowed are the fortuitous coincidences that have brought them together here (and at the inn): they do not decide the crisis but reveal like so many providential hints that the way to a happy outcome is the exercise of free will and rational control that the fortuitous under the guidance of Heaven makes possible.[35]

3. Turning Point   Ch 29

When Quixote re-emerges from his penance in Sierra Morena he has been absent from the narrative for two or three days. In the interval we have followed Sancho to and from the inn, have met up with the priest and barber and have heard out the stories of Cardenio and Dorotea. This is the longest interval in the entire book in which Quixote is hidden from the reader. Only once before has he disappeared from view (Ch 6) and in that interval, in which he slept and rested, the priest and barber carried out the scrutiny of his books. Following that brief absence Quixote set out with Sancho on this his second sally. Now his behavior and condition suggest that his imaginative excess has been played out as a result of his penitential trial. We may even surmise that this trial has exhausted the psychological need for adventure as well as the physical possibility for them. If, then, Quixote's thrust for adventure has expended its momentum, what course shall his story take? Having reached the point of maximum thrust, the course of adventure would necessarily swing back and return to its starting point, his village in La Mancha. Thus, his emergence from the Sierra is the major turning point in Part One. Since it cannot be his own will and resolve that determine that Quixote must now return to his village, the motives for returning will appear in terms that, though new to the story, are derived from the fictional motives for which he carried out his penance.

The 'cause' of the penance was entirely gratuitous, but its purpose was "to win renown and fame" equal if not superior to any literary figure who had undertaken a similar trial: ". . . tengo de hacer . . . una hazaña con que he de ganar perpetuo nombre y fama en todo lo descubierto de la tierra" (I.25, 303). [I intend to carry out . . . a deed that will win me everlasting fame and renown over the whole face of the earth.] What he construes as its purpose—to win fame and renown in literature as 'mad lover' (i.e.;, Orlando, Amadís)—is of course depicted in chivalric books as the *result* of actions of literary heroes. On emerging from the Sierra, Quixote can be said to have acquired this fame and renown. His absence has served as a gestation period for this conceit which now endows him with a new configuration.

Removing the protagonist from the foreground appears to have been the necessary circumstance for Cervantes to introduce this new turn of events. That Quixote should take on the dimensions of a renowned, literary knight was nearly predictable from the way his parody of chivalry began in chapter 2, ". . . cuando el famoso caballero don Quixote de la Mancha, dejando las ociosas plumas. . . ." [when the famous knight Don Quixote of La Mancha, quitting his downy bed. . . .] It is one more conceit that fulfills his illusion of himself. Yet there had to be an occasion for it and his absence serves as the necessary hiatus to propose that as a result of his penance Quixote is now famous and renowned for it. It is the indispensable structural conceit in the scene in which Dorotea as Princess Micomicona approaches and requests a boon of the mock hero. "Y si es que el valor de vuestro fuerte brazo corresponde a la voz de vuestra inmortal fama, obligado estáis a favorecer a la sin ventura que de tan lueñes tierras viene, al olor de vuestro famoso nombre, buscándoos para remedio de sus desdichas." I.29, 364 [And if the valor of your mighty arm be equal to what I have heard of your immortal fame, it is your bounded duty to succor this luckless woman who comes from lands so faraway, drawn by the scent of your great fame to seek from you a remedy of her misfortune.]

Unlike previous scenes with a comic likeness to the chivalric originals, this one turns on the fiction that Quixote is now a knight with a renown similar to Amadís's. At one more point the exemplary story unfolds to reveal the generic nature of the hero and the process of his transformation: his 'fame' materializes from the 'fictional' nature of his illusion, from his literary madness. That Quixote should be a 'famous' knight renowned for his deeds is the indispensable core of his fiction as knight. It is both an image of himself and an illusion born of his deepest cravings and expectations. And yet as the story began by elaborating the fiction of his fame as an aberration of his mind, now it proceeds to enlarge upon it as a fiction that can be entertained in the mind of others. The 'fame' of Don Quixote in the real world of the hidalgo and his friends, the priest and barber, Sancho and Dorotea, is the nuclear core of his chivalric illusion.

In other words, the 'Quixotic fiction' is the inevitable issue or consequence of the exemplary story and the means by which the story sustains and enlarges upon itself. Looking back to the beginning of Part I, we can see that, from the moment Cervantes introduced the style of a chivalric romance in an exemplary account, he instituted the process by which he complicated structurally and stylistically an almost plotless story. The exemplary plot would remain simple, reduced to the most general of lines and intrigue. The book's complications of structure and style would arise from the literary motivations of Quixote and become progressively intricate. Quixote's chivalry would be the first 'fiction' to emerge from the story; the others would emerge as the illusory fiction of his fame as knight took hold. That Quixote has won fame and renown through his deeds and exploits is a burlesque outcome of Cervantes' parody, but likewise the indispensable element of structure that will permit the author to expand his story by incorporating other fictions.

In more than one sense, then, Quixote is a creature of fiction; his entire depiction depends on maintaining the illusion that he has won renown by performing chivalric but ineffectual deeds. What he has performed or carried out is only the illusion or fiction of himself as knight. Yet this tergiversation, which would be intolerable in almost any other narrative, is here not only tenable and necessary, but even compelling, because the story has already established that the condition by which Quixote's fame is presumable and derivable is that he is ineffectual in the real sense. His effect is literary, fictional, not real. His actions cannot exert on social or physical reality the 'heroic' effect that his madness attributes to them. He has not remedied (and will not remedy) one single case of injustice or wrong in the real world. This is not just the theme of the story or the effect established by Cervantes' narrative technique; it is the idea governing the design of interlocking levels of fiction, of a narrative structure of fiction-within-fiction. From the character of a comical exemplary story who was merely interesting (to Ch 15), he has developed into the entertaining character who elicits our sympathetic responses. While preforming deeds that are a travesty rather than an imitation of chivalric actions he entertains with greater efficacy than the 'real' heroes of chivalric literature. Cervantes, that is, has subverted the effect a romance of chivalry was intended to produce (to entertain its readers or listeners with stories of efficacious deeds) by producing a hero who is intrinsically and comically entertaining by consistently failing to be efficacious in this way, because his chivalry is only an illusion of his madness.

Quixote will now come in contact with characters drawn from various levels of Spanish society and who come forth with a "storied" personal affliction. Their narratives will be played out and resolved around him, but he will not be the agent who acts or intervenes to bring about that resolution. Yet his presence alone is efficacious for bringing about the conditions that propitiously permit a resolution. It is in this way that his mock identity will come into its own, as reality and as 'fiction.'

When Quixote agrees to aid Princess Micomicona, and the party of priest, barber, Sancho, Dorotea and Cardenio leave the Sierra, the course of narrative has not only turned homeward, but due to the element of Quixote's 'fame' has been turned inside out with respect to what is real or parody. The change is apparent in various details, most of all in the change of clothing. Quixote has put on his clothes and armor. Dorotea abandoned her boy's disguise and dressed herself as a great lady. Cardenio has been shorn of his rags and beard. The barber has put on a disguise with a beard in order to play the part of a chivalric squire. These changes of dress, costume, or disguise indicate that the parody of chivalry has become a ritualized hoax and Quixote the victim rather than the instigator.

The most obvious complication that accompanies the enlargement of the story into fiction-within-fiction is the replacement of Quixote's incentive for adventure by this carnival illusion in which, like the fool figure of tradition, he is the object of hoaxes, replete with costumes, masks, and impersonations.[36]

4. Sancho at el Toboso: Triangle   Chs 30–31

The great vehicle by which the interlocking fictions are introduced and sustained has been of course dialogue. Yet so skillful is Cervantes in producing the illusion that each of his characters expresses in his speech a personal point of view and an inimitable personality—the character literally speaks for himself—one can overlook the skill with which he unfolds the story from the flow and turn of Quixote's and Sancho's dialogue. In chapter 25 Quixote told Sancho he was sending him on an errand to Dulcinea: "Loco soy, loco he de ser hasta tanto que tú vuelvas con la respuesta de una carta que contigo pienso enviar a mi señora Dulcinea." (I.25, 306) [Mad I am, mad I shall remain until you return with the answer to a letter that I mean to send by you to my lady Dulcinea.] There followed that amazing series of exchanges on who Dulcinea is. "—¿Que la hija de Lorenzo Corchuelo es la señora Dulcinea del Toboso, llamada por otro nombre Aldonza Lorenzo?—Ésa es. . . y es la que merece ser señora de todo el Universo.—Bien la conozco. . . y sé decir que tira tan bien una barra como el más forzudo zagal de todo el pueblo. . . . I.25, 311–12 [—The daughter of Lorenzo Corchuelo is the Lady Dulcinea of El Toboso, otherwise called Aldonza Lorenzo? —That is she . . . and she deserves to be mistress of the Universe. I know her well . . . and I assure you she can pitch the iron bar as well as the strongest lad in our village. . . .] Up to then Sancho had heard much talk about Dulcinea, but it had been all abstract (i.e., "she deserves to be mistress of the Universe"). Hence his amazement to learn that this ideal, distant lady is really a peasant girl. In disclosing who Dulcinea is Quixote opens the way to Sancho's intrusion in his intimate affairs. Sancho had no choice but to agree to set off to El Toboso to deliver the letter Quixote wrote down in a notebook and read aloud (but failed to turn over). Their dialogue is on the surface vivid, vehement and comical. Apparently the dialogue is all the story consists of. But in fact Cervantes is such a powerful creator of fiction that through dialogue he creates not only character but the very structure of his book as fiction.

By devising a message that Sancho is to deliver to Dulcinea, and a verbal description of his penance (Ch 25), Quixote intended to carry out one more imitation of chivalric practice. The decision to subject himself to fasts and other penitential trials if carried out solely for his sentimental satisfaction would not have led to the consequences that his decision to inform Dulcinea about it through Sancho will produce. Further, so that his penance should have for him the desired, meaningful effect, Sancho must return with a favorable message from Dulcinea. The success of the penance is contingent on it. In this way the intimate and sentimental side of his devotion to Dulcinea becomes exposed and the consequences turn out to be decisive. When informed by Sancho that his master expects a reply from Dulcinea, the priest and barber seize the opportunity to deceive him with the ploy of a false message. And Sancho, once prodded and prompted, will fabricate an entire fiction of his interview with Dulcinea. Her supposed reply and request, that Quixote leave the Sierra and set out for El Toboso, is the first in an entire chain of events and deceptions that will lead to the scene on the outskirts of El Toboso in chapter 10 of Part II and beyond.

Quixote was obliged by his own conception of the sentimental relations between knight and lady to enlist Sancho's aid as messenger and intermediary. In doing so he unwittingly made Sancho indispensable to his relations with Dulcinea, recreating the triangular situation that is so prominent in *Amadís de Gaula*, where the squire Gandalín plays the role of messenger and confidant between Oriana and Amadís.[37]

Sancho and Gandalín are poles apart as literary or chivalric personalities. But Cervantes needed only the suggestion from *Amadís de Gaula* to elaborate his own version of the triangle of conflicting personalities and loyalties that develop when the servant of the knight or lady (squire or damsel) is given a major role as intermediary and confidant. Behind the triangle in *Amadís de Gaula* we can discern the influence of the most complicated situation of this sort in chivalric literature, the case of Tristan and Isolde and their servants Brangain and Gurvenal. Gandalín's loyalty is foremost to his master, and he cannot understand or fathom Amadís's submission in body and soul to Oriana. And once Oriana and Amadís are united in love and then marriage his role is reduced and then terminated. From their story Cervantes took the suggestion that, in order to approach Dulcinea (whom Quixote invented), the mock knight needed to send Sancho as an intercessor and messenger. From this he further suggested (as parody) that in doing so the knight was jeopardizing not just the tender and intimate nature of their relationship but the very identity, indeed existence, of the lady Dulcinea. All of this transpires through the dialogues of chapters 28 to 31.

Sancho's account of his trip to El Toboso and interview with Dulcinea is a 'big fib' that qualifies for status as a fiction because it is drawn according to Quixote's expectations. But what we see now happening as story in their dialogue in chapter 31 is that Sancho has placed himself between Quixote and Dulcinea. From a kind of intruder into their relationship that he was at the start, he is now indispensable.

>—Llegaste, ¿y qué hacía aquella reina de la hermosura? A buen seguro que la hallaste ensartando perlas, o bordando alguna empresa con oro de cañutillo para este su cautivo caballero.
>—No la hallé—respondió Sancho—sino ahechando dos hanegas de trigo en un corral de su casa.
>Pues haz cuenta—dijo don Quijote—que los granos de aquel trigo eran granos de perlas, tocados de sus manos. Y si miraste, amigo, el trigo ¿era candeal o trechel?
>—No era sino rubión—respondió Sancho. I.31, 382

>—You arrived; now, what was the queen of beauty doing? Surely you found her stringing pearls or embroidering some device with golden threads for this, her captive knight.
>—No, I did not—replied Sancho. She was winnowing two bushels of wheat in the backyard of her house.
>Why, then—said don Quixote—you may reckon that each grain of wheat was a pearl when touched by her hands. Did you note, my friend, the wheat, was it the white or brown sort?
>—'Twas neither, but red—replied Sancho.

Through evasion and malice Sancho is forced to invent and describe a Dulcinea who is, ostensibly, Aldonza Lorenzo and entirely plausible by what Quixote disclosed about her in chapter 25. The result is a realistic picture and mental image of Dulcinea that will impose itself on Quixote's mind and senses. It replaces the abstract image of the ideal lady he has painted earlier. Some traits are pure malice on the part of Sancho, who takes a certain pleasure in prevaricating on his master's suggestions:

> . . . bendigo y bendeciré [mi fortuna] todos los días de me vida, por haberme hecho digno de merecer amar tan alta señora como Dulcinea del Toboso.
> —Tan alta es—respondió Sancho, que a buena fe que me lleva a mí más de un coto.
> —Pues, ¿cómo, Sancho? . . . ¿haste medido tú con ella?
> —Medíme en esta manera—. . . que llegándole a ayudar a poner un costal de trigo sobre un jumento, llegamos tan juntos, que eché de ver que me llevaba más de un gran palmo. I.31, 383

> . . . I bless [my fortune] and shall bless it all the days of my life, for making me worthy of the love of so high a lady as Dulcinea of El Toboso.
> —So high is she—answered Sancho, that she's a good hand's breadth taller than I am.
> —How is that, Sancho—said Don Quixote—. Have you measured yourself with her?
> —I did, like this—Sancho answered—: for when I was helping her raise a sack of wheat onto an ass, we came so close together that I couldn't help seeing that she was taller than me by a good span.

Unwittingly, Quixote has allowed Sancho to interject himself as indispensable to his relations with Dulcinea and the third party in a chivalric triangle. Quixote needed a witness to his penance, and preferably that very witness should report on his actions to Dulcinea. For this reason Sancho's lie about her reply will carry the force of Quixote's expectations. The result—Sancho's ascendancy and his new role as intermediary—leaves Quixote vulnerable to deceit and machinations and confirms the comic principle of the story that determines that each theme will retrace motion from Quixote's imagination to Sancho's corporeality.

> Y, finalmente, me dijo que dijese a vuestra merced que le besaba las manos, y que allí quedaba con más deseo de verle que de escribirle, y que, así, le suplicaba y mandaba que . . . saliese de aquellos matorrales y se dejase de hacer disparates, y se pusiese luego luego en camino del Toboso . . . porque tenía gran deseo de ver a vuestra merced. I.31, 384

> And, finally, she begged me to tell you that she kissed your hands, and that she was more eager to see you than to write to you, and that she begged and commanded you . . . to leave these bushes and briars and give up your mad antics, and set out at once on the road to El Toboso . . . for she had a mighty desire to see you.

The entire subject of a trip to El Toboso and interview with Dulcinea is a deception played on Quixote. Yet even as a fiction it has been described as an event that was plausible in the most realistic terms. The 'fiction' never happened, never took place as an event or turn in the plot, but it effectively 'happens' in the form of dialogue. And its effect on the story or on Quixote is as complicated as if it were an intrigue and action in the plot. Thereby its full status as fiction. Sancho has 'invented' a peasant Dulcinea with physical features that only he could have conceived, and now moreover he is Quixote's indispensable access to her. Quixote's image of Dulcinea has been compromised irreversibly by Sancho's fiction.

5. The Inn: Castle, Stage, Palace   Chs 32–47

When the party arrives at the inn, Quixote's first request is to be taken to bed. His weary state would explain why he does not misperceive where he is. He falls asleep for an interval of several hours. He will not be awake and part of the action until after the conclusion of *The Curious Impertinent* and the scenes that reunite Cardenio and Luscinda and Dorotea and Fernando and just before the captain Ruy Pérez and Zoraida arrive at the inn. His absence, however, is but a matter of hours, whereas during his penance he was out of sight for three entire days. And since his 'fame' has now replaced his incentive for adventure, the process of his transformation will be borne out explicitly by the mechanics of fiction-within-fiction. As an object of practical and festive hoax he has acquired the fictional efficacy to preside over the storied lives of the secondary characters.

The setting has moved indoors, to various rooms in the inn. The narrator will omit any reference to the historian Cide Hamete or to his 'history' throughout the remaining mass of narrative, and his technique becomes predominantly a dramatist's. According to Quixote's illusion and the hoaxes perpetrated on him, the inn is a castle and 'enchanted.' But the dramatic coincidences that bring about the resolution of the subordinate plots provide an analogy to stage comedy (where the conventional ending is the marriage of reunited couples) and convert the inn into a theatrical stage. A further analogy with its contrasts will connect these scenes of reunion and resolution with the magical 'palace of love' where according to literary tradition the love problems of distraught or alienated couples are resolved by magical means.[38] Quixote's comical mock chivalry contrasts with the serious conflicts and actions of the protagonists who surround him. Their autonomy enables them to surmount the obstacles impeding the way to the happy outcome of their stories. Quixote's illusion that his presence or valor is responsible, or that his virtue has effected a magical solution, will indicate that the autonomy he exercised over his actions up to the turning point (Ch 29) has been exchanged for the new configuration of his 'fame,' for the efficacy of his 'fictional' self.

So his absence really underscores in a different light how his pathological state, the course of his madness, that is, serves as the main or plot frame for the fictions now to be introduced. In his absence he provokes yet another discussion on the effects of reading chivalric books (Ch 32). All of the characters who have come in contact with Quixote join in, except of course Sancho. Each character voices his own subjective opinion and illusion about them, so we have not just the negative side voiced by the priest and barber, Dorotea and Cardenio. The innkeeper and his wife, his daughter and Maritornes, though illiterate, have heard books of chivalry read aloud, and express their personal tastes and liking for their contents. The scene and dialogue are among the most ingratiating written by Cervantes. The innkeeper mentions his supply of books and the priest asks to see them. The illusion conveyed is that nothing here is fictional. It is life as full or artless as realism can make it.

In the valise brought out by the innkeeper the priest finds three printed books and a bundle of papers, i.e., a manuscript. This is the material form of fictional and nonfictional narrative, counterpointed to the lives and 'real' characters who sit around the table and discuss and evaluate it from opposite points of view. Two of the books are romances of chivalry, *Don Cirongilio* and *Felixmarte*. The other is a historical narrative about the deeds of the Great Captain, Gonzalo Hernández de Córdoba. The priest argues against the nonsensical marvellous and fantastic in chivalric books because they produce a fraudulent product and in favor of a verisimilar mode of narrative based on historical events and persons because it is acceptable to reason and a critical morality, and moreover supported by experience. This mode, because directed to the intellect, can reduce the marvellous and fantastic to plausible explanations and even to didactic, utilitarian ends of what is right and wrong. None of this convinces the innkeeper. He retorts that chivalric books give real pleasure precisely because their fantastic and marvellous elements are depicted as real. The priest of course echoes the narrator's own position. His arguments are meant to convince the protesting innkeeper that chivalric books cannot give real pleasure because they were composed with little or no critical design. The questions is left in suspension (to be taken up by the priest later in his conversation with the canon from Toledo). For now the question of design as indispensable to verisimilar, hence superior, fiction has been laid down. The manuscript in the valise is the *Novel of the Curious Impertinent*, which the priest will now read aloud. There is another novel in manuscript in the bag (hidden in the lining); it is not mentioned until much later (p. 559). Its title is *Novel of Rinconete and Cortadillo*. This is the second of three instances in Part I in which Cervantes alludes to himself and his works. In chapter 6 the priest mentioned *Galatea* and its author. In chapter 40 the captain will describe "the soldier something de Saavedra." The characters who sit around the table and listen to the *Novela* exist as fictional creatures in a given reality, depicted as a moral and social world of maximum plausibility. The frame situation appears to be entirely verisimilar because nothing 'fictional' happens but daily life. It is of course a literary effect striven for by the narrator and sustained by the tensions of the exemplary course of Quixote's madness. Within this plane and 'order' Cervantes will now introduce his highly fictional *novela*. By design the maximum plausibility of the frame contains the relative plausibility of the *novela* as a relationship between 'orders' of fiction. The procedure suggests: how is one fiction containable within another? And the answer: by a 'critical ordering,' by design. There is, then, a direct relationship between what tensions in a narrative aim at and what they demand of our credibility, the suspension of our disbelief. Hence the plausibility of the exemplary story as of any of the 'orders' of fiction that follow depends on how the various elements of narrative are 'ordered' or pressed to engage and suspend our disbelief. As a generalization, we may say that Cervantes centers the tensions of his narratives around a 'crisis.' The eight narratives outlined on Chart II can be put into three groups, according to the crisis they embody.

1) 'crisis of sentiments.'
2) 'crisis of events.'
3) 'crisis of conscience'.

The narratives built around the first are the sentimental stories of Cardenio and Luscinda, Dorotea and Fernando and Don Luis and Clara. *The Captain's Tale* takes its shape from a 'crisis of events.' A 'crisis of conscience' gives shape to the *Novel of the Curious Impertinent*.

6. Novel of the Curious Impertinent   Chs 33–35

Among the major sources uncovered by scholars for this novel are two legendary situations, the test of a wife's fidelity by means of a magical wine goblet, from which a husband would be unable to drink if his wife had been unfaithful to him, included in *Orlando furioso*, and an ideal and heroic friendship between two males, also retold by Boccaccio in the *Decameron*.[39] Both situations involve a test. In the case of the second, the test comes about when one of the friends, out of loyalty and gratitude, surrenders to the other his beloved or bride when he learns she is desired by him. From these legendary materials Cervantes produced a story that for its approach to and insight into human nature, and the craft of fiction that proposes to depict it, is as 'modern' today as in 1604. It is most significant that he called it a *novela*, not just because its form and length correspond to the Italian short prose narrative (*novella*, plural, *novelle*), but because its means and ends as prose fiction, or its plausibility as a fictional account of human nature, were inscribed within this form or kind. Its themes, characters, and intrigue are removed from the Spain of Quixote's adventures and located in the Italian city of Florence about a hundred years before. This distance in time and space to the scene in the inn is commensurate with its 'closed' structure, its calculated arrangement of disclosures, from the part assigned to the narrator to the unrelieved enclosure of the characters in Anselmo's house in Florence, which on other terms might appear implausible. The narrator's appeal to our 'suspension of disbelief' is then relative to what the *novela* attempts to depict as well as how it carries out its aim, i.e., its strategy.

In the *novela* as Cervantes knew it and shaped it, the relationship between character and events is nearly the inverse of what it is in a *tale*. In the *novela*, for the way their motives and actions are depicted, we see and believe that characters determine events and the outcome. In any given narrative these two elements come into play. But the distinction that Cervantes imposes between *tale* and *novel* (*'cuento,'* '*novela*') is that in a novel the intrigue becomes a complication stemming predominantly from character, whereas in the tale a complication of events become the intrigue.

The *Curioso* is then a *novela* because it depicts characters who of their own free will and with their moral or psychological resources or deficiencies determine a course of action as an exemplary depiction of human conduct. At one end it exposes an abnormal, even pathological compulsion only to carry it forward to its most enlightened moral implications. The ultimate test of its plausibility is not whether it tells a believable account of adultery and the dissolution of three apparently virtuous and honorable characters, but whether it is a true and meaningful account of the human capacity for good or evil.

Anselmo, Camila and Lotario are three beings endowed by nature and Providence with all that they need to ensure their happiness: wealth, beauty, intelligence, honorable social position and ties. These two Italian males are such close friends they are known to all as the proverbial "good friends." Anselmo has married Camila whose devotion to him promises an untroubled marriage, and Lotario, ever loyal, respects his friend's new marital obligations. Nothing in their existence—nothing external to their character, that is—is a threat to their continual happiness. But despite this, and contrary to what he appears to be, Anselmo is possessed by an abnormal obsession; though he has no reason to doubt his wife's fidelity, she has not been put to the test. He convinces himself that he must be unhappy so long as he does not have tangible, that is sensory or sensible, proof of Camila's fidelity. What better remedy than to have Lotario, out of loyalty to him, pretend to seduce her, as an 'experiment,' and thus satisfy his 'curiosity' and ease his conscience. The seeds of destruction have been sown in the diseased soil of Anselmo's conscience out of his deficiency as husband. His 'impertinent curiosity' has become all-compelling when he reveals his scheme to Lotario and proposes and then pleads that out of loyalty to him, and as the one remedy that can cure him, his friend pretend to seduce Camila. Lotario grasps the awful implications of Anselmo's proposal in every respect. At first he is stunned by the revelation, for he realizes that despite their close friendship there is a part of them completely unknown to the other. And even a part of themselves that is unknown to themselves, we add. For how can the Lotario who so genuinely tries to dissuade his friend from such a dishonorable course with the most telling moral and rational arguments know what he is himself capable of, when, out of compassion for Anselmo, he consents reluctantly to take up the scheme, in the hope of curing him by an honest deception? The triangle of constrained loyalties is played out as an account of crossed, mutual deceptions, and the great passions of fictional intrigue: jealousy, injured self-pride, guilt and sexual attraction. But these passions are aroused, released and impelled to the final calamity by a crisis of conscience induced by Anselmo's diseased curiosity.

Because he was unable to repress in his mind and imagination the thought that his wife should be tested, Anselmo in his conscience committed an 'adulterous deed' even while expecting that Camila would resist Lotario. His diseased soul was convinced that to have his wife tested by another man was necessary for his honor, when in fact the very idea is not only dishonorable but of course adulterous. From the beginning, then, what he imagined then desired and finally requested was a betrayal of his marriage and the friendship, so that inevitably he becomes the victim of his obsession.

Lotario is the loyal friend and carries out Anselmo's wishes but deceiving him, until Anselmo learns the truth and berates him for his dishonesty and disloyalty, at which point Lotario's masculine pride and sense of honor are irreparably injured and his egotistical motives take over. Camila is the resisting, faithful wife until, assaulted by genuine passion aroused in Lotario by her beauty and in the absence of her husband, she succumbs to elicit desire, flattery and vanity. The intrigue of the novel illustrates the theme that error and betrayal in conscience alone is sufficient to destroy, totally, honor and the trust and loyalty of marriage and replace them with perfidious deception. The unloosed chain of mutual deceptions from scene to scene as disclosed by the narrator has originated in the soul-error of Anselmo. He assumed that ostensible proof of Camila's loyalty—sensible or sensory evidence of her fidelity to him—was sufficient proof to establish that she was or was not faithful in the absolute sense. Hence the 'impertinence' of his curiosity or obsession. He applied it not only to a question reserved to the Absolute or Divine, and for humans 'impertinent' to usurp, but he applied it in a totally superficial way, for he wished to be satisfied by external, 'sensory' or empirical evidence, by what he heard and saw, by 'appearances.'

Hence the narrator's strategy and the intrigue of enmeshed scenes and events set in motion by the corrosive power of illicit passion are made to illustrate the novel's interlocking themes in the scene when, passively, and utterly duped by Camila, Lotario and Leonela the maid, Anselmo, satisfying his voyeuristic streak, watches and hears from behind curtains the scene and action that now materialize from his deepest inadequacy. What he sees and hears convinces him that he has a most faithful wife and the most trustful friend. What he sees and hears he believes to be the absolute proof he desired. The illusion of virtue is theatrical, but beneath Camila's performance is the truth of her corrupted conscience. Out of desperation and guilt she slashes herself with a dagger and bleeds. Her blood is the ultimate, 'sensory' proof (not of her fidelity, but) of Anselmo's initial error and self-deception. She is the more pitiable victim by far, for she does not know nor ever learn how the two males deceived her. The fact is that the whole affair has become so endemic with deceit and wile, corrupted loyalties and guilt, that pretense and truth appear inextricable. Out of the resources of his craft the narrator can sharpen the significance of the scene to a fine edge.

> Atentísimo había estado Anselmo a escuchar y a ver representar la tragedia de la muerte de su honra; la cual con tan estraños y eficaces afectos la representaron los personajes della, que pareció que se habían transformado en la misma verdad de lo que fingían. I.35, 436 [Anselmo had stood listening and watching with rapt attention to this tragedy representing the death of his honor, and performed by the players with such strange and moving passion that they seemed transformed into the very characters they were acting.]

It is just after this scene that the reading of the novel is interrupted by Sancho's cries about Quixote and the wineskins. It is the obvious moment to reflect on the connection between Quixote's madness—altruistic, and Anselmo's obsession, entirely self-consuming and egotistical.

The outcome seems inevitable, for once the intrigue is played out—through Leonora the truth of Anselmo's dishonor is known in all of Florence, Camila and Lotario flee—the narrator's strategy is to bring his themes to their consummation with Anselmo's discovery of the truth; so bitter, so regretful does it weigh on his conscience that it literally kills him in the act of writing... *"yo fui el fabricador de mi deshonra"* I.35, 445 [*I became the maker of my own dishonor*]. It is recognition of his error of conscience that kills him. Both victim and culprit, as jealous and outwitted husband Anselmo not only acknowledges his curiosity was impertinent (i.e., the title is attributable to him), that he has been the cause of his downfall, but must confess his total guilt, pardon his wife, all-but-sentence himself to death, and finally expire, all as the last act of a remorseful but illuminated conscience. The completely anti-heroic nature of Anselmo, his moral inadequacy as husband, delegating his honor to his friend, is consummated in the final act of conscience of his remission and death. He has been an 'experimenter' who deceived himself foolishly into believing he could control this 'human experiment' and was in turn deceived, bringing upon himself his dire ruin. In different ways Camila and Lotario also find death a means of expiation.

The *novela* concludes with the complete enclosing of its fictional beings in a world of moral cause and effect. It has dealt with moral error and miscalculation to great psychological depth in an exemplary depiction of personal motives and forces with a finality and manner commensurate with its 'order' of fiction. The error develops from a crisis affecting all three principals, but for Anselmo so serious that by its very nature it can be resolved only as an 'act of conscience,' admission of his error and guilt and for Camila's infidelity, his repentance and punishment, attainable only through death. Here we have the most obvious parallel between Anselmo and Quixote as protagonists of their respective 'exemplary novels.' Quixote's error is that he believes he is a real knight. When he recovers his sanity at the end of Part II, he confesses his error and the admission is tantamount to dying. He 'lets himself' die, as the final 'autonomous act.' But Quixote belongs to another order of fiction and much superior to Anselmo's for reasons too complicated to elaborate on here. Cervantes wrote two *novelas* about jealous and inadequate husbands (or rather, one 'curious,' the other 'jealous,' Carrizales in *The Jealous Extremaduran*), who become victims of their own misconceived schemes and end up exposing their wives to adulterous deceit.[40] In both he contrived a great artifice to place the blame for the wife's infidelity on the husband. In this respect he is certainly one of the more original nonconformists of his or any age.

7. Fernando and Dorotea

No sooner is the manuscript of the *novela* put away than a group of travelers arrives, their faces concealed by masks. They are Don Fernando and his companions with Luscinda whom they have abducted from a convent where she had gone to hide from him. Following the *novela* with its theatrical scene we have another, but this one by contrast offers or permits an 'open' happy solution to the narratives of Cardenio and Dorotea, adequate to their 'sentimental story.' The four characters come together fortuitously, their reunion under these circumstances is providential, but as they and the narrator himself point out, not the event but the force of rational and moral persuasion on individual conscience can restore order among wronged affections. The solution is then 'novelistic' by Cervantes' requirements, though the means to it are largely theatrical.

The combination of fortunate coincidence, masked faces, expressive sighs, fainting spells, and profuse tears is dramatic emphasis of the sentimental nature of the conflict of alienated affections. Yet the real conflict takes place below the expressiveness of these means, and there, also, rest the logic and verisimilitude of the action. The dramatic grouping of the four principals is all-important, from any of their movements to the next; for, again, voice, glances, tears, gestures and motion may describe or express what the characters think, feel, and say, but it is their moral force as free, rational beings on an individual basis that affects the solution. That is to say that the plausibility of the solution rests on an act of conscience. Don Fernando's, of course. It is he who must be convinced to relent, to accede, to make a 'change of heart,' and here, so to speak, on stage, in a matter of minutes. But Fernando is the least introspective of the principals, the one up to now least inclined to look inward. Dorotea with her energetic resources of character precipitates the change.

Looks, voices and action revolve around Fernando. When Luscinda hears Cardenio's voice from behind the door, the nobleman reaches out and forcibly restrains her. She struggles to free herself, and his mask falls off. Dorotea recognizes him and faints: Fernando in all his ferocity as the violent, lustful nobleman. The priest rushes to revive her, removing the veil from her face. Fernando recognizes Dorotea and the sight of her face mortifies him. We can only surmise the inner turmoil he is going through as Dorotea now recovered falls to her knees and vehemently and eloquently implores him to release Luscinda and restore her to Cardenio; to keep his word to her, restore her honor and accept her as his wife. With the instinct of a woman who knows her cause is just, she does not reproach him for dishonoring her nor abandoning her, but appeals to his self-respect as nobleman on high principle, by humbling herself. She appeals then not to his guilt or even repentance, but to his most generous instincts as a nobleman. She will sway, persuade and convince him because her arguments make of her love, dependency and devotion to him not just a moral reason for reparation but the truth of intellectual persuasion as well. She pleads, weeps and sobs out of apparent desperation, yet the verbal vehemence of her discourse is a measure of her intelligence and energetic self-possession. It is as if she is determined to show this proud aristocrat how right he was to seek her out, that though a farmer's daughter, her natural distinctions—intelligence ('discretion'), beauty, virtue—are equal to his nobility. Her outpouring is the righteous vehemence of virtue offended, an outpouring of her conscience directed at his. Now "full of confusion and fright," moved by the truth of her pleas, but still torn between passion and reason, he relents, opens his arms and releases Luscinda who falls as if fainting.

Cardenio rushes to embrace her. But at the sight of Luscinda in Cardenio's arms the nobleman feels renewed rage and jealousy. He is still the nobleman who can bear no opposition to his will. He makes a move to unsheath his sword, then Dorotea flings herself at this knees, restraining him. Now she implores that he desist from any action that Heaven would disallow, to temper his rage and show his noble generosity, to subdue passion and follow reason. In this way her implorations reveal what he undergoes inwardly; he must subdue those self-seeking passions he has vented, lust, rage, jealousy, and through shame and horror restore the claims of honor, generosity and self-respect in his noble breast. By her love and humility she offers up to him a moral picture of his true self that he cannot deny. At this point her words cease and the narrator's strategy enlists the other characters in the way of a chorus to make explicit that Fernando must resolve to "conquer himself."

> ... todos rodeaban a don Fernando suplicándole tuviese por bien de mirar las lágrimas de Dorotea, y que, siendo verdad ... lo que en sus razones había dicho, que no permitiese quedase defraudada de sus tan justas esperanzas. Que considerase que, no acaso, como parecía, sino con particular providencia del cielo, se habían todos juntado en lugar donde menos ninguno pensaba; y que advirtiese—dijo el cura—que sola la muerte podía apartar a Luscinda de Cardenio ... y que en los lazos inremediables era suma cordura, forzándose y venciéndose a sí mismo, mostrar un generoso pecho, permitiendo que por sola su voluntad los dos gozasen el bien que el cielo ya les había concedido ....
>
> En efeto, a estas razones añadieron todos otras, tales y tantas, que el valeroso pecho de don Fernando—en fin, como alimentado con ilustre sangre—se ablandó y se dejó vencer de la verdad, que él no pudiera negar aunque quisiera;

y la señal que dio de haberse rendido y entregado al buen parecer que se le había propuesto fue abajarse y abrazar a Dorotea, diciéndole:
—Levantaos, señora mía. . . . I.36, 453–4

> . . . they gathered around Don Fernando, imploring him to be moved by Dorotea's tears and, if she was speaking the truth, . . . not to suffer her to be defrauded of her just expectations. They begged him to reflect that it was not by chance, as it appeared, but by a special providence of Heaven that they had all come together in such an unexpected place; and to bear in mind—the priest said—that only death could part Luscinda and Cardenio . . . and in these irremediable cases it was wisest for him to restrain and conquer himself, and show a generous heart by allowing these two, of his own free will, to enjoy the good fortune which Heaven had granted them . . .
> In short, they added so many compelling arguments that Don Fernando's valorous heart—which was, after all, nurtured by generous blood—softened, and allowed itself to be conquered by the truth, which he could not deny if he would. And the sign he gave of his surrender and acceptance of this good advice proposed to him was to stoop down and embrace Dorotea, saying:
> —Rise, my lady. . . .

From this moment forward Fernando acquires his new and definitive 'storied' character that will make him the witty and engaging accomplice in the hoax played on Quixote. From the treacherous nobleman of Cardenio's narrative and the inconstant but sought-for husband of Dorotea's he emerges, so to speak, as himself, as a consequence of this redeeming act. Luscinda is restored to Cardenio, but as a now happily reunited couple they are divested of their fictional cast. Cardenio has at last showed courage before Fernando, when he took Luscinda protectively in his arms, but it was Dorotea who precipitated the outcome. So now Fernando takes over the center of their story and not only for his high rank. Just as it was his self-serving passion that set in motion the chain of cause and effect that drove Cardenio and Luscinda apart, and Dorotea to seek him out, so now his conquest of his passionate self as a free act of conscience permits the complete and happy solution. As fictional causality their story rests on the individual's freedom to seek out and strive for, despite all barriers, an ideal sentimental relationship. Cardenio would have willingly perished in his search and blamed others for his failure. Dorotea had the self-possession never to give up. Fernando finds his at last in Dorotea, through the rejection and dramatic purgation of pride and the lust it conceals that a providential event made possible.

There is then an indispensable connection between the narrator's technique that depicts the scene in the way of dramatic encounters on stage and the 'order' of fiction that it establishes. A character must be depicted—hence the resemblance to theatrical performance—exercising (of his or her own free will) those impulses of reason and imagination that affect the solution to the conflict. There is an analogy on this level between Fernando's conversion and Anselmo's confession. They conform to an act of conscience, which is how Cervantes conceives and represents a 'novelistic' solution. While using theatrical techniques, he pursues ends different from those of the dramatist, for he conceives the outcome of his plots in terms of reason and illuminated conscience, the opposite of the histrionic scenes of death and vengeance, or exaltation of passionate love in the manner of Lope de Vega. The freedom of individual conscience to affirm or deny becomes indispensable to the end toward which he aligns and subordinates all elements of story. The *novela* read in the preceding scene showed how Anselmo committed an error of conscience, was enormously deceived, and too late recognized his fault. The analogy noted above is even more emphatic for the fact that once the masks fall off every element of deception is eliminated from the scene, and the 'truth' of his actions is overwhelming evidence to his senses in the moments Fernando ponders his decision The *novela* has a 'closed' form. Here strategy provides an 'open' solution, and for this reason the Cardenio-Luscinda, Dorotea-Fernando complex belongs to the 'order' of 'story.' In both cases Cervantes brought the conflict involved forward to a solution that rejecting external factors like the magical, marvellous, or circumstantial, depends on a decision of his characters.

8. The Captain Ruy Pérez and Zoraida

Before they appear Sancho has roused Quixote from his sleep and vented his despair at having seen Princess Micomicona 'transformed' into a mere noblelady and bride of Don Fernando. Quixote now re-appears, his strange outfit and bizarre figure causing renewed amazement. Once more the contrast he makes for his mad illusion certifies that he belongs to another 'order' of fiction. He approaches Dorotea with exaggerated courtesy and inquires whether she has 'changed.' Fernando looks on. Her reply is a vivacious play on the two levels of fiction, one real, the other fantastic. She can truthfully say that she is the same person as before as that her affair has been turned around for her having entrusted her cause to Quixote. Alongside Fernando, whose idea of his person and social worth are prescribed by birth and position, Quixote forms a social contrast; alongside the captain Ruy Pérez who now enters with Zoraida he forms a most instructive literary one.

As in the case of Cardenio and Dorotea, the initial picture is indicative of their fictional cast. He wears the blue outfit of a Christian captive from Algiers, leading the donkey on which she rides, draped in a Moorish cloak and her face veiled. Despite his clothing he has the distinguished appearance of a well-built man just a little past forty in age. She is a girl, much younger, perhaps nineteen. They suggest, ever so slightly, Joseph and Mary; the pictorial suggestion is borne out by the difference in age and her devotion to the Virgin. From the moment of their appearance they form such a contrast in age, race and culture (between them and the other characters in the inn) they excite the interest and wonder of fabled beings. They have in fact emerged from another order of life and experience with its own historical ties of blood and belief, customs, and perils, and from another 'order' of fiction as well with its own inherent design of conflict and causality, of desire, motive and reward. We learn in due course (from his narrative) who they are and why like a picture from a mythical past this man of mature age and bearing leads this exotic Moorish girl protectively like father and husband.

By parentage and upbringing Zoraida is a Muslim and speaks only an Algerian dialect of Arabic. She is the daughter of a wealthy Moor in Algiers. She lost her mother at an early age. One of her father's women slaves taught her (secretly, we suspect) the rudiments of the Christian catechism, inculcated her with a strong desire to become a convert, and inspired in her a great devotion to the Virgin Mary. After the death of the slave woman, Zoraida had visions in which the woman urged her to go to a Christian country where she could worship the Virgin on whose great love she could depend . So deep was her desire to become a Christian and so intense and pure her faith in the Virgin (despite her meager acquaintance with Christianity) she prepared a plan to escape from Algiers secretly with the help of Spanish captives and her father's wealth, entrusting to them her person and her hope in the face of almost insuperable obstacles, for as a Moorish daughter she lived secluded from affairs of the world and the evil conspiracies of slave traffic. For any Christian slave in

Algiers such an escape is an impossible dream. The captain Ruy Pérez is the Spaniard she chose to aid her in her plan. The greatest obstacle to her freedom was her father. In the captive she has found a man so noble and devoted to her that as a husband he will replace her father in her affections.

The captive's name is not revealed until much later, by the priest (p. 517): Ruy Pérez de Viedma. Eighteen years ago serving as a Captain of infantry on board a Spanish galley at the naval battle of Lepanto (fought October 7, 1571, between the Christian and Turkish fleets off the coast of Greece) while leading his company he was separated from his men on board the Turkish galley they were attacking, wounded and taken prisoner. Up to the time Zoraida selected him to put her plan into effect he had been forced to row as galley slave and then to languish among thousands imprisoned in Algiers for almost half of his life. Her intercession, then, has been the union of an all-but legendary figure of a girl who for her passionate faith and love is a miraculous intercessor and redeemer with a Spanish captive who for his privations and patience in adversity is worthy to love and serve her as her future husband.

Zoraida's 'storied' character is derived from legend, which accounts for the idealized nature of her spiritual conflict and the abstract, even naive treatment of her motives at every turn. Ruy Pérez is likewise not based on any psychological study of the inner forces that inure men to pain and adversity, nor even on his part in an intrigue about imprisonment and escape. He is in the way of a historical personage who for his heroic deed at Lepanto and suffering at the hands of Spain's enemies deserved the intercession of Zoraida. Their narrative is, in short, an account of how noble characters prove their personal worth by surmounting adverse events. Within the terms of its own plausibility, what they mean as characters is subordinate to what happens to them, to events, for in this way are traced their idealized responses along a chain of events so prodigious or fabulous as to be nearly miraculous. Their narrative has the internal organization of a *tale*.

9. The Captive's Tale   Chs 39–41

When the company (on stage, so to speak) sits down to dinner, Quixote seizes the opportunity to give the second of his discourses, this one on the old debate between "Arms and Letters." On the level of Cervantes' representational techniques his discourse is the thematic introduction to the captive's tale. In terms of referential meaning Ruy Pérez represents "arms" and the jurist his younger brother, with whom he is reunited just after concluding his narrative, the cause of "letters." Quixote's discourse is then by design a structural parallel to their appearance, in the first instance fortuitous, because as yet no one among those at the table can suppose that (even because of his captive's outfit) he has had a military career with the rank of Captain. Quixote sits at the head of the table, but it is Fernando who presides over the scene. On his instigation the captive consents to tell his account, and after he concludes it Fernando makes the important critical comment on it.

"En un lugar de las montañas de León tuvo principio mi linaje . . . "[My family had its origins in the mountains of Léon . .] From the moment he begins to speak the captain takes on the likeness of the teller of tales of an oral tradition nearly as old as humanity itself. It can be said also that he preserves the anonymity of this narrator, though the account is personal. He corresponds to the archetype of the survivor of adverse events by miraculous escape who has lived to tell of it.[41] The fact that he remains nameless and enigmatic up to the point the priest reveals his name is indicative of this impersonal and even mythical role. For its tone as for its form and content his narrative is serious and solemn and in complete contrast to Quixote's comical adventures. As a tale its strategy is to unify and justify as historically 'true' the containment of a legendary situation within an autobiographical account. The captive who tells of his experiences is the narrator of Zoraida's conflict, motives, and experience. He is as devoid of self-analysis as of self-consciousness. Because of this personal bias the Zoraida we know from his tale cannot be precisely the girl we see in the inn.

In the tale she is the idealized lady of his gratitude and near idolatry. As narrator he is as 'unconscious' of his efforts and effects as that his autobiography is composed of motifs from folklore and legend strung on a historical thread. Compare his naive claim that it is all historically 'true' with the design of the narrator of the *Novela* of the *Curious Impertinent* who declares his fiction (artifice) to be morally 'true.' The strategy of the two narrators is as different as their corresponding 'orders.' The narrator of the *novela* depicts motives and actions from an objective point of view that corresponds to our analytical response. The captive's intention is to impose on our response his subjective and idealized portrait of Zoraida. For this reason their fabled escape to Spain is subordinate to the plausibility of *why*?—of the motives that bind them to one another. The tale then depends for producing its effect on a totally different set of principles. The most obvious is of course that it is heard as a true historical account by the other characters sitting around the table. Though it is autobiographical, the captive does not emerge as a 'character' until midway through it. Up to that point he has laid down three distinct layers of narrative on which to construct the verisimilitude of fictional intrigue in the remainder. The first layer is the account of his family background and separation from his father and brothers, an elaboration of a motif from folklore. Each of the three brothers selected a different career ("letters," i.e. law degree, commerce, and military) based on the proverb "*Iglesia, o mar, o casa real.*" They separated from home and from each other as young men. The motif sets in motion our subconscious expectation that they will be re-united, as well as the theme of self-abnegation as moral counterweight to wealth. The separation (true to the nature of folk motifs) has been complete; never once in all these years has he been in touch with his father or brothers. "Éste hará veinte y dos años que salí de casa de mi padre . . ." [This will be the twenty-second year since I left my father's house . . .] Ruy chose a career as soldier and made his way to Italy where he enlisted in the imperial army of Philip II. It was the year 1567.

The second layer of narrative is in the way of a soldier's memoir. Between 1567 and 1571 Ruy served in Italy and Flanders and was promoted to captain just before he was taken captive at Lepanto. As a galley slave he witnessed (from the enemy's side) the Spanish attacks at Navarino (1572), and the Turk's siege of Tunis and La Goleta (1574). This part of the account is based on Cervantes' own experience; he fought bravely at Lepanto where he was wounded (not captured) and took part in the campaigns of Navarino, Tunis and Goleta. It is more difficult to draw the lines on which Cervantes idealized his own experience. Apparently the captain's rank is in the way of vicarious fulfilment of his own expectations. When Cervantes was captured by Algerian pirates in September 1575 he was on his way back to Spain with letters from important persons recommending his promotion to captain. His captors read them as evidence that he was a valuable prisoner and set a high price for his ransom. He was a captive in Algiers from 1575 to 1580.

A complete analysis of points of similarity and contrast would be fascinating for what we could find as biography turned into fiction. The task would fall short of its objective, however, because just after the point where history and biography coincide in the mention by the captive of "the soldier something de Saavedra" (I.40, 486), the legendary and purely imaginary take over to make a tale whose idealized content has an entirely different connection to Cervantes' own experience. What Cervantes did and lived through at Algiers has all the ingredients of adventure and intrigue of suspenseful fiction. On four occasions he attempted to escape, devising and organizing schemes for liberating whole groups of men. All failed because of bad luck and the treachery of informers. To those who knew him he had the qualities of a true hero. Various documents disclose that he impressed his captors and his companions for his dynamic qualities: fearlessness, intelligence, tenacity, sense of honor and ability to take charge and lead.

The fictional captain is quite different. He was brought to Algiers from Constantinople by a new owner around 1575. He mentions having attempted "a thousand ways" to escape while at Constantinople, but the impression we get is that he endured his years of captivity with mournful, heroic resignation. The reason is artistic. In the tale his situation must appear depressingly hopeless, in order to make Zoraida's intervention miraculous. Nor has the captive been able to communicate with his family. In Algiers he is as much the prisoner of events as of his captors, the Turks. The third layer is the transition from history to legend. It covers the interval between the last date mentioned (1574), Ruy's arrival in Algiers (feasibly in 1575) and the appearance of Zoraida and escape to Spain fifteen years later. In this interval Ruy underwent the change to a mature man of about forty-two, confined to the misery of a captive's life. Of course this interval is necessary in order to depict his liberation in the present year (1589), but in his tale it forms a hiatus almost devoid of narrative material. In any case the transition brings us from the early years of his captivity to the time of Zoraida's appearance. Because his rank is captain his captors have confined him in a bagnio with other noblemen held for ransom, though for him there is no hope of ransom. At this point the figure of Zoraida appears from behind blinds of a window overlooking the bagnio.

Her appearance is prepared by an elaborate composite of narrative formulas and devices, in order to magnify her legendary aspect. By waving the reed and dropping her messages and money at his feet she signals her choice of him over the other noblemen in the bagnio. This part of the account surely resembles a day dream visited on a hopeless captive. A mysterious, beautiful and rich woman offers a means of escape and a large sum of money to procure it and even herself in marriage, inspired by an intense faith and devotion to the Virgin.

This idealized girl is based on a legend about the daughter of a wealthy Muslim living in Algiers in the years 1575–80 (the years of Cervantes' captivity there), known to scholars as "the legend of the daughter of Agi Morato."[42] This legend was doubtless a creation of the imagination of Spanish captives, based on rumor but of course assumed to be true. Yet this 'historical' legend is a more modern version of earlier medieval legends found in the (French) Carolingian epics (dating from the Crusades) about a Sarracen princess who falls in love with a Christian captive, betrays her father and her religion, liberates him and flees with him. It is also related to universal folk motifs of 'miraculous release and escape of a prisoner' and 'escape with the enemy's daughter who falls in love with prisoner,' as well as to legends of the Virgin Mary who effects an escape through the favors she shows a Moorish girl. The name of the historical daughter of Agi Morato (Hadji Murad) has not come down to us; her father was a renegade Christian. Perhaps for this reason a legend recalling pious hagiographical accounts about miraculous conversions was attributed to a historical personage who became successively in her adult life the wife (and widow of the first) of two prominent Muslims. Cervantes re-told the same legend in one of his plays.[43] Zoraida in the tale is probably based on what he knew and recalled about the historical personage in her youth. Perhaps he never saw her, but her legend attracted him powerfully.

From the first she wields over Ruy and his companions a spiritualized attraction. Inspired by love for "Lela Marien," she, a total stranger, inspires in them reverent trust and complete devotion. Physically she has the exotic beauty and chastity (and rich jewels and garments) of a sex goddess, but she excites no sexual or erotic impulses (nor her wealth any greed), only the most spiritualized feelings a male may feel for a woman. She not only provides the plan for escape and the money to put it into effect, from her person and spirit emanate the bonds of trust, confidence and hope that bind them all to one cause. An ideal trust binds them to her and to one another. This feature is more revealing of Cervantes' mind recalling his own frustrated efforts at escape than of the dangers such a plan was likely to encounter in the moral squalor of betrayers and renegade informers. Her garments, like her physical beauty, are the external attributes of an almost divine power that inspires in Ruy a worship of her: "me parecía que tenía delante de mí una deidad del cielo, venida a la tierra para mi gusto y para mi remedio" I.41, 497. [She seemed to me a heavenly goddess come down to earth to bring me happiness and relief.] Under her influence the tale becomes an account of ideal harmony and love between Ruy and Zoraida, ideal Christian devotion and trust and loyalty between the captives and the renegade on whom all depend, as they surmount each obstacle to freedom. So complete an idealization of the plausible is a 'truthful' product of a narrator unconscious of his efforts.

Its sober meaning is centered in Zoraida's separation from her father. When Ruy, following her instructions, goes to the garden by the sea and meets Agi Morato and talks to him, Zoraida comes out of the house and at last shows herself to the Christian slave in all her radiant beauty. Of course she is deceiving her father, but for motives fully justified within the tale. When her father goes off to drive away the Turks who are stealing his fruit, but then suddenly returns, interrupting their secret conversation, she pretends to faint, collapsing into Ruy's arms. Zoraida in this scene deceives her father as dispassionately as Camila deceived Anselmo. The two scenes were created by the same author Cervantes, but one as '*novela*' the other as 'tale.' Camila's motives and intrigue were corrupt, Zoraida's are courageous and pure, divinely inspired. Zoraida deceives, betrays and abandons her father (not wishing him any harm of course) on the level of intrigue; as the serious meaning of the tale her actions reveal the force of Christian faith that, while demanding the rupture of ties of kinship, will replace them with superior spiritual ones. Zoraida has the courage to leave her loving father in order to reach the sanctuary of faith and love in Christianity. Her motives, so to speak, are given to her by this conception of story and faith. She surmounts the trial of separation not to prove her faith, but the terms of idealization in the tale.

The scenes of separation at sea are among the most solemn written by Cervantes and of the entire contents of *Don Quixote* the most serious in the sense that their morality is unproblematical. Here the movement of fiction-within-fiction has receded to a point and frame of narrative so completely antithetical to Quixote's comical chivalry as to contravene its 'perspectivism,' the relativity of its situations.

Zoraida's plan was to disappear or steal away from her father while he slept. When because of the commotion he awoke and gave the alarm, it was necessary to take him prisoner and put him into the ship. Now Zoraida must face her father and witness the suffering she heaps upon him. Their parting must be for her a painful ordeal, a martyrdom. Of course this is the idealized response aimed for by the captive as narrator. He does not question her motives, nor why, if her faith is so compelling, she has not attempted to convert her father rather than betray him to his enemies. It is futile to attempt to reduce her actions and motives to moral and psychological analysis within the frame of legend in the tale. They are there caught up into the ascending line of Ruy's idealization. Their plausibility is precisely and no less than what he says it is, a heavenly emancipation through woman's love and faith. Those critics who fail to see the subjectivity of this portrait and submit it to analysis as if it were a characterization in a novel by Cervantes are misapplying their talents. Zoraida is not drawn on the same novelistic lines as Dorotea, Marcela, or Camila. She is a creature of legend, in only one instance brought forward to the larger frame of exemplary story. Her motives are no more improbable than the whole gamut of incidences taken from folk literature, like Ruy's prolonged isolation from his family.

Her faith in Lela Marien can survive the ordeal and even the curse she hears from her father's lips. She flees from him for the sake of the true faith. Heaven itself is disposed to show this. The very chain of cause and effect of flight across the sea unfolds from the human side as a ritual of separation and from the divine as a miraculous manifestation. Here the scenes are told with representational techniques resembling the style (and content) of epic narrative. The northern winds over the sea do not permit them to sail directly to Christian shores. Only when they are ready to release Agi Morato do the winds turn favorable. In his despair at hearing his daughter has become a Christian, he leaps into the sea to drown. They pull him back into the ship and finally set him and the other Moorish prisoners ashore on a remote promontory of Africa, where they can find their way back to Algiers but not raise an alarm that will endanger the Christians's plan to escape. The cove where they anchor is called, by chance, "*La Cava Rumía*," "the cove of the sinful Christian woman," so named by Moorish sailors because they consider it an evil omen to anchor there. But for this band of Christians the cove is a providential haven: "para nostros no fue abrigo de mala mujer, sino puerto seguro de nuestro remedio" [for us it was no wicked woman's shelter, but a secure haven of refuge]. Here they have a (ritualistic) meal and then offer prayers and supplications to God and the Blessed Virgin. They prepare to set Zoraida's father free, and now the winds turn favorable: "No fueron tan vanas nuestras oraciones que no fuesen oídas del cielo, que, en nuestro favor, luego volvió el viento, tranquilo el mar" I.41, 506–7. [Our prayers were not in vain, for Heaven answered them; the winds changed in our favor, and the sea grew calm.] At this point father and daughter separated.

The significance of arrival and now departure from this cove named for the also legendary 'sinful woman' suggests that Zoraida for her faith is a divine-like figure who has been singled out to redeem Christian Spain from the stain of La Cava, as the Virgin purified mankind from the sin of Eve.[44] The event thus points to the inner hierarchic and even hagiographic meaning of her legend. Through Zoraida the Holy Mother has intervened to rescue Ruy and the Christian captives. The captain is perhaps as unaware of the meaning his depiction of events proposes as he is lacking in self-awareness.

From the shore Agi Morato in his affliction first heaps maledictions on his daughter and then utterly debasing his person implores her to return, his voice dying over the waves. In all of Cervantes' fiction there is no scene more solemn and heart-rending, and no figure more desolate than this father lamenting his loss and none more deserving of our compassion. Zoraida cries out to him these words he is unable to hear. They bear the poignancy of a personal will seeking its lasting sphere of freedom beyond the ties of blood or religion and indeed of every social restraint, at whatever cost of suffering.

> —Plega a Alá, padre mío, que Lela Marién, que ha sido la causa de que yo sea cristiana, ella te consuele en tu tristeza. Alá sabe bien que no pude hacer otra cosa de la que he hecho, y que estos cristianos no deben nada a mi voluntad, pues aunque quisiera no venir con ellos y quedarme en mi casa, me fuera imposible, según la priesa que me daba mi alma a poner por obra esta que a mí me parece tan buena como tú, padre amado, la juzgas por mala. I.41, 507

> —May it please Allah, dear father, that Lela Marien, who has been the cause of my becoming a Christian, may console you in your grief. Allah well knows that I could not have done other than what I did, and that these Christians owe

me nothing for my good will, for even if I had wanted not to come with them, but to stay at home, it would have been impossible, so eagerly did my soul hurry me towards a deed which I feel to be as good as it seems evil to you, dear father.

Her reply neither pleads for nor accepts forgiveness. In this one instance her 'storied' legendary character assumes the novelistic outlines of an 'act of conscience.' Her personalized conflict is resolved by the urgency to follow a way to the radical fulfilment of her womanhood. She is disposed to break even the most solemn bonds in her search for self-fulfilment. Cervantes bestows on her here the same radical personalism he gives to Quixote, Sancho, Marcela, Dorotea, etc. It is wrong, however, to attempt to strip her of the legendary cast the entire tale is meant to provide for her. To be sure, in novelistic terms she may appear exposed as an extreme case of nearly pathological alienation centered in a personality disorder, with complete overtones of neurotic narcissism, and fanatical behavior. Even as a devout, passionate girl she lacks the warmth and humanity of a truly spiritualized creature. Indeed, she and Ruy form the most extreme example of the pattern we have seen in Marcela/Chrysostom and Dorotea/Cardenio of a spirited and dialectical female and a male subjected and dependent on her incentive.

Why did Cervantes depict as divinely inspired an act that is by human standards cruel and desolate? The meaning of his fiction taken as a whole is both the practice and the plea for tolerance and compassion in matters of religious beliefs and controversy. The answer can only be that in the tale Zoraida as a figure of divine intercession makes possible a miraculous escape for Ruy and the captives. In re-creating a legend close to the events of his own captivity Cervantes saw his own ransom and liberation in 1580 as nearly miraculous. The moral subjectivity of Ruy Peréz' account is a reflection of his own inner ordeal and an attempt to illustrate it in idealized fiction. We can discern how his requirements for narrative provided in the center of the tale's illustrative means and ends a representational manner (the scenes in the garden and at sea) that perhaps contrary to his original intentions pressed the traditional outlines of motives and intrigue into a focus of novelistic intensity.

Zoraida brought with her into the ship a box full of gold whose value could make all of the fugitives rich. Had they reached Spain with this treasure their material cares for the future would have been assured, but this outcome would not be illustrative of her and Ruy's moral worth. Before reaching Spain they were attacked by French pirates. Because he knew that their lives and freedom were more important than the treasure, the renegade threw the box overboard. The pirates sank their ship, robbed them, and allowed them to reach the southern coast of Spain divested of all but their freedom. In this way the tale illustrates that the treasure was the material, expendable, form of their 'ransom,' to be surrendered for the freedom they find in Spain. Thus, the 'crisis of events' that began with the scene in the baño is finally resolved. The captive and Zoraida have reached Spain divested of all material possessions (the money the pirate leader gave them paid for the animal on which she rides). A picture of virtuous poverty and self-abnegation, they are traveling north to León, hoping to be reunited with his father. She has yet to be baptized and Ruy is not certain she will be well received by his family. At its close the tale becomes inconclusive precisely because its characters must now face the world of realities in Spain, the world of the frame story.

In Fernando's comment Cervantes aptly defined it as a *tale*: a narrative about astonishing, 'unheard of events,' that fills one with wonder and suspense, intended to produce the effect that its enjoyment can be repeated exactly:

>—Por cierto, señor capitán, el modo con que habéis contado este estraño suceso ha sido tal, que iguala a la novedad y estrañeza del mesmo caso. Todo es peregrino, y raro, y lleno de accidentes que maravillan y suspenden a quien los oye; y es de tal manera el gusto que hemos recebido en escuchalle, que aunque nos hallara el día de mañana entretenidos en el mesmo cuento, holgáramos que de nuevo se comenzara. I.42, 514

>Indeed, captain, the way in which you have told your strange adventure has been as remarkable as the novelty and strangeness of the events themselves. Everything in it is marvellous and rare, and full of astonishing incidents that fascinate the hearer; and such has been our pleasure listening to the tale, we would be glad to hear it all over again even if it took until tomorrow morning to tell it.

Compare this comment with the priest's about the *Novela*. The priest objected to a profound improbability at its center. Fernando, who is not his equal as literary critic, assumes that the tale, despite its fabric of improbabilities, is true though terribly strange. The captain appears in the frame story as the survivor of astonishing fiction. His tale traces an entire trajectory of adventuresome events that depicts him as one chosen by divine will to prove through adversity his heroic and fabled status among mortals. Moreover, his adventures have been 'true to life,' historically real. His heroism is real or effective in the historical world, yet he does not feel himself to be nor does he see himself as heroic. He lacks any literary pretensions. And this is the enormous difference between him and Quixote. Cervantes made Quixote a mock and ineffectual hero and gave him not only the inner awareness of being heroic in comical form but the entire literary apparatus of fictional heroes as the basis of his heroic consciousness as well. Any of this he denied the captive, who, however, like himself, lived up to the heroic ideal in real life.

Thus we see Zoraida and the captain move from the mythical picture of their initial moment through his dynamic but idealized depiction of their escape in the tale to their 'fabled' roles in the frame story. They will accompany his brother Juan Pérez to Seville where arrangements will be made for their wedding. One may speculate in the context of 'story' or novel whether Zoraida will have an easy or hard time adjusting to life in Spain as a *conversa*, a convert, or how Ruy will fare as her husband. We can imagine for ourselves the future relationships between the old, melancholy soldier and the exotic, passionate girl. What we expect is that it will preserve her chastity (this is the meaning of the initial picture); though husband, he is above all her idolatrous protector. Elsewhere I have explained my hypothesis that in them we can discern the germ of the Quixote/Dulcinea relationship, and as such what can be called the *'Ur-Quixote,'* the predecessor whose idealized picture the book subverts.[45]

10. Mambrino's Helmet: Hoax as Adventure   Chs 42–46

The recognition scene between the two brothers leads to the final turn and climax of Quixote's stay in the inn. He now re-emerges as the central figure. The interrelated narratives trace an 'order' of fiction as a serious treatment of life in contrast to his comical chivalry. They trace irrevocable actions to a finality and resolution. By contrast Quixote's actions and his 'fame' are gratuitous, and their depiction can contain the serious narratives because it does not aim at treating conclusively the powerful and irrevocable situations they deal with: the life and death constraints of young persons in search of an ideal partner and the social and family ties that must be accomodated in order to ensure their future happiness. These narratives are serious and instructive for what they disclose of young lives at the threshold of maturity. Quixote's story is comical because his very idea of chivalry is a fiction that emulates their situations with no pretense to a corresponding finality. Their seriousness provides the significant social setting in which to depict the hidalgo as a mad hero acting out his role in the center of a social grouping. In turn the complicity of their characters will elevate the whole idea of a chivalric adventure to the level of a hoax, the next variation of the gratuitous act. While striving for the effect of an utterly farcical confusion caused by Quixote's fantasy about the basin and the saddle bags, the narrator will now carry his story forward by merging various techniques of story and stage to produce a synthesis that can be called 'dramatic novelty' (the simultaneous development of novelistic plots, as if on stage) or 'epic comedy' (the treatment of epic materials on stage in comic form).

The lines of four subordinate plots with their characters move separately and converge in the confusion over the basin: the innkeeper and his wife, his daughter and Maritornes, who know about Quixote from his first visit to the inn and particularly the night spent in the loft; Fernando, Dorotea (also cast in the role of Princess Micomicona), Cardenio, Luscinda and their companions; the captain Ruy Pérez and Zoraida, now reunited to his brother, the *oidor* or judge, who is on his way to Seville and overseas with his daughter Clara; unknown to the judge, Luis a young nobleman disguised as a muleboy has followed their coach and in turn is pursued by his father's servants who want to force him to return. Much of the comical effect in the climactic scene over the basin is produced by the purely coincidental between the subplots and Quixote's mad illusion. Sancho is alongside his master as part of the center. When the barber from whom Quixote took the basin shows up, it will be Sancho he attacks physically. Quixote has called the basin the "enchanted helmet of Mambrino," after an episode from Ariosto (I.21, 253). It will be recalled that he was wearing it when he attacked the guards and released the galley slaves.

He is presumably wearing it when he stands guard that night in the moonlight and when, again, a nocturnal adventure turns erotic. The earlier episode (I.16) in the loft with Maritornes depended on what Quixote's senses conveyed to his imagination. Now, taking their cue from that incident, Maritornes and the innkeeper's daughter are provoked to playing a trick and hoax on him. The inversion is indicative of how the entire structure of adventure has been turned inside out. Quixote is again painfully victimized and again he blames it on enchanters. When the servants who are following Luis arrive at dawn, they find him tied by the arm to the straw-loft and his shouts awaken everyone in the inn. Later he refuses to draw his sword and go to the aid of the innkeeper because this fight is 'not his thing,' not his adventure. Is he a coward? No. The narrators's strategy is to evade depicting him aiding anyone, even an innkeeper.

The basin he wears as a helmet is the only weapon or piece of armor given any prominence in the story and the only one with a name. Some critics have seen this as exemplifying the imaginary (cerebral) aspect of Quixote's chivalry. Whatever interpretation we place on it, his obsession with the headpiece is part of the strategy to reduce his material ineffectualness to a comically positive one. When the victimized barber arrives and reclaims his saddle bags from Sancho, the dispute over the basin is provoked just as Luis reveals his love for Clara to her father. The solution to their love story is laced and tied to the quarrel and its outcome. The reason becomes evident later. "The helmet of Mambrino" becomes a collectivized or 'totalizing' fiction, a jest and a hoax played by one social group on another and a melee to which the entire casts of the subplots are drawn and none escape. The dispute breaks into fist fights when the troopers of the Holy Brotherhood show up. They precipitate the melee by arousing Quixote's choler. There is no better metaphor for the process than the chemical one.

> . . . don Quijote puso mano a su espada y arremetió a los cuadrilleros. Don Luis daba voces a sus criados, que le dejasen a él y acorriesen a don Quijote, y a Cardenio y a don Fernando, que todos favorecían a don Quijote. El cura daba voces, la ventera gritaba, su hija se afligía, Maritornes lloraba, Dorotea estaba confusa, Luscinda suspensa y doña Clara desmayada. El barbero aporreaba a Sancho, Sancho molía al barbero, don Luis, a quien un criado suyo se atrevió a asirle del brazo porque no se fuese, le dio una puñada que le bañó los dientes en sangre; el oidor le defendía, don Fernando tenía debajo de sus pies a un cuadrillero, midiéndole el cuerpo con ellos muy a su sabor; el ventero tornó a reforzar la voz, pidiendo favor a la Santa Hermandad: de modo que toda la venta era llantos, voces, gritos, confusiones, temores, sobresaltos, desgracias, cuchilladas, mojicones, palos, coces, y efusión de sangre. I.45, 544

> . . . Don Quixote drew his sword and attacked the troopers. Don Luis was screaming at his servants to leave him and help Don Quixote, and Cardenio and Don Fernando, for they all had sided with Don Quixote. The priest kept shouting, the landlady was screaming, her daughter was weeping. Maritornes howling, Dorotea stood frightened, Luscinda was perplexed, and Doña Clara

fainted away. The barber was mauling Sancho, Sancho pounding the barber, Don Luis, whom one of his servants dared to seize by the arm to prevent his running away, hit him so hard that his teeth were bathed in blood, the judge was defending him, Don Fernando had one of the troopers under his feet and trampled him to his heart's content; the innkeeper bawled again at the top of his voice, pleading for help for the Holy Brotherhood: so the whole inn was full of wails, shouts, screams, confusion, fear, alarms, disasters, slashes, punches, cudgling, kicks and effusion of blood.

Once the argument comes to blows it becomes an unequal 'civil' combat that, while scrambling the social hierarchy, pits the side led by aristocrats against the troopers of the Holy Brotherhood and the lower 'working classes' who have but common sense on their side. The vertical hierarchy (nobles, hidalgos, professionals, artisans, servants) is melted down to a horizontal mass feuding over a ridiculous question of names.

Still it is important to understand just why narrative ends are pursued by means of representational techniques of comedy. Unlike similar scenes on stage, the confusion is real, not acted. The illusion it provides is proper to narrative, not to the stage. Quixote instigates it, puts himself in the middle of it, and confirms it as authentic 'Quixotic fiction.' By its own logic and chemistry this comic confusion produces its narrative meaning: out of the discord of social relations reduced to riot, Quixote emerges as a hero figure who incarnates its tergiversation of values. What he could not be shown accomplishing in fact through the course of adventures leading to Sierra Morena, he is shown accomplishing as a result of a jest or hoax, establishing his effectuality as 'fictional' in a world of cause and effect shaped to his illusion. The serious meaning extracted is that Quixote's chivalry is endorsed for what it is, a literary fiction, presented self-consciously to the reader as such.

As a result he may now appear as a genuine chivalric character for the manner in which he is depicted: the hero who incarnates the values of a fictional world. Though fraudulent with respect to real life, he is fictitiously genuine and entertaining in a way Amadís could never be. By humoring or opposing and thus endorsing his illusion, the priest, barber, troopers, and the rest have given his mock chivalry the aura of epic narrative as well, since the world around him has begun to pretend to take the shape of his illusion. In turn, by imposing on it the meaning of "discord in the camp of Agramante," Quixote lifts the hoax to the status of a real life adventure. Adventure as a hoax must appear to be the inevitable result of Quixote's gratuitous actions; that is, the sense of adventure must depend on a gratuitous chain of cause and effect (why the basin is called a helmet, etc.) in order to produce the genuine illusion of 'fiction-within-fiction.' All of this is due to the narrator's elaborate representational techniques that combine theatrical and narrational devices to transform Quixote and his illusion into a reality layered with social meanings.

For its various elements the Don Luis/Clara plot is another 'sentimental' story acted out and fortuitously resolved in the way of stage comedy. The young nobleman has disguised himself demeaningly for the love of a girl beneath him in wealth and social position. There is in fact no obstacle to their marriage (but their own innocence). By abandoning his father's home the boy has already overcome his father's possible objections, and the *oidor* is ready to consent to an advantageous marriage for his daughter. Nevertheless, the very threat of possible obstacles was sufficient to arouse fear in the two lovers, and once freed of their anxieties, the outcome reveals a young hero who for his merits and devotion is entitled to his chosen bride.

Three separate hoaxes have been played on Quixote. The most elaborate and sustained is the one designed to curtail any more adventures and get him home, his aid to Micomicona. The second is the love adventure at the hole in the hay loft, and the third the argument over the basin and saddle bags. Hoaxes, played or acted out, have become for their gratuitous nature the process and paradigm by which Quixote's delusion is turned outward as a fiction with a social meaning. Just after the outcome to Luis's and Clara's anxieties, provided by Fernando's rank and influence, the final hoax to be played on Quixote in the inn is put in motion: the prophecy of his future marriage to Dulcinea. This is pure comical hoax promising for Quixote in mock terms what has become real for the 'sentimental' adolescent couple. It is designed and played out to convince him that, though a spell has been laid on him by enchanters, by submitting to phantasmal captors he ensures his triumph. The barber, the priest, and the rest, including the troopers, Luis's servants and the innkeeper, disguise themselves and cover their faces with masks to produce the necessary fantastic illusion. Their 'purpose' is nothing more than to get the demented hidalgo back to his village and to his bed in the hope of ameliorating or curing his mind. The hoax as literary fiction has, however, its own inner purpose. A chivalric illusion has been improvised in the manner of stage costumes and roles to resemble a carnival hoax. With Quixote the fool figure at its center and believing the deception to be reality, the hoax not only acquires the status of fiction-within-fiction but in doing so simulates both carnival festival and the literary illusion of the knight overpowered by enchantment. Quixote is bound and placed in a cage, locked in (like a madman or prisoner) and transported on a cart pulled by oxen, a vague allusion to Lancelot's shameful ride in a cart (a degrading vehicle for knight or horseman). Since he feels or imagines himself powerless to resist, he is convinced he has been enchanted.

Hence the carnival hoax is not just a semblance of mock reality in a burlesque narrative, but the means by which its perpetrators are made to authenticate Quixote's illusion of himself. What started out (Ch 2) as an autonomous parody has taken on the structure of a hoax, which is both semblance and reality. He is the hero of a fiction that depicts the fictional hero in society. The process of fictionalization has been turned inside out, and in a way that vastly expands the referential and figurative meaning of Quixote's actions and illusion. His narrative has acquired the 'totalizing' effect of the classical epic without the learned apparatus prescribed by theorists, for the hoax is representational, realistic, or mimetic art elevated to the status of artifice, the self-conscious 'imitation' of life by art. Here again Cervantes took over and transmuted an old device of popular storytellers (tricks, deceptions) into a major artifice of modern fiction.

11. Return to Village   Chs 47–52

The last five chapters complete the second phase of Quixote's transformation in Part I, the phase that began when he emerged from Sierra Morena and ends with arrival back in the village. He emerged from the Sierra 'famous' in his illusion and his 'fame' became the indispensable structural condition for the hoaxes and deceptions improvised and carried out by others. In the inn the social grouping around him confirmed his fictional efficacy by elevating him to the status of mock epic as well as mock chivalric hero. The synthesis of techniques of narrative and stage comedy is a design that leads to and sustains his comical apotheosis in the melee over the helmet of Mambrino. The force or comic attraction of his madness compels or invites others to accept his illusion as the only way to deal with him, thus establishing the reciprocity between hero and community of epical narrative. When the troopers had to give up any attempt to arrest him, he succeeded in imposing his autonomous and fictional personality over social reality in a concrete measure. Yet, like chivalric and epic heroes who are or resemble the semi-divine, he must feel and be depicted as isolated from his social dependents. Though he incarnates their values and desires, he is unique among them for his elect status and his nexus to the supernatural. The hoaxes played on him are designed to trace a ring of cause and effect around his illusion of both isolation and relationship. When, believing himself to be enchanted, he allows himself to be placed, locked and transported in a cage like a madman, felon or beast (or, rather, like the fool figure of carnival ritual), the stage is set for the completion of his 'fictionalization' in Part I. The homeward journey is a comical retracing of the return phase of various story patterns, folk, chivalric, epical. The hero returns to renew his strength, or to plan new strategy, or his return provides for recapitulating his exploits, or to establish a new point of interest and suspense for his next outing.

While Quixote travels in the cart, the priest and now a fellow traveler, a canon from Toledo, converse on the books that have 'caused' his madness. These two ecclesiastics are among the most appealing of Cervantes' minor characters, perhaps because he attributes to them some of his own literary preferences. Their conversation is 'theoretical criticism' on the highest level possible in Cervantes' time, and although it includes the most explicit, overall censure of chivalric books, it revolves around the larger question of public standards of taste as reflected by poetic works, and for this reason Lope de Vega's new and popular *comedias* are compared for their defects to chivalric books. It is, then, the occasion for recapitulating the censure of chivalric books as well as the relation of the hero to the work that depicts him.

The canon and priest agree that chivalric books degrade public taste because they depict hero-knights in a manner offensive to an enlightened rationality and moral sense, because they deal with the fantastic and marvellous on implausible grounds.[46] Reason and moral sense demand an imaginative literature that is a truthful (i.e., realistic) imitation of human nature, speech and social reality. This 'mimetic' mode would be transparently instructive, both didactic and pleasurable for its avoidance of abstract (dogmatic, doctrinal) extremes that produce symbolism and allegory. It would merge fictional causality to reason and excite wonder and astonishment precisely for its design, its enlightened appeal to our credibility. By bearing down on the bad qualities of chivalric books and Lope de Vega's plays, their talk postulates the very procedures that describe Cervantes's own exemplary narrative, his depiction of Quixote's mock adventures, as well as the inclusion of the subordinate narratives and their 'critical' ordering. In short, his fusion of popular and learned attributes of story telling. But to see this one has to compare their theorizing with Quixote's reply to the canon.

Sancho meanwhile tries to convince his master that his confinement in the cage is not enchantment but the work of the priest and barber who are envious of his fame. Doesn't he have to relieve himself, urinate or evacuate? Then he is not enchanted. Of course it's up to Sancho to apply this test. At this point their dialogue is not just a retracing of the idea of 'enchantment' according to comic movement from Quixote's imagination to Sancho's fixation on physiological acts. Sancho's arguments and Quixote's reply resolve for now what Quixote's enchanted state means in terms of adventure as sense experience. Enchantment is palpable as an arrestment of the senses. That he needs to get out of the cage to relieve himself does not negate the arrested state of his sensory illusion. His reply to the canon illustrates down to the smallest detail how he feels, hears, sees chivalric illusion to be sense experience as big as life.

From the priest and canon we get such views on chivalric books as authors or critics might discuss between themselves. When the canon reproaches him for reading them and entreats him to take up more 'truthful' books, ridiculing any idea of enchantment, the Quixotic character replies out of the very process of his fictionalization. Quixote describes and justifies chivalric books for their effects in terms of 'real life.' He does not think in terms of 'invention,' 'verisimilitude,' 'didactic content,' but in the dynamic terms of what books can inspire and imbue. They are not just 'historically' true; their 'truth' can induce a man to become similar to their exemplars of heroic valor and daring; they can arouse through emulation heroic qualities potential in him; they can transform him into an exemplary hero. His reply retraces their theoretical approach to the very depiction he has undergone according to his illusion and will. The Quixotic hero construes his own fiction in the moral-physiological terms of the clinical narrator:

The Quixotic Fiction 131

> Y vuestra merced créame, y como otra vez le he dicho, lea estos libros, y verá cómo le destierran la melancolía que tuviere, y le mejoran la condición, si acaso la tiene mala. De mí sé decir que después que soy caballero andante soy valiente, comedido, liberal, biencriado, generoso, cortés, atrevido, blando, paciente, sufridor de trabajos, de prisiones, de encantos; y aunque ha tan poco que me vi encerrado en una jaula como loco, pienso, por el valor de mi brazo, favoreciéndome el cielo y no me siendo contraria la fortuna, en pocos días verme rey de algún reino, adonde pueda mostrar el agradecimiento y liberalidad que mi pecho encierra. I.50, 586

> Believe me, sir, I repeat, and read those books, and you will see how they banish away your melancholy and improve your temper if it happens to be bad. I can say of myself that ever since I became a knight-errant I am valiant, courteous, liberal, well-bred, generous, polite, bold, gentle and patient, and an endurer of toils, imprisonments, and enchantments; and although only but a short while ago I saw myself imprisoned in a cage like a madman, I expect, by the valour of my arm, if Heaven favors me and fortune is not against me, to find myself in a few days king of some kingdom, in which I can display the gratitude and liberality enclosed in this bosom of mine.

The Quixotic sense is that chivalric books are 'real' life. They challenge one's potential. To make his point Quixote recounts one more chivalric adventure, the descent of "the Knight of the Lake" to its fantastic world. It is of course fiction-within-fiction and illustrative of Quixote as narrator and even inventor of a fable (and a contrast to the captain and his tale). But his narrative is really striking for the way each detail down to the last of the knight picking his teeth is disclosed as an absorption of the senses. Quixote as narrator sums up the potential of chivalric books as sense experience. For its scenes and themes the "adventure of the Knight of the Lake" anticipates his dream experience in the cave of Montesinos.

In the next scene he is matched against the pseudo-goatherd in the most physical way. He listens to the goatherd's story more than sensitive to the way he contrives to make of a vulgar incident a stylized 'pastoral.' It is a reprise of the pastoral narrative on the low-brow level. Marcela inspired in Chrysostom an all-consuming erotic attraction on the high-brow level of aristocratic pastoral. Leandra is attracted sexually to the colorful soldier who robs and seduces but does not violate her, perhaps because his braggardness concealed impotence anyway. Recall that Eugenio first appears chasing his wayward she-goat called *Manchada* (Speckled). That he has taken up tending goats (not sheep) is indicative of the low level of the affair he embellishes as a 'pastoral' story. The key then is the female figure. Leandra is very nearly the opposite of Marcela (not to mention Zoraida). With her father's consent she was free to choose from among her suitors the one most to her liking, but being fickle and lacking the moral strength of Dorotea and Luscinda, she allowed her sexual attraction for the showy and deceptive soldier to ruin her chances for an honorable marriage. This story would seem to have no solution, least of all the one Quixote proposes. Oblivious to the misogynous turn Eugenio gives to the story at its close, Quixote offers to rescue Leandra from the convent where her father has confined her. Eugenio's insulting reply arouses the choleric outburst and awful vilification ("yo estoy más lleno que jamás lo estuvo la muy hideputa puta que os parió"I.52, 597) [I am fuller than ever was the whore's daughter that bore you]) that bring on Quixote's worst moment and comical humiliation, the dog fight with Eugenio over the picnic spread. The hero is brought low and deeply humiliated as the second sally draws to a close. Why? To assert his comical ineffectualness? To denigrate his self-esteem publicly? To punish his vain pretension (as the canon and priest would say)? Perhaps all of this. But also to reassert in the face of his disablement by the other characters the hero's obligation to stand up to humiliating reversals. Part I closes with the hidalgo back in his convalescent's bed, but even before then, anticipating the end of Part II, he dies in a mock way, when the villager whacks him on the shoulder and knocks him unconscious. Over his motionless body Sancho utters, comically, a lament with a panegyric of his virtues. When he recovers, Quixote replies to Sancho's entreaty with the last words he declares in Part I: "Será gran prudencia dejar pasar el mal influjo de las estrellas que agora corre" I.52, 601 [It is prudent to wait until the evil influence of the stars that now reigns passes away.] To the end he is, so to speak, in character. The heroic conscience with which his madness endows his foolish actions obliges him to interpret reversals in terms of preternatural forces. Like the epic hero he is obliged to be heroic, to remain constant to his sense of mission in the face of adversity. The low point of Quixote's return to his village is the indispensable nadir to his reemergence in a third sally.

12. Part Two: Third Sally   Chs 1–8

It does not get underway until a connective back to the action of Part I can establish new terms for Quixote's fictionalization. The book

Cervantes published in 1615 is as much a sequel as a new and different story. Yet the illusion he wished to establish from the first page is that his story continues after only a month's interval. This would be a simple matter of a purely fictional duration if it were not also the case that Cervantes now took as a new point of departure the popular success of Part I and the notoriety of his characters in the real world by incorporating this situation directly into his fiction.[47] The hidalgo learns that while he convalesced and as if by magic and prophetically his adventures have appeared in the form of a published book, in some eight editions, and that he and Sancho, even Rocinante, are so well known by the public they are thought of as celebrities. The interval of one month of fictional duration is thus made to condense the book's success in the years between 1605 and the time when Cervantes began to compose the sequel, around 1610. After a month Quixote is sufficiently recovered to undertake another sally, yet he does not—rather, he will not—start off immediately nor, as before, improvising as he goes along. Now he and Sancho do not start off until certain preparations are carried out by them and certain deliberations by the narrator. The situation can be explained as a consequence of the popularity of the published book of 1605 and of the fame and success that Cervantes himself had acquired in the historical world of 1615.

The connective introduces the new proportions of Quixote's fame. In the opening chapters he is confronted with the news that a book depicting his and Sancho's adventures has been published, circulated and commented on by the public at large. A fictional character is confronted with his reputation and fame as such in the real, historical world.[48] This novelty has been commented on at length in literary criticism since 1800 as an instance of Cervantes' 'irony' and 'self-conscious' manipulation of his story that not only breaks deliberately the illusion of fictional reality but also manages to insert 'the book of 1605' into 'the book of 1615,' and vice versa, the obvious instance of fiction-within-fiction. The action of Part I is recalled in Part II in the form of a printed book known to many, yet the sequel is a continuation of it and bound by its fictional time. All of this we recognize as a consequence of the manoeuvre carried out much earlier, precisely at the turning point in Sierra Morena. Quixote was 'famous' in the story, and in his own illusion (and in the narrator's techniques), before he became famous or notorious as a result of the popular success of Part One. While the news of his fame as the hero of a new chivalric history shocks Quixote as unexpected, it seems inevitable in the structure of his fiction. For now his fame as a celebrity in the real and historical world will complete his depiction as a hero related to, and moving within, a given social reality, so that as the new course of adventures unfolds he will take on by degrees the attributes of a mythical character: his story will become as much a mock chivalric reality as an homage and celebration of his person and fame, that is, of his characterization. The 'revised' title of the sequel confirms this: "Second Part of the Ingenious *Knight*. . . ."

The Quixotic fiction becomes explicitly the celebration of the hero it depicts. Looking back from the vantage point of these opening chapters, we can see that this turn of affairs is a consequence of a narrative process that began by simulating Quixote's illusion of himself, disclosing from within the mechanics of his fictionalization. But complementary to this process was another, the process by which the supposed authors of his history (but of course Cervantes) assumed an ostensibly greater degree of omniscience. Looking forward, we can anticipate that the story will now aim at the illusion of Quixote as a restorer of heroic virtue to society, a comical hero who, though ineffectual in the material sense, entertains while performing in the efficacious way of fictional hero-knights. Likewise, Cide Hamete as the self-conscious narrator on an epical scale will now come into his own. Hereafter, for the sake of convenience, we will refer to the two authors, Cide Hamete and 'second author,' simply as the narrator.

The preparations now indispensable (Chs 1–7) involve placing Quixote and Sancho within this new 'order' of fictional illusion. In the opening scene with the priest and barber Quixote converses on affairs of state and his proposal that knighthood and indeed one single knight could take care of the menacing Turks is like the first note of the motif of the hero-knight entrusted with the defense, even deliverance of a nation. The proposal convinces the priest and barber that he is still mad. But if he is disqualified before he even begins, what nation or society will the hero deliver or redeem? A fictional one, of course. In the next scene with Sancho he shows concern for his reputation and the public's reaction to his attempt to restore the forgotten order of chivalry, his deeds and valor. Sancho can report on local opinion only, and what he says is in the way of satirical commentary on the hidalgo's pretensions. Another villager and neighbor knows a lot more, he says. What this villager knows turns out to be (of course) Quixote's literary fame (his mock fame, that is).

Like the historian of his exploits in chapter 2 of Part I, this new character all but materializes out of Quixote's fame. Samson Carrasco, who is a wag and student of theology with a mischievous disposition, on greeting the hero in the flesh, drops to his knees and exclaims, mockingly: "Give me your hands to kiss, your magnificence . . . for your worship is one of the most famous knights-errant that has ever been or shall be. . . ." His words go to the core of the fiction.

> —Deme vuestra grandeza las manos, señor don Quijote de la Mancha; que por el hábito de San Pedro que visto . . . es vuestra merced uno de los más famosos caballeros andantes que ha habido, ni aun habrá, en toda la redondez de la tierra. Bien haya Cide Hamete Benengeli, que la historia de vuestras grandezas dejó escritas, y rebién haya el curioso que tuvo cuidado de hacerlas traducir de arábigo en nuestro vulgar castellano, para universal entretenimiento de las gentes. II.3, 59 [Blessed be Cide Hamete Benengeli, who has left us the history of your great deeds recorded, and thrice blessed the man of taste who took pains to have it translated out of Arabic into our vulgar Castilian for the universal entertainment of mankind.]

Thus the hero is confronted with the ulterior purpose of his depiction. From his first appearance Samson's role is that of a mock adulator of Quixote's public image and instigator according to it, so that he replaces the priest and barber as schemer and hoaxer. We can think of him as indispensable to the action and to the story's 'inside' purpose because he knows Quixote and Sancho primarily for having read about them. He can intervene in the story because he knows all about their illusions and motives. He is familiar with them as . . . a reader. This is of course another instance of the blurring of the lines between fiction and reality. It is part of Samson's role to furnish details of the public reaction to Part I and to provide a little critical review of it (Ch 4) that shows how far Cervantes had moved in critical concepts and insight from the discussion between the canon and the priest at the close of Part One.

The three characters discuss the work in print (even the work in progress) and its dual authorship as if to declare their absolute autonomy and independence from any authorial control. This device of 'characters in search of an author' (made well known in our day by Unamuno and Pirandello) is not so much introspection into the process of creation by the demiurge-novelist as a re-casting by him of the illusion of authorial omniscience he means to establish and sustain. Quixote's illusion of himself as knight-errant has been confirmed by a reading public, so that now, in order to maintain the illusion of him as a public hero, the narrator allows him a wider freedom by withdrawing to a greater distance. Cervantes has invented and introduced Samson, who intervenes in the action on the basis of his knowledge of Part I and in this respect can be thought of as a surrogate who, filling the space vacated, simulates the author's invention and control. Quixote needs to consult him about plans for the new sally and the wag advises him to travel to Aragon and the city of Zaragoza, where the annual jousts and festival of Saint George's day (April 23) will be held "within a few days." Samson Carrasco (a mock Hercules) will intervene in the action by design. He provides Quixote with a destination and incentive according to plan. The illusion to be sustained now is that Quixote for his knighthood is a public figure and celebrity in the contemporary world of 1610–1615, and Samson is the character who not only fixes the connective back to the action of Part I by announcing the existence of and reception to the published book but who, for his mocking personality, frames the exemplary depiction of Quixote within a mythical configuration. Ostensibly a friend and admirer, he urges Quixote and Sancho to depart (to the consternation of the housekeeper and niece) in order to follow up with his own little scheme.

Sancho's preparations are even more involved. He takes leave of his wife Teresa with a full explanation of his purpose; he intends to acquire an island of which he will be Governor, become rich and famous and marry off his daughter Teresica to a nobleman with a high-sounding title, all of which amazes and distresses his wife. This scene in chapter 5 shows that Sancho, too, is under pressure to live up to a new image of himself. He speaks and thinks in a high-falutin' way, so that in speaking to Teresa he takes on the role and speech of instigator of illusions that is Quixote's when he talks down to Sancho. And the sense of importance he gains, supposedly knowing that an admiring public considers him as important and as entertaining as his master, encourages him to demand to be paid wages for his services, a demand Quixote is for now in a position to refuse.

13. Dulcinea Enchanted   Chs 8–11

Cide Hamete's buoyant exclamations on beginning chapter 8 are a far contrast to his hero's depressed state. Author, Samson, Sancho, even Rocinante and Dapple, urge him on, yet he heeds what he perceives to be malignant omens. Why—with a new course of adventures before him—are Quixote's spirits so low? There are two answers. One points back to the exemplary depiction of his pathological state in Part One. The other prepares us for his ensuing mythical enlargement. Though Quixote has convalesced, his mind and spirit have not recovered from the depression that set in at the close of Part One. The acute melancholy that prevailed over the choleric side of his temperament has become almost endemic. His choleric outbursts in Part I were accompanied by violent exertions because they brought on a release of imaginative flight; he was most imaginative when choleric and violent. When his melancholic side prevails (as now), he almost lacks imagination and becomes reflective, meditative, his 'gravity' or seriousness the deep sadness of inverted megalomania. The lines of his clinical characterization trace a parody of heroic depictions along both sides of his temperament. He is both a hero of violent and exalted action (choleric side) and of feeling, of meditative insight and even a little introspection (melancholic side). The adventures in which he exultantly and imaginatively 'transformed' reality into a fantastic flight (windmills, sheep) were brought on by a release of choler. Now in his depressed and meditative state he resembles the reflective epic hero (Aeneas), weighted down by his sense of mission or of fate, as if struggling through gloom and shadows against unseen enemies. Already we have seen that in his dejection he attributes reversals to the work of evil enchanters who oppose and oppress him out of envy for his virtue and fame. The low state of his spirits, his pathological state, is the precondition for what happens in El Toboso. The decision to set off for Dulcinea's village is both a carry-over from the action of Part I and a new requirement.

They set out at nightfall and arrive there the next night and search futilely for "the palace of Princess Dulcinea." We recall that in the dialogue of chapter 31 Sancho made up a fiction of his meeting with the villager Aldonza Lorenzo and described a scene in terms both realistic and malicious. Quixote was persuaded to leave the Sierra with the ruse about Dulcinea's reply to his letter: he should not delay in coming to see her. Sancho described a peasant girl with mannish features who perspired while winnowing wheat in her back yard, and although Quixote protested that Dulcinea was a lady of beauty and a princess he accepted the reply as genuine. They are here now to fulfill her request, but Quixote has either forgotten or ignores that Dulcinea is Aldonza and leads Sancho through streets in the dark in search of a palace. Not he nor the author nor Sancho even mentions the daughter of Lorenzo Corchuelo. The story has come a long way from the episode in Sierra Morena, to be sure, yet why did Cervantes omit any reference to Aldonza now that at last he has got his characters to El Toboso? One explanation is that Aldonza is no longer necessary as a pretext for Dulcinea. To have had Sancho look around for her father's house now would only have spoiled the story. In his fixation Quixote imagines Dulcinea as an opulent princess. As a dichotomy to this image the narrator intends to introduce and fix a different image of Dulcinea as rank peasant, and she is not Aldonza. From his distant omniscience, he means to replace Aldonza with a new and even more repulsive peasant, as if to exacerbate Quixote's depressed state.

Perhaps in no other episode does Cervantes conceal his craft more slyly. He has already aligned various elements of story to suggest the secretive, even illicit nature of Quixote's love and subjection to his lady, like nightfall as the hour of departure and the nocturnal atmosphere for the preliminary dialogue and arrival in the village. In his madness Quixote expects to see and address the lady of his most intimate illusion and to receive from her the favors that will recharge his spirits and chivalric calling. If his illusion and madness impel him towards this ideal lady, they also conceal and protect him from a too direct exposure to her; the very hour he chose to arrive here is a subconscious evasion. In the dialogue on the road he protests when Sancho repeats that the girl he talked to was a peasant winnowing wheat. That false and defaming image of her he attributes to detractors and enemies, one of which might be the very author or recorder of his exploits. As a fine lady Dulcinea's tasks would be to weave a cloth of gold and silk threads, like Garcilaso's nymphs.

> Y desta manera debía de ser el [tejido] de mi señora cuando tú la viste; sino que la envidia que algún mal encantador debe de tener a mis cosas, todas las que me han de dar gusto trueca y vuelve en diferentes figuras que ellas tienen; y así, temo que en aquella historia que dicen que anda impresa de mis hazañas, si por ventura ha sido su autor algún sabio mi enemigo, habrá puesto unas cosas por otras. . . . II.8, 94 [In such work my lady must have been employed when you saw her, only that the envy that some wicked enchanter bears against me changes and turns all things that give me pleasure into shapes different from their own, and so I fear that in the history which they say tells of my deeds in print, if by chance the author is some enchanter my enemy, he has probably changed one thing into another.]

If Dulcinea has appeared as a peasant, the explanation is that she had been 'transformed' by envious enchanters. His obsession with 'transformations' is at the core of his madness, not just because they explain those violent clashes with reality he meets with, but because the obsession itself is the very nuclear process of his fictionalization. At the close of chapter 8 he concedes that secular fame like knighthood's may involve humiliations that unlike the fame of saints or friars would defame one. In El Toboso Quixote seeks confirmation of his image of a 'princess Dulcinea' because it corresponds to a new public image of himself as the famous hero of a published history. He pursues it madly in the dark, oblivious to the inconsistencies that Sancho points out to him: what palace? what princess? and at this hour of the night? The description of El Toboso by night, deserted streets, weird silence broken by brays, grunts and miaows, insinuate his inner depression and feelings of inadequacy before this lady who, ostensibly, will infuse him with ardor.

At daybreak, despairing like the pathological case that he is, he eagerly accepts Sancho's suggestion that they give up looking for the palace and retire to the outskirts where "you can hide in some nearby wood"; Sancho would return by daylight to find Dulcinea. Sancho has in mind another deception like his previous lie. With that lie he made himself indispensable as intermediary and this is the role he intends to play now. He adds that he will plead with her to permit herself to be seen "without any damage to her honor and reputation." Behind his inventiveness one can discern Cervantes' strategy. What is at stake is not whether Sancho will get the upper hand, but whether Quixote can live up to the public image of himself as chivalric hero.

They retreat to the outskirts and the countryside, where Quixote hides in a clump of trees. He is convinced he must conceal himself in order to keep his relationship to her secret and intimate. Sancho, despairing on his own, needs to extricate himself from the tangle his lies have got him in. Quixote sends him back to the village with the order not to return without having delivered a verbal message.

> Mandó a Sancho volver a la ciudad, y que no volviese a su presencia sin haber primero hablado de su parte a su señora, pidiéndole fuese servida de dejarse ver de su cautivo caballero, y se dignase de echarle su bendición. . . . II.10, 104 [He ordered Sancho to go back to the village and not return to his presence without first speaking to his lady on his behalf, begging her to be so good as to allow

herself to be seen by her captive knight and to deign to bestow her blessing on him. . . .]

Despite the disclaimer that begins chapter 10, the author is 'setting up' Quixote with the hero's own words. In his desperate need Quixote demands that Sancho deliver the request that "she allow herself to be seen by her knight." He demands a visual, material presence. Sancho sets to work on this. He could have returned after a suitable interval and cleverly invented another lie while reporting that he saw and spoke to a princess Dulcinea and delivered the message, and even provided a suitable reply to deceive his master, mimicking his chivalric style as he does later. But that would be a case of Cervantes repeating himself. Everything concerning Dulcinea has been maintained up to this point as illusion, image and 'fiction'; now she will materialize with all the attributes of 'fiction' as sensory experience. When Quixote ordered Sancho to produce a real Dulcinea, he made inevitable the hoax that will victimize him.

Sancho leaves him and sits under a tree beside the road to argue with himself. His soliloquy is really a dialogue and argument between his two attitudes toward Quixote; it reveals both his clever malice and his simple and crafty mind. It is transparently Cervantes' means for retracing comic movement from Quixote's idealism to Sancho's own sensory data. Sancho knows that what happened to them on the way back to the village that Quixote can be deceived into believing a hoax despite all evidence to the senses if one resorts to enchantments to explain it. In the first instance he reasons that telling Quixote he saw and spoke to Dulcinea will be enough. This Dulcinea has of course to be a peasant girl, though he will describe her as a princess.

> Siendo, pues, loco, como lo es, y de locura que las más veces toma unas cosas por otras, . . . no será muy difícil hacerle creer que una labradora, la primera que me topare por aquí, es la señora Dulcinea; y cuando él no lo crea juraré yo; y si él jurare, tornaré yo a jurar . . . o quizá pensará, como yo imagino, que algún mal encantador de estos que él dice que le quieren mal la habrá mudado la figura por hacerle mal y daño. II.10, 106-7

> Well, since he's crazy, and so crazy as to mistake most times one thing for another, . . . it won't be very difficult to make him believe that the first peasant girl I run across about here is the lady Dulcinea, and if he doesn't believe it, I'll swear, and if he swears, I'll outswear him . . . or perhaps he will think, as I imagine he will, that some wicked enchanter of those he says holds a grudge against him has changed her shape to do him wrong.

The Quixotic Fiction 141

His plan is to give Quixote a verbal report, to deceive him again with words, and he waits until afternoon to return to him. But then at the very moment he gets up to rejoin his master, he sees the three peasant girls on their she-asses riding toward him. The coincidence makes it possible for him to rush to Quixote with the news that Dulcinea is approaching, to produce a Dulcinea in the flesh. From his distance and control the author has allowed Sancho himself to inscribe these three females into comic movement, for they all-but-materialize out of his rude, peasant-infested mentality. They belong as well to the folk and mythological tradition of a sinister triad of ugly and evil women that includes witches, harpies and gorgons.[49] Their appearance provides him instantly with not one but three females and their mounts to show Quixote as Dulcinea and her damsels. The trick is Sancho's; the coincidence is the author's; together they confront Quixote with the gravest challenge yet to his illusion.

Although his techniques and story are turned around now to the reverse of how he started back in Part I (Quixote's fantasy is all but inert), Cervantes is consistent in pursuit of the theme of 'transformation of sensory reality.' Only Quixote can change the reality of the senses into fantasy and fiction. Here in utter stupefaction before the peasant girl Sancho calls and describes as Dulcinea his senses are overwhelmed, but they in no way distort what is before him. And yet he, not Sancho and his crude rhetoric, will 'transform' this figure into Dulcinea. Only Quixote can effect the indispensable transformation. He has gotten down on his knees beside Sancho and addresses this figure as Dulcinea.

> Y tú . . . ya que el maligno encantador me persigue, y ha puesto nubes y cataratas en mis ojos, y para sólo ellos y no para otros ha mudado y transformado tu sin igual hermosura y rostro en el de una labradora pobre, si ya también el mío no le ha cambiado en el de algún vestiglo, para hacerle aborrecible a tus ojos, no dejes de mirarme blanda y amorosamente. . . . II.10, 110–11

> And you . . . now that the malignant enchanter persecutes me, and has put clouds and cataracts into my eyes, and for them alone, and for no others, has changed and transformed the peerless beauty of your countenance into the semblance of a poor peasant girl, if he has not also turned mine into the appearance of some spectre to make it abominable in your sight, do not refuse to look at me softly and amorously. . . .

Many pages have been written on the supreme comic realism of this scene without the least attention to the central element that connects the whole (the peasant's odor and speech, Sancho's crude hoax,

Quixote's courtly speech and grotesque posture) into unforgettable story, into fiction, that is. Quixote's madness can of course provoke violent clashes of sense experience and he can impose on physical, real objects his verbalized fantasy, all as a Cervantean 'representation of reality.'[50] But the core idea, the mythos of 'transformation' that focuses the whole into superb narrative, is not a part of that physical reality and has no place in it. It is pure mythopoetic fantasy usurped from chivalric romance. Precisely what is *not* represented as reality because it is madness, imaginative and extrasensory, is what serves to delimit and define reality here. This is precisely what Cervantes' style is all about. From this moment the fiction is established that Dulcinea is enchanted, because Quixote believes she is.

This scene on the outskirts of El Toboso sets in motion the structural fiction that will unify at one of its deepest levels the entire course of Part Two. Sancho has wilily pulled off his major deception as mock sense experience, but it is Quixote who believes Dulcinea is enchanted as a full reality of the senses, and it is his conviction that will impose and endorse this hoax as the cutting edge of the Quixotic fiction to come. An enchanted Dulcinea corresponds to the most powerful of themes in chivalric romance: the abduction of the knight's lady by dark mythological and magical forces and the ordeal to rescue her made encumbent on the hero knight. The most important example from medieval chivalric romance is also the most important antecedent for *Don Quixote* in this as in other respects: the abduction of Queen Guinevere and her rescue by the young Lancelot. By initiating the third sally with his powerful theme Cervantes has undertaken to sustain Quixote's madness on a new and inimitable level of comical storytelling, raising it to a veritable celebration of the poetic essence of chivalric romance. Quixote must inevitably feel driven to disenchant his lady and this personal or private obligation will be drawn in conflict with his public image and social role as deliverer or redeemer, all of this bound inescapably to his relationship with Sancho.

Once again the 'fiction' that recharges and compels Cervantes' story forward has issued from Quixote's illusion. Yet this fiction would seem to devastate that illusion, it is so contrary to his expectations. Or is it? Wasn't his dejected state, when he interpreted one omen after another as evil, an anticipation? With his failure to find the palace and Dulcinea in the dark the incentive passed to Sancho, and Quixote resigned himself to the passive condition that exacerbates his pathological depression. In the scene with the three females his senses are acutely alive, but not to ignite his imagination to the image of 'Princess Dulcinea' with all the verbal and poetic vehemence we have seen previously. His senses succumb inertly to the coarse villager's physical presence. His senses tell him plainly the girl is not Dulcinea. Why, then, does he believe Sancho? Why does he let Sancho's crude description of what is not there persuade him? Because having forced Sancho to produce a real Dulcinea, he was in turn compelled to heed the description of the peasant girl before him as the princess of his delusion. Despite the shock, he could not deny his expectations. When he sees Sancho kneel before the girl, he does likewise. He cannot deny this girl may be Dulincea because to do so would deny that she exists. Addressing her, he reasserts his dignity and integrity, even as he accepts the horrible humiliation, for beyond the flat-faced peasant he addresses the ideal lady. In the act of acknowledging that this girl is not the ideal lady but her deformed shape he effects the fiction of enchantment, ". . . now that the malignant enchanter persecutes me . . . and has changed and transformed the peerless beauty of your countenance. . . ." In other words, he accepts the peasant girl as Dulcinea deformed because he must remain in character. Or his madness must impel Cervantes' story from within.

Immediately following the narrator can mimick his mad illusion and call the peasant girl Dulcinea as if she were genuine. His self-conscious stance exonerates him from the ridiculous outcome by simulating Quixote's illusion: "Apenas se vio libre la aldeana que había hecho la figura de Dulcinea, cuando, picando a su *cananea* . . . de manera que dio con la señora Dulcinea en tierra . . . y quiriendo don Quijote levantar a su encantada señora en los brazos. . . ." II.10, 111 [No sooner did the girl who had played the part of Dulcinea find herself free, than she prodded her hackney . . . so that the animal plunged my lady Dulcinea to the ground . . . and when Don Quijote wishing to lift his enchanted lady in his arms. . . .] It is Quixote (sic) who is guilty of a ridiculous parody of chivalric romance. Having established the fiction of a peasant as tranformed lady, the narrator does another manoeuvre. In her flurry to get away from the weird man who accosts her, the girl pricked the animal she was riding so harshly the beast galloped across the field and flung her to the ground. Quixote rushed over to aid her—it was then he smelled her foul breath—but she got up, leaped on the animal and rode off with her companions. Her hurried getaway is his last and most impressionable image. The episode closes with a caper brought on by the whim or 'autonomy' of the she-ass and is the first of a series in which an animal's behavior is made to galvanize the action. These animal motifs were ominously announced on Quixote's entry into the village by night. The series begins here and climaxes with his triumph over the lion, to resurface with the ape's antics. Quixote's actions are made to revolve around these animal antics, his own chivalric purpose and incentive now implicated by his lady's predicament.

In the aftermath of the devastating scene, dejected, he lets Rocinante take his own way, when a wagon bearing a group of costumed players—masked Death, a Devil, an Angel, Emperor, Queen, Cupid and a clown—crosses the road. At the sight of this cast of characters Quixote can assume that a fantastic adventure is in store. But then the player dressed as the Devil explains the reason for their appearance. They have just performed "The Parliament of Death" (*Auto de las Cortes de la Muerte*), a play for the feast of Corpus Christi, in one town and are travelling to the next for another performance. His explanation dispels any suggestion that their appearance is in some way allegorical. Again a senseful reality that provokes Quixote's illusion now refutes and disappoints him. The clown's dancing and bells frighten Rocinante so that, like the she-ass previously, he gallops across the field so violently he falls and throws Quixote to the ground. Sancho jumps down from Dapple and rushes to help him. The clown (now imitating Quixote's ride to the ground) leaps on Dapple, frightens him and makes him run off a stretch. Roused to vengeful anger for this affront to his person, Quixote threatens the players with violent punishment, only to retreat when they defy him like a squadron armed with stones. With this sorry humiliation a new course of adventures of fantastic and carnivalesque proportions begins. The hero knight is challenged on an epical scale by a senseful reality with a potential for real or mock triumph or bitter humiliation.

14. The Structure of Illusion

The effect is comic pathos on an upward trajectory. For Quixote's will-to-achieve becomes both deeper and problematic as each encounter assumes not only the semblance of his literary illusion but by degrees its necessary and imminent fulfilment. This is of course

Cervantes' craft at its inimitable best. His purpose and effects (whether we think of them as satirical or novelistic) are no longer merely to create and sustain the illusion of mock chivalric adventures as in Part I, but the more novel and subtle illusion of senseful reality itself depicted as fiction. His comic realism is transparent on the scale of the epic with the substance of ceremonial ritual, legend and myth, but of course in their comical, that is, popular and mimetic form, the make-believe and inverted world of carnival with its mock transformations and the antics of performing animals. The structure of Quixotic illusion and its pathos are implicit in the narrator's self-conscious stance.

The third sally starts off with a profoundly dejected hero, yet its course is an upward trajectory. From the disillusion over an enchanted, misshapen Dulcinea the action expands upward along a progression of chance encounters that recharge his audacity and self-confidence and renew his sense of mission: a challenge from and combat with "The Knight of the Mirrors"; then "The Knight of the Green Coat" and victory over the caged lions; then two episodes that increase his self-esteem and polity and depict him as an unexampled sociable knight, the visit to a country mansion and the rustic wedding of Camacho. Then to conclude this the initiatory phase of his mythical enlargement as redemptive hero, he goes down to the cave of Montesinos and returns to describe a journey to the underworld of enchanted spirits where the 'mythos' of chivalry lies entombed. His account is the prototypal Quixotic fiction—the fiction whose structure epitomizes all the others about him—for it is told by the subject himself and discloses the underlying themes of the story to come: his public image and role as redemptive hero are jeopardized by the predicament of his lady and his private obligation to disenchant her. These encounters take place against a backdrop of Spring and its ritual of festivals and on an itinerary that swings south to the location of the cave of Montesinos in La Mancha, to swing north again later toward the Ebro and Zaragoza. They comprise the first portion of the overall movement of Part II and lead to the central episodes of mock apotheosis for Quixote and Sancho at the palace of a veritable Duke and Duchess in Aragon.

This trajectory would seem to parallel and even repeat in various respects (and in some cases down to details as we shall note) the narrative movement of Part I: a series of individual feats in the countryside leading to prolonged collective or totalizing hoaxes that effect a comical apotheosis of Quixote and Sancho and climaxed by a hoax that effectively disables the hero, followed by the inevitable return to the village. The approximate correspondences between the two sequences and trajectories are shown on Chart III. Some very discerning critics have written on this recently in most illuminating ways. But the third sally is not so much a parallel linear unfolding of fictions retracing the adventures in the second sally of Part I as a new configuration into which the latter have been integrated and as it were thrust forward. This will be most apparent in the 'order' of the fictions or encounters that now emerge. In them narrative techniques are pressed to bring Quixote into his own as mythical.

15. Knight of the Mirrors   Chs 12-15

A 'triumph' over a real but mysterious knight raises Quixote's spirits to a new level of self-confidence. Of course it is a hoax turned against its perpetrators, but as a hoax it is fictional on the new, enlarged scale. A little discourse on the warmth of animal friendships as seen in the touching affection Dapple and Rocinante have for one another precedes and introduces the nocturnal encounter. Because Quixote's victory is (once more) owed to an animal's antics, the discourse is meant to be instructive in more ways than one. In his self-illusion Quixote is not only effectual but invincible. Such an outcome can only be the result of the lengths to which Cervantes will press his representational techniques to depict and even saturate senseful reality according to his hero's illusion.

The encounter with the Knight of the Mirrors is a parody of episodes in chivalric stories in which two knights, their identity unknown to one another, fight as strangers only to discover they are friends. We recall that the second sally in Part I began with the attack on the giants turned into windmills, a reversal that set in motion the recourse to 'transformations,' and was followed by violent physical combat with the Biscayan, a victory over a real, fire-breathing adversary made possible by the panicky mule. This third sally has begun in a similar way: a disastrous encounter with three peasant girls and a new call to affront the envy of wicked enchanters, followed by an exhilarating triumph, or the next best thing, owed to an animal's antic. This adversary is also full-bodied, Herculean even, and moreover a real knight in a fine outfit (and accompanied by a

The Quixotic Fiction

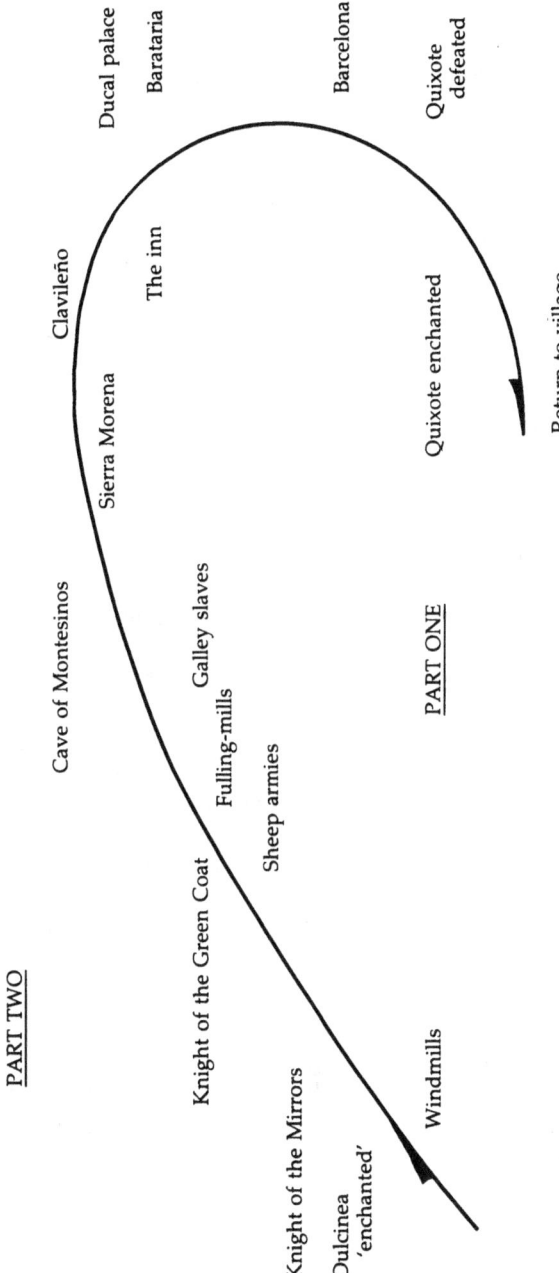

squire); over his armor he wears a cassock sprinkled with little discs of glittering mirrors while the size and weight of his lance are enormous. He not only has the appearance of a spectacular and formidable chivalric challenger, he possesses inside, seemingly enigmatic knowledge about the knight Don Quixote, about his prowess and his fame, even about 'what makes him tick' (i.e., his madness and psychosomatic complex). Quixote's fame has preceded him, so to speak, and has made this encounter inevitable.

Its plausibility (or implausibility), even for readers in 1615, are kept in suspension until the final disclosure, in the spirit of the models parodied. But even then Sancho and Quixote do not get to the bottom of the hoax. Whereas 'transformations' might explain it to their senses, their minds reject with disbelief the evidence that their friends conspired to victimize them.

They had settled down with their animals to spend the night in a secluded wood when a voice in the dark awakened Quixote: a knight in heart-rending tones addressing his lady who, if he is to be believed, is as cruel as she is beautiful. This lady, Casildea de Vandalia, has in her cruelty compelled him to seek out and challenge all the knights-errant roaming about Spain to acknowledge her as the most beautiful lady of the world and he has defeated them all, including all the knights in La Mancha. The stranger, perceiving Quixote's protestations, comes forward and introduces himself as a companionable, afflicted soul. They greet one another as knights mutually afflicted with misfortune, love for an idealized lady. It would seem that La Mancha is a very different place by night. Before it is over Quixote will hear from the stranger's lips the incredible 'fiction' of his defeat and will be brazenly challenged by him for a *second* time.

The disclosure of who this knight is "surprises" almost everybody, though various clues were given out along the way: his size and shape, his verbal mockery and fabrication about Casildea, his self-styled imitation of Hercules, and some details consciously dropped by his squire. Narrative strategy has been to align mimetic technique and authorial control to both simulate Quixote's illusion of an eventful challenge and combat and yet stage and disclose it as a hoax. Everybody, including the narrator it seems, is dumbfounded to learn it is . . . Samson Carrasco.

The friend and neighbor, wag and adulator, put on a knight's outfit, enlisted another neighbor and peasant Tomé Cecial as his squire, and disguised together they succeed in tricking Quixote and Sancho with their make-believe. Samson had planned all along to catch up with and provoke Quixote into a fight by brazenly challenging his knight's honor at its most sensitive, his loyalty to Dulcinea, as an effective way of curing his madness. His strategem is to provoke Quixote into a fight with lances because he is sure to defeat him with his superior strength and guile, break his illusion, and compel him to return to his village. It is all a plot hatched by Samson and the priest and barber with Tomé as accomplice.

So Samson's friendly encouragement at the outset was mischievous and deceptive. He planned a betrayal, yet to be effective it had to take the shape of a 'fiction' drawn around Quixote's illusion and Sancho's garrulousness. His plan didn't work, though he effectively deceived Quixote, and inadvertently accomplished the exact reverse of what he intended. The mock challenger turns out to be a greater fool. He takes a terrific blow when his horse refuses to budge in the face of Quixote's charge, is unhorsed and falls with all the big weight of his armor to the ground. So Quixote was able to achieve a real though lucky triumph. Samson and Tomé were 'done in' by the very length to which they went to deceive by creating a senseful deception and semblance of adventure. Their disguises, like the over-sized lance and the enormous nose on Tomé's face, were meant to instill terror and intimidate; their hoax was over-sized to ensure over-kill. Their efforts are, however, matched by the narrator's to depict not just senseful experience but for all its realism a veritable saturation of the senses on an extravagant scale. Not only is Samson's outfit with its many mirrors designed to heighten Quixote's illusion by sparkling with countless reflections of his image in the morning sunlight, and the ulterior design of Samson's fabrication designed to instill—mockingly—symbolical and mythological meanings into their encounter,[51] even the food and drink the two squires enjoy is on the exaggerated scale of a peasant's ritual feast down to the over-sized rabbit cooked in the pie, which Tomé maliciously packed to the size of Sancho's appetite. The narrator's self-conscious stance is transparent in the very titles he invents for the stranger, first "Knight of Woods" because that is the way Quixote perceives him in the dark, and then by daylight "Knight of the Mirrors."

How is one to interpret Samson's defeat? Obviously the narrator's obsession with instinctual friendship between the two horses and Dapple suggests that Samson is a victim of his own baser motives in the desire to pursue and "cure" Quixote. Moreover, he is boastful with false pride. His mock praise of Quixote is out of base envy. He is a 'false' friend and pays for it in the senseful reality of terrific pain in the kidneys and the humiliation of having to humble himself before a mad fool. In chapter 15 he expresses the now real and bitter desire to get back vengefully at the vainglorious Quixote who hit him but is too mad or simple-minded (or free of guile) to believe or even imagine that his neighbor Carrasco is capable of tricking him. Sancho, too, was taken in by the trick. Samson's motives are completely beyond him, and Quixote's explanation that the defeated knight looks like Samson because of wicked enchanters is the one he has to believe. Unlike Quixote, Sancho was intimidated as well as fooled by his counterpart. He was duped by Tomé's sly provocations as surely as he was terrorized by his false nose.

By unhorsing Samson and frustrating his scheme, Quixote has prolonged his fiction and the exemplary story indefinitely, at least for the present. But the very name "Samson Carrasco" is ominous and structured into the fiction. In it two ideas are joined: a mock hero with the size, shape and strength of the biblical Samson and the tree (kermes or shrub oak) which when cut down to a stump recoups to burst vigorously with new strength.

16. Knight of the Green Coat   Ch 16

With Samson laid out flat on the ground, Quixote drew his sword and pointed it to his face, prepared to strike the death blow. His 'triumph' bears comparison with the fight with the Biscayan noted above. There he struck a blow with his sword on the head and pillow stunning his adversary and brought copious bleeding from the nose and ears; he drew blood, yes, but not because the sword blade cut into flesh. And here he abstains for good reason from piercing the flesh of unlucky Samson. Quixote's sword is understandably the object on which Cervantes can bring to bear the theme of his ineffectuality as heroic and his effectiveness as fictional. It is not only in the nature of a mock weapon, its *in*effectuality is also an ethical theme.

As indicated on Chart III, the appearance of the Knight of the Green Coat is roughly parallel to the episode of the galley slaves in Part One. Because they have in common approximately the same position in the upward movement and disclosure of individual feats, they are two encounters strategically placed in the narrative for their ethical significance. In one he carries out and in the other performs a 'gratuitous act,' and while the circumstances are not as dissimilar as they might appear, the narrator's purpose in each is entirely different. Freeing the galley slaves is on the surface at least an altruistic act of Christian compassion. Facing the lions in a display of selfless but heroic courage is an act of sheer megalomania. Here the proportions of what is 'fictional' about the encounter with the man in the green coat brings into opposition two conceptions of character and the moral values they incarnate. The sword drawn to attack the lions epitomizes his pathological estrangement drawn comically identical to heroic daring.

From an encounter with a stranger who isn't to one with a genuine stranger who has never heard of famous Don Quixote or even read a book of chivalry and for whom a live 'fictional' knight is an object of amazement. Yet they are both country hidalgos, social equals, who are ethical opposites. Their encounter is sustained by techniques of representation that, while simulating Quixote's illusion, depict a senseful reality in which no deception, no trick will contradict what things, persons and animals appear to be. The techniques and the realistic illusion are the opposite of adventures staged or played as hoaxes. As in the case of the episode of the galley slaves, no distortion, no hallucination is allowed to complicate or compromise the ethical significance immanent in their chance encounter. It is under such conditions that 'fiction' becomes one and the same with illusion.

Don Diego does not wear a disguise and everything about him eschews the slightest notion of guile or deception. The elegant green outfit he wears (dyed and cut as prescribed by custom for travel) suggests a man so refined in his taste for good clothes and grooming as to be slightly ostentatious for his age.[52] It provokes Quixote to address him as "Señor Galán. . ." ["Sir Gallant. . ."]. The elegant outfit is both declarative and denunciatory. From the beginning Quixote senses the interest this man of his own age and social class may have for him. In his social equal he perceives a moral challenge. His manner is both courteous and slightly provocative, *"Señor Galán. . .,"* he calls out. The stranger in turn is not just astonished but amazed at Quixote's battered outfit. Urged on by the other's gaze and unbelieving expression, Quixote introduces himself as "The Knight of the Rueful Countenance" and the rest, all to the further amazement of the stranger. He is provoked by the stranger to give the most self-conscious description of himself we have heard up to now, for the public image as living hero of a published book requires a courteous tolerance to reactions of disbelief. Quixote's vainglory shows through his sincere modesty. Concealed in Don Diego's courteous silence and then disclosures of disbelief is the certainty that the self-styled knight suffers from some mental disorder. Quixote has to beg him to disclose something of himself.

Does the stranger sense the challenge and provocation?—He says: "Yo, señor Caballero de la Triste Figura, soy un hidalgo natural de un lugar donde iremos a comer hoy, si Dios fuere servido. Soy más que medianamente rico y es mi nombre don Diego de Miranda." II.16, 153 [I, Sir Knight of the Rueful Countenance, am an hidalgo and native of a village where, please God, we shall dine today. I am more than moderately rich and my name is Don Diego de Miranda.] His self-introduction is truly as amazing as Quixote's; it is a social, psychological and moral portrait. It is likewise a literary portrait whose significance cannot be reduced to a mere formula.

Like Quixote he is a country hidalgo, and like him makes no exclusive claims to having 'pure' old Christian blood in his veins. Yet his life style incarnates the most prized virtues of the hidalgo establishment; he is affluent, a family man, married and apparently well adjusted domestically and his wife Doña Christina shares his personal and social tastes; he has fathered a son who is a credit to him; he is a devout Catholic. He has every reason to be satisfied with his share of the world's material goods and the enlightenment his religion provides. He is, alongside Quixote, an almost self-complacent conformist of the times. Quixote could not have met up with a more meaningful counterpart. In his illusion he supposes he has met up with another chivalric personality, but what we hear from Don Diego repudiates any such idea.

The stranger has been provoked to make an assessment of his life style and personal and social qualities which is both self-congratulatory and self-effacing. It belies his own version of what is virtuous and worth striving for. Excluded are the obsessive Quixotic concerns for honor and fame. His personal ideal is a certain moderation, 'prudence,' revealed in the way he enumerates his traits and qualities. He eschews violence and does nothing to excess (not even virtue). Moderation, it seems, is for him a balance between 'sensation' and 'reason,' between feeling and pleasure and their rational control. He engages in the physical activities of his social class, hunting and fishing, but in the least violent way possible, without birds of prey or hounds, '. . . no mantengo ni halcón ni galgos, sino algún perdigón manso or algún hurón atrevido." [I keep neither hawk nor hounds, but only a tame partridge and a good ferret or two.] (This phrase strikes a particular chord in Quixote.) He owns a respectable library of devotional and historical books in Latin and Spanish and selects with care what to read among books of imaginative literature. Books of chivalry are all but unknown to him. There is a calculated choice in what he enumerates in negative form: he does not pry into the lives of others nor gossip, he dislikes hypocrisy. He is generous, cordial, civil; he shares his table in the spirit of conviviality with neighbors and friends. He believes in 'good works,' is charitable to the poor without ostentation. He hears Mass every day. . . "soy devoto de nuestra Señora, y confío siempre en la misericordia de Dios nuestro Señor." [I am devoted to Our Lady and always trust in the infinite mercy of our Lord God.] His religious life would seem to add up to an ideal of secular Catholic piety, for he makes no mention of dogmas or sacraments (i.e., questions of doctrine and ritual are of little concern).[53]

Quixote is not overly impressed, Sancho is: he runs to kiss the feet of this 'saint in the saddle,' and the sight makes Quixote laugh, visibly breaking his deep gloom.

Alongside Quixote in his fine green outfit Don Diego represents an ideal of private and inner virtue turned outward as the eminently sociable Christian virtues of charity, devotion and conviviality, a kind of secular saint. Or what amounts to the same thing and what Cervantes has hinted at circumspectly: a sedentary paradigm of 'Christian Knight,' a secular form of Christian virtue (*Miles Christianus*). To some it has seemed greatly perverse on the part of Cervantes to have matched him with Quixote, whose illusion (or the narrator's) provides Don Diego with an appropriate title—"Knight of the Green Coat." Is the title meant to be ironical? A knight typified by his *non*-deeds? Is it meant to confer a 'storied' personality or an ironical meaning on him? In other words, what is the literary meaning of Don Diego's self-portrait? Is Don Diego paradigmatic, that is, principally a moral example? Or is he novelistic, a possible subject for a novelist? The values and virtues he represents are evident (this is the point), for they are those consecrated by the Spanish establishment (nobility and property, Catholic religion), and his defects and idiosyncracies minimal.

As a paradigm of 'Christian Knight' he incarnates an ideal of secular piety commensurate for a Spanish hidalgo 'who has everything': 'a bourgeois ethos' for enlightened Spanish nobility of modern times. Even so his self-portrait is paradoxical as much for its moral and historical meaning as for its literary meaning. He may be seen for instance as an example of a Christian conscience 'secularized' of doctrinal or monastic impurities and excesses according to Erasmian teachings. In fact he describes himself very much in the form and style of Erasmus's characters in his Latin Dialogues.[54] And what he describes is indeed a kind of secular ideal of Christian society, but in terms of such moderation and even self-effacement as to compromise the most moving of Christian virtues. He is sensitive, yet in his life there are no great passions, no intense beliefs, feelings, hates, loves, no ambitions, no true self-abnegation. His virtues appear to be moderation and reason, even faith, become devirtualized and devitalized. For all his inner tranquility and self-sufficiency Don Diego is a sensualist and materialist, a maybe 'Christian' epicurean.

By contrasting him face to face (and act to act) with Quixote Cervantes has drawn an axiological contrast and vastly extended the range of this scene's referential meaning; his mimetic art is so transparent in all its features that it would seem to need no further explanation, but then its very transparency invites almost endless speculation and interpretation, again, however, in the direction opposite to the abstract, figurative meanings of allegory and symbolism. Don Diego would seem to be for his devitalized virtues an impossible subject for a novelist, even one with the genius of Cervantes or Flaubert. By his own admission he is not only non-heroic but even non-novelistic. He is 'ethical,' not 'fictional.' One needed to bring him into the orbit of the Quixotic fiction and to match him against its hero to be able to invest his life with novelistic interest and value. The facts of his existence would seem to repudiate any fictionalization. Yet, if the modern novel can be said to have come into existence at a particular moment in literature, I suggest it would be here in the encounter between Quixote and Don Diego de Miranda.

Two country hidalgos so opposite as individuals have so little in common that their social courtesy is the only mutual point of contact. Don Diego's disapproval of his son's enthusiasm for poetry is the only cloud that darkens the happiness of his existence: as heir his son is obligated, he says, to maintain the family's honor and prestige by preparing himself for a career in law or the Church; but no, at the University in Salamanca he's shown a frivolous inclination to take up poetry as a study. Don Diego's tolerance and generosity apparently do not apply to his son (nor his Christian love perhaps). Quixote goes into yet another discourse, this one on the rearing of children and poetry as 'Queen of Sciences.' He supports the youth's choice, yet he has not understood the reality of Don Diego's family problem because he cannot assume the conformist's attitude toward it. In the Quixotic scale of values personal freedom comes before family. His "defense of poetry" reaches a new level of moral and psychological illumination of his ingenio as a disclosure of his pathological state. He discourses imaginatively and lucidly on an abstract subject, yet he does not imagine very much. Don Diego is astonished at Quixote's sagacity and his verbal skill and wonders whether his first diagnosis could be wrong. At that moment the cart appears and Quixote sees it. Now, as if by a flash, his imaginative exaltation has been ignited by the sight, the visual stimulus, of the cart's sudden appearance on the road ahead. He senses a new challenge and an adventure in the making. He calls out to Sancho to bring him his headpiece.

17. Knight of the Lions   Ch 17

"The man in green heard this and gazed in all directions without discovering anything but a cart coming toward them hung with two or three small flags, which made him think that it was carrying the Knight's treasure. . . ." So that the contrast may be complete, Don Diego replaces Sancho as interpreter of senseful reality and dissuader of adventures. The circumstances must show Quixote performing before this sensitive but self-complacent witness an act foolish and mad in every respect but one: the singular one that satisfies Quixote's inner illusion (or that vindicates him as the subject of Cervantes' narrative). Don Diego's asides and exclamations put into focus the view that, unless it be the foolish temerity of a madman, Quixote's baiting of the lions is senseless.

Sancho hands over the helmet with the cheese curds in it. Quixote puts it on and squeezes the curds so that they ooze down over his face and beard: are his brains melting, or why does he sweat so? he exclaims. Technique has called for yet another variation: the hero is humiliated before not after the attack as is usual. The association of soft cheeses with madness has been traditional in folklore,[55] and Don Diego's cutting aside "no doubt the cheese curds have softened his brains" was to be expected. He has heard Quixote speak on a lofty level of eloquent, illuminated humanistic discourse and now, astonished, he hears him order the lion keeper to open the cages for he means to fight the lions as if they were a personal challenge sent by enchanters. As dissuader Don Diego pleads from a prudent, textbook view of chivalric combat and a sane respect for the King's animals: "valor which verges on temerity is more like madness than bravery, what is more these lions have not come against you. . . ." For his good sense Quixote orders him away with the disparaging "Váyase . . . a entender con su perdigón manso y con su hurón atrevido. . . . [Go away . . . and see to your tame partridge and good ferret. . . .] But again Don Diego admonishes him not to attempt an act so foolhardy as to defy God himself. He gives up trying to reason with a madman and retires to a safe distance, so that it is he who suffers a loss of personal dignity; he retreats from the scene not as the prudent man he is but as if he were cowardly.

Quixote's intrepidity has three witnesses and their testimony becomes part of narrative technique. The lions are real and to 'challenge' them would seem to be an act of sheer audacity, uncontaminated by tricks, hallucinations or deceptions, or even imagination itself, an act unfalsified in the light of stark reality. As a gratuitous act to match the release of the galley slaves in Part I it is senseless of course in all respects but one: the illusion of chivalric fame it concedes. By the 'mythos' of his chivalric calling and personality the hero is compelled to carry out an act of courage that has no other meaning than to invest circumstance with his heroic identity. The fact that it is frightful for Sancho, brave for the lion keeper, and foolhardy for Don Diego only heightens the version Cide Hamete interjects; it is he who defines it as 'fiction.' "Tú a pie, tú solo, tú intrépido, tú magnánimo, con sola una espada. . . ." [You on foot, you alone, you bold, you magnanimous, with only a simple sword. . . .] For once his exclamations reflect a heroic image of Quixote. They recall the Vergilian hymn in praise of lion-slayer Hercules (*Aeneid*, VIII, 293ff.). His apostrophe performs the same function as have 'transformations' and hoaxes to effect Quixote's act as 'fiction.'

Like the demented subject that he is, Quixote waits 'intrepid' in front of the opened cage, expecting to leap at the lion, his sword drawn. The lion, confined in his cage in the heat of the afternoon, behaves according to his norm. It is no perverse objectivity of the narrator to mention the hindparts he exposed to his challenger before lying down again. These African lions, after all, belong to a particular species of *Felis leo* in the zoology of fiction. They have shown up in the role of animal adversary (though the male's passive behavior would suggest also the role of animal companion to the hero), whether they perform or not according to Quixote's illusion. Comic technique has here depicted a 'gratuitous lion' to match the gratuitous act and displace the 'grateful lion' of Chrétien de Troyes' story and the medieval chivalric tradition.[56] The comic lion who emerges from his cage, pretends indifference and unconcernedly retreats to the safety of his cage, refusing combat, is one who freely removes himself from the field and 'gives up' to render the knight a 'free' triumph.

According to Cide Hamete (and Miguel de Unamuno), defying the lions is an act of selfless, magnanimous heroic virtue. Even with the no-show stance of the drowsy male lion it amounts to a feat and test of real courage. Reality is itself a structure of illusion. Don Diego's presence and then the lions riding in their cages provoked Quixote to a new outbreak of his pathological exultation. It is the same exultation that obliges him to justify his action self-consciously to Don Diego, for his very words in their measured elegance describe, imaginatively now, his pathological estrangement as heroic immolation.

>   —Quién duda, señor don Diego de Miranda, que vuestra merced no me tenga en su opinión por un hombre disparatado y loco? . . . porque mis obras no pueden dar testimonio de otra cosa. Pues, con todo esto, quiero que vuestra merced advierta que no soy tan loco ni tan menguado como debo de haberle parecido. II.17,166

>   No doubt, Don Diego de Miranda, your worship considers me both foolish and mad . . . for my deeds testify no less. But, for all that, I wish you to note that I am not so mad or so lacking in wits as I must have appeared to you.

Don Diego's intervention and testimony are essential to depicting it as a personal feat that, pathology aside, transcends purely social values and is heroic for its gratuitous nature. Don Diego, for the values and conformist virtues he represents, cannot of course 'see' it in this way, and to suppose that it reveals heroic virtue would defy his mind altogether. Perplexed anew by Quixote's pseudo-rational explanation, he can only offer guarded praise. He is, so to speak, non-fictionalizing as he is non-heroic and adverse to humor and to jesting: his scale of values could not recognize Quixote's illusion as real, and even less as 'fiction.' He cannot fathom his motives or exposure to danger and death in the quest of 'fame' because he cannot fathom a desire rooted in a fictionalized meaning and conception of life. But this is precisely his role in the episode. Not having any 'inside' knowledge about his madness or the printed volume of Part One, he is an uninformed, impartial spectator who judges Quixote's actions and words for what they are, not as pretense, or imitation or entertainment. But one feels that his amazement at what he hears and sees would not be any less if he had read through Part One.

Quixote's illusion of himself as brave knight is now confirmed in the title he gives himself, "Knight of the Lions," though the animal he challenged merely ignored him: he has shown those qualities traditionally attributed to the male lion (ferocity, fearlessness, strength), because he assumed the stance of heroes who verily faced lions and either fought and killed them or subdued them, like the Cid, by their glaring intrepidity. His triumph is, again, illusory, fulfilment of illusion within physical and sensuous reality, or better still 'fictional,' thanks to the animal who performed according to the right variation of comico-satiric design.

18. Camacho's Wedding   Chs 18-21

Victory over the drowsy lion pits him against the heroes of history and legend who subdued lions and magnifies his personality by projecting his career onto the scale of the literary epic. It is not so much that Cervantes has devised a prose version of epical unity imposed on an episodic action with its subordinate plots and characters as that he has devised a structure of narrative that unfolds to confirm the hero in his illusion: he moves and acts within a senseful reality of auspicious events immanent with the literary pattern of the classical epic. How he acts depends very much on how he is treated by those who come into his presence, and for now he is given no cause to react violently. He is greeted and welcomed as an odd but distinguished guest. Called on to display his most sociable qualities, courtesy, discretion, rhetorical skill, he shows himself an exemplar of dignified social conduct. His madness has turned inward as self-examination even, as exterior reality becomes not only tolerant but increasingly sympathetic to his illusion. The quest of adventures seems suspended in a season of ritual and festival in a rural landscape of Spring. A world now seemingly impregnated with his fame is festivally prepared to celebrate his chivalric identity.

Since the structure of illusion is now one and the same with the epic structure of thematically aligned episodes, Cervantes can develop the classical themes of country life and rural peace (*beatus ille*) and then a country wedding without removing Quixote and Sancho from the center: their senseful experience is lifted to the order of encomium and festival. Don Diego leads them to his home where they stay for four days: there no incident is more important than the senseful fulfilment of their separate needs and illusions. Sancho at last enjoys food and lodging to his satisfaction. Quixote is greeted and treated with respect and dignity in a household whose routine can hold no adventure more telling than the conviviality of good manners, good food, conversation and comfort. Don Diego, his wife Doña Cristina and the son Don Lorenzo, as their hospitality shows, fulfill in their separate happiness and self-contentment the social and moral virtues of country life imbued with Christian moderation. Quixote's chivalry as a 'science for living' is an idea nearly alien to their personal order and domestic tranquility. Yet the son Don Lorenzo is susceptible to Quixote's extravagance when he hears himself praised as a superlative poet. It is he who comes up with the apt description of Quixote that evaded his father: "él es un entreverado loco, lleno de lúcidos intervalos." II.18, 173 [He is mad in patches, full of lucid intervals.] They provoked him into two revealing expositions of his knighthood and its utopian nature as a social program of personal obligations to others (where the subject of arms and fighting hardly appears). He could not have spoken in such terms to Sancho or Carrasco, or to anyone he has met up to now. But also he did not offer his help to these sensitive hosts as knight-errant, for their material well-being on his own social level had put his chivalry on the defensive. Not in deed—attacking the lions—but dialectically his utopian chivalry is set as a counterpart to the 'happy mediocrity' of their serene but self-enclosed materialism.

Don Diego is a Manchegan hidalgo with only the remotest analogy to a prototype from the mythological world of epic adventures. Taking leave of him, Quixote decides to set off for the nearby cave of Montesinos to investigate and learn "the origin and true sources of the seven lagoons called the Lakes of Ruidera." These regions of La Mancha will be made to disclose their "origins" concealed in mythological fables and legends; the geography of adventure is about to reveal primordial mysteries. Don Lorenzo recited his sonnet on the Ovidian couple "Pyramus and Thisbe" and this poem with its artifice that impressed Quixote is the thematic introduction to the episode of Camacho's Wedding. They are led to the village of the wedding by the two students and two laborers met on the road, the first set of guides who lead the way to the cave.

"Camacho's Wedding" bears comparison to the episode of Chrysostom and Marcela in Part I, but here Quixote's new configuration has imposed a 'fictional' or hoax structure on a story of 'real' shepherds. In the first a rejected lover committed suicide and Quixote and Sancho are present at his burial when the cold and chaste Marcela appears to exculpate herself for his death. In the other a rejected lover Basilio commits suicide to the horror of the bride, priest, and wedding guests and with his last breath pleads to be united to her apparently in death. The first is a situation of 'crossed lovers' fatally separated by her desire not to love. In the second Basilio and Quiteria are separated by her father's decision to marry her to the rich Camacho. In the first narrative illusion maintains a somber, elegiac representation of the tragic erotic. The second is sustained on various levels of representation to produce a festive, mock death as the 'fiction' by which love wins over material interests and celebrates its triumph, a consummation of Quixotic illusion attested to in the well-known adaptations of this episode to film and the ballet.[57] Each is a 'fiction-within-fiction' but the second, by recapitulating the first to a point, assumes the explicit outlines of a Quixotic fiction.

The very phrase "Camacho's Wedding" betrays pejorative but festive mockery of an outwitted bridegroom (and even the priest who performs the ceremony) who bears the huge cost of a sumptuous country feast but is cheated by the bride. The core of the episode is a celebration of fraudulent 'fiction': Basilio's mock suicide raises to its own level of grotesque celebration of solemn marriage and funeral, of love, wit and artful fraud, a happy outcome to a romance fable. The mythological model in the background is the story or myth of the Babylonian lovers Pyramus and Thisbe (*Metamorphoses*, IV) with its outcome of mutual suicide brought on by the visual evidence of the beloved's blood, and the horrible spectacle of real blood brought off as a dramatic artifice recalls a similar practice in classical Roman drama.

The Quixotic illusion of an adventure is commensurate in the senseful, or rather, horrible but false bleeding that brings success to

Basilio. The various levels of representation, real, mimetic and deceptive in the lavish wedding feast correspond to the levels of sensory adventure for Quixote and Sancho, and their dialogues bear out the thematic correspondences to their separate characterization. The sensory perception—visual, olfactory, auditory—of the lavish scale and variety of the feast and then its gastronomic pleasure becomes Sancho's experience. Quixote's is the esthetic spectacle of dances, costumes, decorations, songs and poetry, and the dramatic and allegorical masque performed, together with the dialectical argument between "Love" and "Interest." Yet it is Sancho who provides the rustic, hyperbolic description of the bride, as it is Quixote who takes the bleeding Basilio in his arms.

Thematically the episode resolves the contest between "Love" and "Money," the lovers' choices and parental authority, wit and artifice on the side of poverty and against affluence, in favor of a natural love and union of two young lovers. In this case 'artifice' is the natural ally of truth and reason. Quiteria's word, her consent—when she is prepared to be separated from him forever—really decides the contest (or legitimizes the trick), for it is her true love for Basilio that seals their union. Basilio's stratagem depends on the horror caused by the sight of his body bathed in blood. When he falls transfixed by his dagger, Quixote takes him in his arms and holds him there for the long interval of his feigned dying gasps (he cannot be laid out on the ground), and pleads his cause. It is his belief in the truth of what he hears and sees that 'turns the trick' on Camacho. Compare this situation to his disinterest in the cases of 'happy love' resolved in Part One. Quixote is at the center of the action again when he takes up his lance to defend the lovers from Camacho's followers while Sancho seeks refuge in the cooking-pots. He plays the role of mediator when violence threatens, and we recall he played a similar role in the fencing contest of the two students met on the road, when also their boasts turned to a duel in which Corchuelo ('force') was bested by the other's 'art' or 'skill.'

Basilio employs his wit (*ingenio, industria*) and daring as well as athletic ability to bring off a stratagem that 'rescues' Quiteria from the ogre-like Camacho. Their story is a 'fiction' structured to the illusion of a lover who effectively liberates his beloved from an unhappy fate. They are the first of a series of paired lovers whose story in Part II retraces the prototypal situation of the "separated lovers" Quixote-Dulcinea (see Chart V).

19. The Cave Adventure: Prototype   Chs 22-23

The dialogues between Quixote and Sancho are for their thematic, linguistic or idiomatic features the great unifying arc of narrative suspended over events and their chain of cause and effect. The abundance of Camacho's feast provoked lively exchanges on the most basic of human needs and those realities ritualized in the celebration: the physiological needs, food, drink, sleep, and the social obligations between master and servant that provide for them. Quixote's monologue over snoring Sancho is a connective of the same order. For their themes these dialogues serve as prelude to the episode of the cave. To see this, one must stand back from the flow of dialogue and note that, as the main thrust of the narrative, these dialogues are very nearly autonomous in the sense that the narrator and Cide Hamete do not and cannot claim to invent or control them. They are, though dialogues, the most immediate form of narrative for their mimetic nature. The adventure in the cave is the prototypal Quixotic fiction for various reasons, the main one being that Quixote himself is the narrator of it—in the form of dialogue with his audience, Sancho and the scholar guide. In this form it is an 'autonomous fiction' within the book, not attributable to either the narrator or to Cide Hamete who disclaim any responsibility for it. Indeed, what Quixote says he saw and heard in the cave is not, so to speak, 'part of the book'; it does not 'happen,' except as discourse, or illusion. The experience itself appears only in narrative form; and not only was it solitary, he disappeared from view of all, including the narrator. For all these reasons the archetypal Quixotic fiction is formed in the deepest part of his character, where his psychology, morality and physiology interact. Moreover, for its prototypal status it must be suspended in the narrative uniquely as a 'fiction' in the form of dialogue.

It emerges from so singular a combination of motives as to appear as the one single adventure in the book he deliberately sets out to accomplish. It arises directly from his motives, not from a chance encounter or circumstantial sensory stimulus. He revealed to Don Diego his decision to go down into the cave and alone, of course. But he needs a guide to show the way to the entrance. His immediate purpose is the one he explains in the invocation to Dulcinea: "voy a despeñarme . . . en el abismo . . . sólo porque conozca el mundo que si tú me favoreces, no habrá imposible a quien yo no acometa y acabe." II.22, 209 [I am about to plunge in the abyss . . . only to make the world recognize that if you favor me, there is no impossible feat that I may not accomplish.] What remains unstated is what he expects to find in the cave, beyond "confirming the truth of the marvels that it is reputed to contain," 205. There is no mention of a literary model either for or to instigate a purpose or end, as in the penitential episode of Sierra Morena. Nor does Sancho have any place in it (at least until he interjects himself into it later). The literary models of course existed, but for his own purpose Cervantes has chosen to omit any reference to them: the level of parody is to be implied (i.e., Quixote's subconscious) or alluded to mimetically.

It is then the only adventure undertaken with 'premeditation.' Yet he needs an accompanying spirit to show the way. It is of course Cervantes' design that the scholar-guide he enlists is curious about the 'mythological origins' of the local geography and knowledgeable about books of chivalry.[58] The guide's books are whimsical popularizing compilations of pseudo-humanistic if not vulgarizing 'scholarship' and addressed to the undiscriminating. But Quixote will be instigated by their eccentric 'transformations' and 'inventions' and the guide's promptings to fabricate a fiction revolving around 'metamorphoses' and in which the guide himself has been transformed into a pseudo-academic in the form of Montesinos. In the first instance the guide is indispensable to lead the way to the location of the cave and to interject the subject of his books into Quixote's subconscious mind. They arrive there with the necessary provisions at about two in the afternoon (again the effect of the afternoon heat), and after ritualized invocations and farewells, and with a rope tied around his waist, Quixote is lowered into the cave. He disappears into the earth and for the first and only time out of view—*of everyone*, characters, narrators, or readers. This point is fundamental to the verisimilitude of what his account will mean as physiological disclosure, literary fabrication or psychological self-characterization with its psychoanalytical content.

His religious prayers, invocation to Dulcinea, and the ominous send-off Sancho and the guide provide are the realistic semblance to a ritualistic pattern of words and actions that will emerge from his account. The entrance is covered by a thick growth of brambles so that Quixote has to draw his sword to hack an opening to the cave, and from within crows, jackdaws and bats fly out and knock him to the ground. A bad omen that only assures him he is on the right track. It is all a clear reference to Aeneas who (on the instigation of the

Sibyl) draws his sword when he prepares to enter the underworld, the classical Hades (*Aeneid* VI,vss. 260 ff.). Quixote lowers himself into the cave, calling out for more rope, until Sancho and the guide let out all of it (about 500 ft.). At this point they lose contact with him for about half an hour, then, fearing the worst, they tug at and hurriedly recover all but the last fifty feet of it. One deduces that the distance Quixote penetrated into the cave did not exceed forty feet. They pull him to the surface and need to shake and turn him over to arouse him from a sleep so deep he seems to be unconscious. When he opens his eyes and speaks he recriminates them for having awakened him . . . not from sleep, but from "the sweetest experience and most delightful vision any human being has ever beheld." What he describes from the first moment has been a full sensory revelation of waking life: "Now indeed I know that the pleasant things of this life pass away like a shadow or a dream, or wither like flowers of the field. O unhappy Montesinos! O sorely wounded Durandarte! O unlucky Belerma! . . ."

About an hour later, having satisfied thirst and hunger, he tells what he saw and did in the cave. The first thing he did was to explore the upper part of the cave, until he fell asleep, only to awaken again in the midst of a pleasant meadow. What probably happened is that he became drowsy for lack of the proper amount of air, or oxygen, and fell asleep and would have lost consciousness altogether if he had not been pulled out when he was. Most critics today are disposed to treat his narrative as the account of a dream. I object to this on grounds that he does not tell it as a dream. Perhaps he did dream, but what he dreamt is not the account. And whatever resemblance we may suppose his account has to dreams and dreaming, the fact remains that his narrative is verbal because imaginary, which is not the case with dreams. From a scientific point of view neither dreams nor reality are verbal—only our means of understanding them are. Dreams and dreaming are not imaginary, nor are they verbal; their enigmatic, problematical, or mysterious nature is due to the fact that they take place below the level of conscious states. What Quixote tells is a wakeful, sensory experience in the form of an invented fable, a fiction, which may resemble a dream or a vision. As make-believe or fiction it is structured according to a literary pattern of words and actions. As the prototypal Quixotic fiction it is structured according to his deepest illusions. The assumption that it is a dream is only one basis for judging it as possible, or verisimilar experience. What, then, is the literary pattern?

From time immemorial entry into and existence in caves and the underground have been connected with beliefs about Man's origins, with rites, superstitions and magic, with myths of access to the world of the dead, or with profoundly prophetic or mystical experiences and revelations. We can suppose that Cervantes was acquainted with many features of cave-lore as known and interpreted in sixteenth-century Spain, with both popular and secularized versions of legends and tales handed down by tradition and the learned literary versions of historical legends, hagiographic accounts and poetry, like the Inferno of Dante's *Commedia*. Among these the account by Saint Ignatius of Loyola of his 'conversion' by the Virgin in the cave of Manresa, and the story of the founding of the monastery of Montserrat (located over a series of caves) as told in the poem *El Monserrate*, which we found included among Quixote's books, are of particular interest. But cave-lore, it would seem, is inseparable, if not from the very "origins" of Man, at least from the origins of his culture.

For among stone age tribes of prehistory it was tribal custom to bury the dead in caves and to believe that their spirits inhabited underground caverns, so that some of Man's earliest religious beliefs and rituals involve communicating with departed spirits in their abodes underground, and the belief in an underground 'paradise' or 'elysium' is undoubtedly bound up with the origins of mythologies. The stone age cultures of the Middle East, we may suppose, passed on to the ancient cultures of the Mediterranean these and similar religious beliefs elaborated in Greek and Roman mythology and poetry. The classical versions of descent and journey of Greek and Roman gods, demigods and heroes to the otherworld no doubt repeat much earlier myths and rituals of the search for an ancestral divinity among the dead.[59] A journey like Aeneas' implies not only a sacred mission but a special dispensation, for the obstacles involved in the journey to the dead are less formidable than those the hero must surmount to return to the world of the living. Various versions of the pagan underworld and journey were incorporated into the Christian version of hell and medieval eschatology, together with beliefs, myths and traditions of the Celtic and Germanic peoples. In Quixote's fabrications Cervantes has drawn on three lines of folk and literary traditions: (1) the journey and descent from the classical epic, (2) the cave adventure from chivalric prose romance, and (3) for his personages, the Castilian lyric-narrative ballads, from which the name 'Cave of Montesinos' derives, and for their afterlife, the vision of a lovers' inferno where many famous lovers of legend and history—in pairs or singly—live on encapsulated in time.

Aeneas' descent to the underworld in Book VI of the *Aeneid* may be thought of as the prototype in epic narrative. At about the mid-point of his mission to found Rome and her civilization, Aeneas lands in Italy at the head of his band of Trojans. As their leader he prepares to descend, alone, to the underworld, whose access is the cave at Cumae, to find his father Anchises and receive from him a revelation about the tasks still ahead. He must have a guide to show the way and enlists the help of the Sibyl (and priestess of Apollo and Diana); he must take a 'golden bough' as an offering to Proserpina, the Queen of Hell; he travels through various regions where the dead live on in ghostly form and sees among them Queen Dido whom he abandoned in Carthage; in Elysium he finds Anchises and receives from him a prophetic revelation of Rome's future greatness; his strength and faith in himself renewed, he leaves the underworld through the Gate of Ivory, one of the twin gates of sleep.

The descent to the underworld in epic narrative is closely linked to ancient rituals of initiation in which communication with the dead is a ritual passage from death to rebirth.[60] The ritual rebirth like Aeneas's renews the hero's purpose and his strength and confers on his mission a transcendental meaning. In the prose romances of chivalry the literary pattern is altered by erotic love and magic and the new, medieval conception of the hero. The knight's quest is a personal one, a search for the adventure that will win for him the greatest fame. In the chivalric versions of the cave one or more royal personages are held in the underworld in a state of enchantment, the work of a necromancer, which the hero is destined to break by virtue of his strength and prowess. These versions no doubt descend from solar mythologies where the hero sun-god liberates his queen or consort, a vegetation goddess, in the year's renewal. It is important to note that Quixote's fiction resembles rather closely two episodes from sixteenth-century prose romances in Spanish. The first is the author's dream in Montalvo's *Esplandián* (1510), in which the enchantress Urganda leads him through a subterrean palace and explains that the personages he sees are Amadís, Oriana and others (the very characters of his earlier work), held deathlike in a state of enchantment.[61] The second is the episode in *Espejo de príncipes y caballeros* (*Mirror of*

Princely Deeds and Knighthood, Bk. II, 1555), by Diego Ortúñez de Calahorra. Rosicler, the Knight of Phoebus, makes his way into the cave of Artidón where this enchanter, before killing himself for love of her, imprisoned and enchanted Queen Artidea; Rosicler kills an enormous bull, a dragon and a giant in an underground palace and releases the Queen from the spell. By his magic Artidón preserved himself as if alive; his breast is opened by a wound exposing his bleeding heart, and he recovers speech to reveal to Rosicler important affairs of his love life. Quixote's fiction then follows the general outlines of the mythological descent to the underworld of the epic pattern of initiation, combining it with the chivalric and solar pattern of an enchantment to be broken and conceives this enchantment in the form of the 'fame' of illustrious personages who are lovers in popular ballads about Montesinos and the battle of Roncesvalles.

The thread of verisimilitude connecting the world above to the fiction in the cave is his claim that the passage from one to the other was indelibly perceptive, conscious and sensory. He fell asleep and then awoke; rubbing his eyes, he felt his head and body to assure himself that he was not sleeping; he sees, feels, hears, thinks. "Despabilé los ojos, limpiémelos, y vi que no dormía . . . me tenté la cabeza y los pechos, por certificarme si era yo mismo el que allí estaba . . ." II.23, 211. Again, sensory fulfilment is the test of adventure. The absolute certainty of its reality is that *he sees himself* in the scenes he describes, which may account for his passivity, for he assumes of course the role of the initiate: the passive, perceiving subject of the ritual.

In the fair meadow where he awoke rose a great crystal palace of transparent walls from whose gateway emerged a venerable old man, Montesinos himself. Each of the images Quixote discloses—the elysian field, the crystal castle, etc., and their thread—are archetypal in the literature of mystical visions and initiatory rituals. Montesinos is the ancestral figure whom he is to consult, but he is also the guide; he is dressed appropriately for this solemn role, yet each of the details pressed to bear out the significance of his appearance becomes a distortion of the ritual, a comical distortion for the unconscious nature of the disclosures. Montesinos approaches to greet him, for he knows who he is and has long awaited his coming: "—Luengos tiempos ha, valeroso caballero don Quijote de la Mancha, que los que estamos en estas soledades encantados esperamos verte, para que des noticia al mundo de lo que encierra y cubre la profunda cueva . . . hazaña sólo guardada para ser acometida de tu invencible corazón y de tu ánimo estupendo." II.23, 212 [It is many centuries, valorous Don Quixote, that we who dwell enchanted in these solitudes have been waiting to see you, so that you may inform the world of what is contained here . . . an exploit reserved to be attempted only by your invincible heart and your stupendous courage.] The adventure in the cave is meant to confirm his elect status as the chosen new champion of chivalry. Its very structure of intimate illusion confirmed as sensory experience calls for a more passive stance on his part. It traces out a design of causality where great, even transcendental, claims may be made for him—he is the hero chosen for the task—the cause adequate to the effect—without his having to prove any bit of it. His very passivity before the great figures of legend confirms, to his fantasy, his elect status and his heroic effectiveness.

Scarcely had Montesinos announced the purpose and meaning of his presence in the cave than Quixote asked, like the naive initiate, whether it was true he had extracted Durandarte's heart with a little dagger (as told in some ballads) and carried it to Belerma. His question is the exact reverse of how he has carried on (in Part I) in the real world, where he transforms factual objects into fantasy. Does it betray a deep craving to make more real, more credible the illusion of adventure confirmed as sensory experience? The poetic tradition never concerned itself with the instrument used to extract Durandarte's heart; it did specify that Montesinos dug the grave in which to bury his body with a small dagger, which would have been the only instrument available. His fabrication revolves around the credibility of the extracted heart, its size, the instrument used, its conveyance to Belerma, its preservation. The extracted and now mummified heart is the quasi-mystical object of his initiatory experience, hence the unconscious struggle to make every detail about it realistic, sensory and verisimilar. Montesinos takes him before the sepulcher; he sees the knight himself laid out on the tomb *in place of* his effigy; not a living body, we suppose, but an enchanted one. As told in the old ballads, Durandarte died on the field at Roncesvalles (the historical date was 778) and was buried there by Montesinos. This then must be his 'corporeal ghost' because his body is intact, except for the heart, and shows no sign of decomposition. But while the body has been immaculately preserved, the separated heart has been exposed to effects of age and putrescence from the moment it was extracted, for Montesinos used salt as a preservative so that, while it has not been reduced to dust in nearly a thousand years, it is now a withered shadow of what it was when Belerma first received it. As guide and ancestral figure Montesinos reveals the intimate story about Durandarte, himself and Belerma but while doing so is shaping another fiction-within-fiction as the ultimate Quixotic fiction for the redemptive role assigned to the hero in it. While explaining the 'mythological' origins of the cave, the lakes of Ruidera and the river Guadiana, the scene at Roncesvalles and the rest, the old man is in fact disclosing the transcendental meaning of Quixote's presence among them. Quixote seeks in the cave a subliminal confirmation of his effectuality as real or fact, yet what emerges from his subconscious is prophetic experience in which proof of his effectuality becomes an ever receding illusion.

What he elaborates is a version of the story as it had developed in popular ballads of an oral tradition, combining isolated details from different ballads to concoct a fantastic and distorted version of events which depends for its unity on his two obsessions: enchantments and fame. The personages from the old ballads are held enchanted in the form of their traditional fame. Durandarte dead, his heart delivered to Belerma who sorrows over it perpetually.

The scene beside the body of Durandarte is the first of two supreme moments of 'revelation,' for here he is not only veritably living the fiction of his fame as knight, he has put himself—or the process of generative fictions in the book have put him 'bodily,' so to speak— beside the great literary figures of chivalry. He matches himself against the very prototype of hero in war and love according to Spanish popular legend: Durandarte, the knight and lover who with his dying breath pleads that his cousin Montesinos remove his heart from his dead body and bear it as a token of undying fidelity to his lady Belerma. Poetic and folk tradition know his plea as the theme 'take out my heart.'[62] Merlin, whether compassionately or out of spite, has enchanted Durandarte in the form that perpetuates and comically immortalizes his 'undying devotion.' He will rest on his sepulcher forever in this form, his right arm over the cavity in his breast, until the knight destined to break the enchantment penetrates the darkness of the cave and breaks the spell.

The transcendental meaning of the scene is obviously concealed in the answer to the question: is Quixote the knight chosen for this great feat? Such a feat would be a real test of the redemptive power of his virtue. The reply is enigmatic: Yes and No. Durandarte's wry reply is

"Paciencia y barajar."[63] Or, "Does it really matter?" Would breaking the spell permit him to recover his heart, return to Belerma and take up life after Roncesvalles? Or permit him to return to the grave? Durandarte, as a surrogate of himself, as a fabrication called up from his own subliminal depths, not only casts doubts over the whole affair but is himself a knight rendered impotent or ineffectual in love. Durandarte admits what the story in the ballads implied, that he was a 'loser' in love and war (and at cards) in a heroic story. He lost his life at Roncesvalles, lost his love because Belerma was unworthy of his fidelity and has lost his heart to no purpose. His indifferent reply is the enigmatic admission of his own and Quixote's impotence which, of course, cannot be confronted directly but evasively, in a fiction in which the test of his redemptive power is put off until a momentous but ever receding time.

As an account of his knighthood reduced to passive essence, his fiction circumscribes a design of cause and effect, reward and punishment, act and fault, lack and want for the inhabitants of the cave, but whose issue is Quixote's own chivalric personality, mission and fame. The great personages of the cave are held in the grip of an enchantment: he is their chosen disenchanter and deliverer. Durandarte lacks a heart (and cannot be at peace without it) and Belerma, though unworthy, needs love; his redemptive immolation can mediate (where?) to repair their want. They are lovers separated by an abysmal fate: his gratuitous effectuality can reunite them. To do so would be tantamount to restoring chivalry to its former glory, confirm his public image and vindicate his mission. It is all vicarious fiction and sensory fulfilment of illusion because the initiate Quixote is but the recipient, the passive recipient of this stupendous revelation. The fiction, like the revelation, is self-fulfilling because as sensory experience his intervention is portentous, yet he need not act. His fabrication is the most transparent disclosure of the structure of illusion and of the process of his fictionalization.

The scene shifts to the passage or gallery where Belerma and her servants pass in procession, wailing and screeching. In contrast to Durandarte's permanent silence, the female half of this fallen, enchanted populace brazenly and loudly grieves in guilt and sorrow. Belerma was ungenerous if not unloving while Durandarte was alive (as the ballads imply), so her punishment is to know in sorrow that he reproved her with his last breath for her aloofness and foisted the mummified heart on her as a sign of her guilt in love. By the logic of association (implied in Montesino's comparison of them) Belerma is a counterpart of Dulcinea, who is also 'cruel,' 'inaccessible,' and 'unyielding' to her lover. In the inverted world of the cave the ideal woman and image of regeneration takes on the ugly features a male in his subconscious may assign to her as a penitential act of his own making.

At this point Sancho asks why Quixote didn't sock and kick the old man for comparing ugly Belerma to Dulcinea, and the guide questions how all this could have happened in so short a time as he was in the cave. Their questions divide Quixote's account into two parts, so that their growing disbelief introduces the second 'revelation': Dulcinea in the underworld. Montesinos pointed out three peasant girls in the elysian field, who were (not riding on animals but) frolicking like she-goats and Quixote at once recognized them as Dulcinea and her two companions he and Sancho saw on the road outside El Toboso. Montesinos could not tell him who they were, but assumed they must be ladies of high category now 'transformed' and enchanted into these circumstances. Sancho protests dumbfounded at this travesty of the facts and his disbelief compels Quixote to reveal the rest of the scene and in a most astounding way.

The peasant girl was wearing the same clothes as on the road outside El Toboso, so she was Dulcinea in her enchanted form. He spoke to her, but she made no reply. Unconsciously he lets slip in the allusion to the scene in which Aeneas sees and addresses Dido in the underworld and she turns away. Like them, Quixote and Dulcinea are now 'separated lovers.' Montesinos cannot of course explain why Dulcinea was enchanted and by whom. Everything in the cave rests ultimately on enigma. But then neither does Quixote the initiate ask *why*? At this point there occurs the second 'revelation.' At the very moment Montesinos is about to reveal when and how Quixote will be called on to break the spell of their enchantment, one of Dulcinea's companions comes to his side and makes the piteous request on her behalf for a loan of half a dozen reals with her cotton skirt as security. The lady must be in some great need, Montesinos says, so give her the money. Quixote can supply only up to four reals, but instructs the girl to inform her mistress that he intends to swear an oath (imitating another hero from the old ballads) to disenchant her. The second revelation is another admission of inefficacy, if not sexual impotence, for even the oath-taking is evaded and left to a future time.

If the first revelation disclosed to him a mission that singles him out as the knight destined to restore chivalry to its former glory, the second discloses the feat he cannot avoid, the feat thrust on him by private and sentimental obligation—the disenchantment of Dulcinea. The two are inextricably linked as the presence of Montesinos indicates, for now the ancestral figure of the cave is witness to her plight and to his promised oath. With its resolution imminent but not forthcoming, the experience ends abruptly and inconclusively (or rather, Sancho's protestations force Quixote to suspend his account), yet for its very inconclusiveness it has recharged his illusion of effectuality by concealing it as an enigma stored in the 'mythos' of chivalry. The very fiction of his redemptive virtue acknowledged by these figures of legend confirms and renews the illusion of his effectuality and fame.

The adventure in Part I parallel to the cave episode is Quixote's penance in Sierra Morena. When aligned and matched, the similarities between them point to their separate meaning and to their strategic position in the unfolding narrative. In Sierra Morena Quixote imitated the 'mad penance' of Orlando and Amadís in a self-conscious and evasive attempt to communicate to Dulcinea his love and submission. He sent Sancho to her with a letter, he supposed, and was left alone in the wild Sierra to live out his illusion. In the cave episode he imitates both consciously and unconsciously the lone hero's descent to the underworld and the cave experience of knights chosen to break the spell of enchantment laid on great personages. His illusion and fabrication is a retracing of a literary pattern in which the hero descends to the subliminal depth of an underworld in order to face a challenge from within to his efficacy and by so doing gain a new insight into himself that will permit him to re-emerge with renewed strength and confidence.

The episode in Sierra Morena turned out to be the deeply subjective experience from which, according to his illusion and the narrative's structure, he emerged with a new fame. The cave episode as illusion and sense experience is explicitly the initiatory adventure that bestows on him a redemptive virtue on a social scale and sets the stage for the forthcoming narrative of a mock mythical Quixote. Both adventures come at a point approximately one-third of the way into the narrative and elaborate from and into a fiction. Both are transparently subjective and involve an unsuccessful (or evasive) attempt to reach and communicate with Dulcinea. In each case the adventure renews Quixote's career, recharges his energy and endows him with greater 'fame.' The story was simplified as a result of the first, now it will become intricately more complicated.

20. Illusion Shattered and the Three Phases of Part Two

The cave of Montesinos is located southwest of El Toboso in La Mancha and geographically is the furthest point south in the itinerary of Part Two. From this point Quixote and Sancho swing north again to traverse the long distance over mountain passes and long stretches of uninhabited country to the river Ebro and Aragon. Their arrival there, and the dunking in the river, closes the first or initiatory phase of Quixote's depiction in Part II. In the vision of the cave future time appears to hold out the promise of forthcoming efficacious adventure, yet what follows is a series of reversals that not only fails to confirm Quixote's illusion, but frustrates and shatters it precisely where the last series of adventures confirmed it. The next three episodes, as transition or contrast to the adventures of the next phase, are individual feats of daring: the puppet play, braying adventure and 'enchanted bark.' They raise his fantasy and will to adventure to a new level, only to dash them in progressively deeper frustration and entangle them in humiliating materialistic concerns. The course of adventure in each of three phases in Part II retraces the rise and decline of the overall trajectory.

The puppet play is by theme and technique an explicit fiction-within-fiction, repeating the scheme of the cave episode but in terms of action, that is, 'live' or direct experience. A performance, it is directed to Quixote's perceptions as a chivalric fiction made sensory experience, acutely visual and auditory.[64] Yet it is not *his* fiction, but a comical and picaresque distortion of a traditional story in its low popular guise. The puppets perform according to Master Peter's manipulation, but this puppeteer is alias Ginés de Pasamonte, the trickster and deceiver (no longer the dangerous criminal) of Part I; having been freed by Quixote, he has turned non-violent. He lives and profits by his wits and by the antics of his performing ape. The puppet play is about Melisendra's liberation by her husband Gaiferos and their flight from Moorish Spain to Paris, a story taken from pseudo-Carolingian ballads in Spanish. Quixote and the rest of the audience hear and see a story acted out in which the knight successfully rescues his lady. With the boy narrator and Master Peter the manipulator, and with appropriate sound effects, the puppets (including the puppet horse) simulate the very mythical situation that is at the heart of the Quixotic fiction: the rescue and liberation by the hero knight of his lady. I have remarked elsewhere that the puppet play is the single instance in the entire book in which Cervantes depicts a knight successfully aiding his lady.[65] But while a member of the audience, Quixote has been, for his illusion and madness, more a participant than a spectator (as his interruptions show); at the moment of greatest tension, in a display of choler, he breaks in with great commotion on the scene, drawing his sword to slash away at the Moorish puppets pursuing the couple. For a fleeting moment of illusion he is their efficacious rescuer. Immediately thereafter he admits his error and consents to compensate Master Peter for damages to his puppets. The ingredients of story then fall into place, according to a new formula: following the sensory stimulus and violent intervention, Quixote admits his error, attributes his deception to the work of enchanters and in humiliation and frustration agrees to pay material damages. He pays now also in order to preserve the dignity of his new public image. The theme of material or monetary interests counter to chivalric disinterestedness, announced in the episodes of Don Diego de Miranda and Camacho's wedding, now surfaces with new implications.

The ass or braying episode moves from a folk theme introduced in chapter 24 by the stranger leading the mule loaded with lances and halberds to Quixote's and Sancho's encounter in chapter 27 with the villagers who have armed themselves against their neighbors with an array of weapons, to defend their municipal honor. Sympathetic to their cause, Quixote attempts to convince them to seek a rational solution to the sensitive and emotional question of their injured sense of honor. He almost succeeds, but then Sancho breaks in and applies his wit ("*agudeza*") and ends up "making an ass of himself," attempting to outbray and thus affronting the villagers. He provokes from one of them a single blow with a pole that knocks him senseless to the ground. Quixote raises his lance menacingly to defend or avenge him, but the formidable array of pikes, crossbows, even muskets, and then the stones they hurl at him, force him to flee the scene, abandoning unconscious Sancho who is loaded like a sack on Dapple's back and in this way allowed to escape. Quixote has not only been mortified, he has been humiliated, by Sancho's wit and braying and by his own retreat. He has fled in panic, even fearing to be shot, from a situation where physically he is anything but efficacious. He retreated in the face of foul play, as he declares, yes, but he also abandoned his squire cravenly to his fate. Despite his eloquence and clairvoyance, he has been made a fool of and he shares with Sancho the attributes of a 'beaten ass,' unlike the incident in Part I where he watched Sancho's blanketing. The outcome plays on overtones of a ritualistic humiliation and beating inflicted on asinine 'scapegoats.'[66] When Sancho recovers from his pain, he reproaches his master for his perfidy and sulking threatens to return home unless he is paid for his services in wages. In the aftermath of his bewilderment, Quixote first relents and then refuses to pay his wages, but berates him caustically for his disloyalty.

Two days later they arrive at the banks of the Ebro and find a fisherman's boat tied to a tree trunk. The empty and apparently abandoned boat and the moving current are the visual stimulus of the kind seen early in Part I, but now in terms of the redemptive role inspired by the vision in the cave. As sensory experience, the journey in the "enchanted bark" over the waters (or equatorial seas) confirms the illusion of his elect status and efficacy. He instructs Sancho to tie the animals to the tree and get into the boat and accompany him. The current drives the hapless boat toward the churning wheels of three mills they see downstream. Despite Sancho's protests, Quixote declares them to be the castle or fortress holding imprisoned the knight or princess he is called on to aid. When the millers covered with flour rush out to keep the boat from the rapids, the sight of their fantastic shapes would seem to confirm Quixote's child-like illusion; he threatens them and draws his sword while Sancho, struck with fear, kneels and prays, until the boat capsizes and wrecks against the wheels and they are dragged out of the water. Once rescued, Quixote consents to pay the fishermen for the loss of their boat provided the millers release the person or persons held captive. "Mad man, what captives and what castle...?" one of them shouts. Soaked and exasperated, Quixote vents his frustration in an admission of failure and impotence that vainly seeks to preserve his new public image.

> —¡Basta!—dijo entre sí. . . . —Aquí será predicar en desierto querer reducir a esta canalla a que por ruegos haga virtud alguna. Y en esta aventura se deben de haber encontrado dos valientes encantadores, y el uno estorba lo que el otro intenta: el uno me deparó el barco, y el otro dio conmigo al través. Dios lo remedie; que todo este mundo es máquinas y trazas, contrarias unas de otras. Yo no puedo más.

Y alzando la voz, prosiguió diciendo, y mirando a las aceñas:
—Amigos, cualesquiera que seáis, que en esa prisión quedáis encerrados, perdonadme; que, por mi desgracia y por la vuestra, yo no os puedo sacar de vuestra cuita. Para otro caballero debe de estar guardada y reservada esta aventura. II. 29, 267

—Enough, he said to himself. . . . One might as well preach in the desert to try to induce this rabble by prayers to do any virtuous act. In this adventure two powerful enchanters must have met in opposition, the one thwarting the other in his designs: one provided me with a boat, the other capsized me. God help us, for all this world is nothing but trickery and strategem, one against the other. I can do no more. And raising his voice, he continued, his eyes intent on the water mills: —Friends, whoever you are, who live in this prison, forgive me; unfortunately for myself and for you, I cannot deliver you from your misery. This adventure has been reserved for another knight.

With this outburst the first phase of Part II comes to a humiliating close. The pattern of a fictitious fulfilment of illusion followed by humiliating reversal is to be repeated with variations at the close of the two ensuing phases. The narrative of Part II moves forward through three phases: after the first or initiatory phase, it rises to the central episodes and phase of mythical enlargement and mock apotheosis (the long stay at the ducal castle, Chs 30–57), to gather its final momentum in the third phase (Chs 58–74) that will bring the mythical Don Quixote to Barcelona to place him, as prelude to his final disablement and demise, on the stage of history, the city and the sea.

III

The Mythical Don Quixote

1. The Ducal Castle: Fiction and Society   Chs 30 . . . 57

With Quixote's and Sancho's arrival and welcome at the ducal estate Cervantes moves his story to the threshold of its consummation and sets in motion what is perhaps the greatest feat of storytelling in modern literature. Any reader who supposed that by now Cervantes had exhausted his themes and resources is in for many surprises. All of the preceding has been but preliminary to what follows. It will never cease to amaze with what wit and skill Cervantes applies his resources and the techniques of his mimetic art to renew and recharge his themes at every decisive turn. He began by exposing Quixote's illusion to the hard facts (blows and cudgels) of sensory experience mistaken for chivalric adventure, then turned that illusion inward to establish and authenticate it as fictional experience; now he will retrieve the hero's illusion of his efficacy by depicting him and his squire at the center of a social reality drawn to large scale—the social experience that exemplifies Spanish society in 1614. In the phase that consummates Quixote's illusion sensory experience is to be confirmed as adventure by the social reality that is the relations between individuals in everyday, contemporary life. With this feat the author Cervantes may be said to have 'discovered' the formula—the Quixotic formula—to the modern novel.

It is then not only Quixote who comes into his own, but Cervantes himself. It is his inimitable genius and wit which oversee the whole of the arrangements made for hero and squire at the ducal estate. The two poles that sustain his manoeuvres are no longer Quixote's madness imposed on sensory reality but Quixote as hero of its fiction and the social reality that will solemnize it in mock ritual and celebration of elaborately conceived hoaxes: fiction and society. In this way Cervantes has undertaken to depict not just the relationship of the Quixotic hero and his squire to their society, but the relationship of fiction itself to the society that acclaims it, produces and consumes it. The ducal household revolving around the Quixotic hero and squire becomes a paradigm of social reality and the function of the fictional hero in it. The pseudo omniscience of Cide Hamete is displaced by the immanence of Cervantes as author, now supremely aware of the uniqueness of his creatures. The Quixotic version of the hero and society is based on the redemptive role Cervantes' wit and skill has intuited and refashioned from the medieval and Christian tradition of chivalric romance. The consummation of his story, then, and the emergence of a mythical Quixote from the process of his fictionalization, come to be one and the same.

At sunset on the day following their dunking in the river, Quixote and Sancho come upon a hawking party led by a lady in magnificent hunting attire, and he sends Sancho to her with the request for permission to approach her. She is not exactly the regal huntress (or goddess of heroic legend) who intervenes to change the course of the hero's fortunes, but she and her husband perform just this role in the story. She receives Sancho graciously. She and her husband may be thought of as prototypal readers of Part I among Spanish aristocrats. Having read about his exploits, the duke and duchess are not really surprised to meet him—the public figure—in the flesh. Quixote's 'fame' has preceded him to this encounter. They invite him and Sancho to their country mansion or summer palace; from the first they describe it to him as a 'castle.' They are motivated by what they have heard and read of his history to treat him according to his illusion but they will play the role of regal hosts with a mixture of cruel ridicule and exquisite courtesy. Their courtesy, good breeding and aristocratic manners conceal a refined perversity to amuse themselves (the vicarious experience of reading *Don Quixote* Part I turned real) by subjecting their guests to subtle, cruel humiliation, taking pleasure even in their own condescension. Their motives will retrace the very design of mock elevation/humiliation (and of fiction-within-fiction) the narrator devised in the preceding episodes, above all in Quixote's encounter with the lion; it is not amiss that he is introduced here with his new title, "Knight of the Lions." Even as their civil treatment of him confirms his illusion, another manoeuvre on the part of the narrator initiates a train of comical miscues committed by Quixote and Sancho by which they heap social mortification on themselves. In the solemn moment of dismounting before the duchess, both fall "on their faces," so to speak, falling to the ground from their respective animals. At no time, not even now, are we to suppose that Quixote's idea of himself as knight can supplant the comical representation of that idea.

Quixote and Sancho are to be subjected to a new test of their 'public' qualities in the very situation that celebrates what they are as characters of fiction. Hence they take on attributes that would seem to be a caricature of themselves. Quixote's social dignity will appear disfigured with clownish attributes and Sancho's ready talk and wit with buffoonish outbursts and conceits. The ducal pair lead them to their 'castle' where they have already instructed their servants to devise a mock ritual to receive them. Quixote is unable to perceive the deception and even malice behind the social ritual and mock adulation. His dignity as hidalgo as much as his illusion as knight conceal from him the ridicule of his person intended in the hoax the duke's lackeys play on him at the entrance, when the duchess declines to dismount in his arms. The ritual and adulation work on his pride; the effect works to endow him with the innocence of a simple fool and madman. His entry into the courtyard is total sensory confirmation of his illusion, yet as senseful reality directed to the onlooker a ridicule of that illusion as subtly refined as the very nature of the social act that recognition of his person has become.

> —¡Bien sea venido la flor y la nata de los caballeros andantes!
> Y todos, o los más, derramaban pomos de aguas olorosas sobre don Quijote y sobre los duques, de todo lo cual se admiraba don Quijote; y aquel fue el primer día que de todo en todo conoció y creyó ser caballero andante verdadero, y no fantástico, viéndose tratar del mesmo modo que él había leído se trataban los tales caballeros en los pasados siglos. II.31, 273–274.

> —Welcome to the flower and cream of knights-errant! And all, or most of them, sprinkled flasks of scented water over Don Quixote and the ducal pair. And this was the first time that he was positively certain of being a true and no imaginary knight-errant, since he found himself treated just as he had read those knights were treated in past ages.

The course of his madness (its clinical unfolding according to the exemplary plot) will be held in suspension throughout the episodes in the ducal palace. This is a new development, because in the parallel to these episodes in Part I (Chs 32–47, the visit to Juan Palomeque's inn) the clinical details of his madness were held constantly before us. A large cast of characters and subordinate plots were made to revolve around Quixote's personality and illusion much like an action taking place on a theatrical stage. The climax to this combination of the techniques of stage comedy with situations and themes from the classical epic and chivalric romance was the discord over the helmet, the totalizing or collective hoax that precipitated a comical apotheosis for Quixote. In what follows Cervantes has surpassed by far his own model and brought off a comic fusion of epic and romance. Not only do the duke and duchess and their household form a similar cast and social hierarchy on a lavish scale, a number of them emerge as unforgettable individuals whose idiosyncrasies deepen the outlines of Quixote's public image. More deliberately now Cervantes organizes his mimetic art around situations and themes taken from the classical epic, above all the *Aeneid*. The chivalric quest is restructured into the epic hero's test. The Spanish term *burla* covers in a general way the tricks, deceptions and hoaxes the various members of the ducal household fabricate ingeniously to amuse themselves and even suggests the cruel perversity of the boldest.[67] What they emulate is not in the first instance some chivalric model like *Tirante el Blanco*, but the ingredients—structure and themes—of the Quixotic fiction. Quixote is subjected to a trial of cruel social humiliation, as a test of his madness, credulity and capacity to take ridicule, so that the sense of his trial by mockery and social cruelty becomes a test of his 'virtue,' of the redemptive power of his innocence. Their ingenious mockery, whether they intend it or not, becomes, for its effect, a celebration of Quixote's mythical efficacy.

Inwardly his social ordeal becomes a trial of purification, not of his illusion, but of his pride, and alluding to the hero's *hybris* in the classical epic. As mimetic technique, the new hoaxes fabricate a semblance of fictional chivalry over the social setting of the ducal perpetrators, so that the line of reference is to the social meaning that Quixote's person instigates among them. The mockers recreate his adventures as hoax or performance, impelled by their own motives or devices. They become thereby surrogate authors of his fiction within a grand design controlled by the narrator's omniscience. The climax comes in the space fantasy of the ride on the wooden horse with Sancho, for here mimetic technique aims self-consciously to attain its own apotheosis. In this way Cervantes will draw complete the idea he intuited in the discord over the helmet in Part I: Quixote incarnates not just the values of a fictional world, but those of the real or historical world of 1614 made fictional. The story (and its fictions or hoaxes) that now moves to celebrate its hero's efficacy in this self-conscious way is designed to portray him as mythical.

At the beginning of Part I, when Quixote on his first sally comes to the inn he assumes to be a castle, he introduced himself to the two women at the entrance by reciting the opening verses of the ballad of Lanzarote (Lancelot), describing the arrival of this knight to a castle where (in Quixote's version) "damsels attended to his person/princesses stabled his horse" (Quixote substituted "princesses" for the *"dueñas"* of the original). On that occasion Quixote took the women (prostitutes on the road) to be *"doncellas,"* "damsels." With that scene Cervantes introduced the theme of *'doncellas'* into the story of Part I which he subsequently elaborated in Dorotea's appearance. At this juncture he makes use of the same ballad to introduce the other half of the theme, *'dueñas.'* But here it is Sancho who recalls the ballad and concocts a conceit, while Quixote is entirely mystified. In the midst of the spectacle and unable to forsake Dapple with a clear conscience, Sancho goes up to one of the duchess's waiting ladies and asks her to stable his animal. The waiting lady is Doña Rodríguez, one of the duchess's more simple-minded servants. With her indignant reply and Sancho's conceit that a *dueña* should stable his donkey, the narrator has drawn an indispensable preliminary to the appearance of another *dueña*, Countess Trifaldi.

Sancho's conceit is both a cruel affront to the duenna's age and dignity and a buffonish show of self-conceit. Their exchange of insults cuts through the ritualistic veneer with which "squires" and "duennas" comply with their social or class obligations. Quixote is mortified; his dignity and courtesy would have forbade that the interjection of the ballad and its theme should come from him. The narrator's intention has been to interject the parodistic notion of chivalric *"dueñas y doncellas"* ("ladies and damsels") in the social spectacle of waiting ladies of 1614 performing their ritualistic (parasitic) obligations, the interjection of 'fiction' into society. From the first the implication is clear that duennas in the palace are vulnerable as objects of satire. As a type they are female scapegoats, and a sexual recrimination of the type is implied in the wicked tongue and distemper shown by this simple-minded woman.[68]

The social ritual of the first afernoon in the palace inflates Quixote's and Sancho's self importance in a way that points to the ulterior design: Quixote must live up to his public image: a model of civility, courtesy, articulate verbal skill, honorable modesty and personal dignity; yet his illusion implies pride, presumption and self glorification. Sancho must be at his most entertaining, witty, loquacious, shrewd yet conceited in his talent to amuse. In this aristocratic environment they must display their best social qualities, because the success of the hoaxes to be perpetrated on them depends as much on their social pretense and comportment as on their gullibility and self-delusion. Once we establish the pre-condition in our mind, we can follow Cervantes' strategy for bringing into one orbit of deception both Quixote's illusion centered in Dulcinea now enchanted and Sancho's illusion that he is fit to govern an island. This is what the narrator is set on accomplishing in the scenes of the midday meal and hours of the siesta of their first day in the palace.

Splendidly but still ridiculously attired, Quixote is led with pomp and majesty to the dining hall where the ducal pair and their spiritual advisor, an ecclesiastic, greet him as honored guest. Sancho is allowed into the room, like a court dwarf. The duke and duchess (perhaps expecting to be amused at his reaction) have not informed the grave ecclesiastic who their guest is; they are playing something of a joke on him. He reacts irascibly when he finds out, for they have imposed on him insensibly. True to character, he over reacts; in him Cervantes has given an indelible portrait of the uncivil, irascible Spaniard: arrogant and scornful of inferiors, a social deformity perpetrated by an aristocratic caste system (this is the meaning of the narrator's harsh introduction of him), yet completely understandable. The talk at the table discloses the social relation between the ducal pair and the priest—they accept his moral authority with condescension—and how Quixote's presence disrupts and brings that relation to a crisis.

The cleric is in no mood to tolerate, much less entertain the Quixotic hero and reprimands and insults him without compassion. In his oratorical reply (a kind of model of Ciceronian eloquence) Quixote assumes the mantle of an affronted but exemplary hero who by the mortification he suffers at the hands of so uncivil a man, has submitted to a purification of his own pride. Cervantes' own attitude toward both may seem ambivalent, but his strategy is to aggrandize his hero at the expense of the distempered ecclesiastic, who refuses to play any part in the deception. He denounces Quixote and the duke's treatment of him on moral grounds; yet his deflation and unmasking are indispensable to introducing the Quixotic fiction on its own terms into the ducal household. The scene is real (i.e., not fantasy, 'fiction' nor hoax) but except for the priest its meaning or purpose (the illusion it provokes) is to recreate or mimic scenes from chivalric romance. As narrative strategy it accomplishes two objectives, both at the expense of the wrathful priest: Quixote's dignity, courtesy and honor are put to the test and vindicated by the priest's bombast and rudeness, and, as a result, perhaps to aggravate the priest's vexation, the duke, on the spot, offers Sancho the governorship of one of his "spare" islands. When Quixote orders Sancho to kneel and kiss the duke's feet in gratitude, the priest cannot bear the affront to his dignity and departs in a rage.

At the meal's close, the maid servants subject Quixote to a *burla* of their own devising. They are probably retaliating for the slight done to their kind when he refused to be undressed by "damsels" as his chivalry prescribed, in his room before the meal. Soaping and rinsing Quixote's beard in the presence of the duke and duchess is another hoax-test of his innocence, dignity and guile. Is the perverse joke meant to ridicule or to confirm Quixote's illusion of his person? However considered, the public washing mimics the very notion of cleaning or purification of the hero's motives. (The kitchen rascals who later attempt to wash Sancho's beard with dishwater provide the low, picaresque version of the same.) Quixote's own beard, heavy with lather—the sign of his masculine honor and virility—has served to introduce the motif of *beards*, the social and sexual taboos attached to male facial hair. For all his dignity, he has been chastised for his social presumption by maid servants, yet his forbearance was such that the duke considered that the maid servants had been disrespectful to *his* person by washing a guest's beard in his presence, so he disciplined them to the not-so-farcical ordeal of washing his. At this point Sancho leaves the room to get his meal in the kitchen. The two are separated, and the story is poised to take a new turn.

The scenes in the dining room and in the duchess's chamber may be compared for their function to the scenes in the inn in Part I (Ch 32), where characters hold a conversation around the table on chivalric books. In both cases Cervantes lays down the basis of credibility for the liberties he is about to take, for the 'order' of life-within-fiction to follow. In the dining room, with Sancho out of hearing, the ducal pair instigate from Quixote a confession about the who and why of Dulcinea, with the result that he reveals to them that he has seen her but a few days before outside El Toboso in enchanted form, as a foul-smelling peasant. In the next scene, the duchess learns from Sancho the other side of the story, Sancho's claim to have deceived his master into believing the peasant girl was Dulcinea in enchanted form. When the duchess turns the table on him and asserts that he is the one deceived, because the peasant girl was in fact Dulcinea enchanted by evil enemies, Sancho tells her what Quixote said he saw in the cave of Montesinos. Unknown to Quixote and Sancho, then (by the tactic of 'divide and conquer'), the duke and duchess (like Cervantes's readers) have the inside information about the episodes immediately preceding arrival at the palace and will devise their deception in a way that simulates Cervantes's omniscient control over his narrative. The deception they have in mind will recreate the Quixotic fiction by attempting 'to make it real,' 'to bring it to life,' within the social ritual of their household. Behind their strategy to implicate Quixote's illusion with Sancho's, is Cervantes's grand strategy for bringing his comic story to its consummation.

2. How Dulcinea Is to Be Disenchanted

Perceiving that Quixote is most vulnerable in his belief that Dulcinea is enchanted, they fabricate the hoax of her disenchantment and thus introduce into the story the other, inevitable portion and direction of a chivalric quest, the liberation of the knight's lady from evil forces. At this juncture in the story Quixote could not have 'invented' nor Sancho introduced this notion. As on two previous turning points, in Sierra Morena and at El Toboso, the fiction of Dulcinea assumes the shape of an outrageous deception. Then as now its success depends on Quixote's belief in the power of 'transformations.' In the next round of hoaxes Cervantes has found his subtlest technique yet for sustaining the comical dialectic of elevation and glorification of his hero and invalidating, vicitimizing and disabling him. Now that a mock reality has confirmed their separate illusion, the incentive for adventure passes from Quixote and Sancho to the ducal household, and so a representation of sensory reality as adventure misconceived becomes a mimetic representation of itself.

The ducal pair decide to combine their usual social pastime—the hunt—with the new one, amusement at the expense of Sancho and Quixote. They have at their disposal the services of an 'ingenious' mayordomo or steward, who, in the great Italian tradition of his art, arranges and stages their court diversions. For all his delightful wit and cunning this man does not (nor can he) emerge as a character on his own (he remains anonymous), because he is really an authorial surrogate. The hoaxes devised by him turn out to be Cervantes' subtle means for imitating not just the structure and direction of chivalric romance, but his own narrative procedures.

Cervantes' strategy is to have the mayordomo devise a 'Quixotic adventure'—one that corroborates and fulfills Quixote's illusion of himself—while he assumes the task of depicting the social reality in which his fictional creatures have become mythical celebrities. They participate in the boar hunt as the social outsiders that they are, Quixote with pretentious courage and Sancho with comical cowardice. As objects of social diversion, they 'perform' as themselves, and are victimized (not unlike the slain animal adorned with wreaths) by their hosts because they are victims of their delusion. The war-like excitement of the hunt is followed by the nocturnal spectacle planned and staged by the mayordomo. A twilight procession of fires, wagons and figures is awe-inspiring spectacle directed to the senses, an infernal replica of war: sounds, torches, color, marvellous horrible shapes, recreating the 'phantom army' of folk tradition.[69] Its obvious sense is 'otherworldly' and 'penitential' and it imitates Cervantes's own techniques for representing sensory reality as laid down in Part One. It is fiction comically and self-consciously recreated in life. And as witty hoax (unperceived by the victims) it is also directed to the onlooker's and reader's mind as 'extra sensory' meaning. Taking his inspiration from Quixote's vision in the cave, the mayordomo stages a version of the chivalric netherworld, bringing four famous enchanters out of retirement, Lirgandeo, Alquife, Arcalaus, and Merlin, the arch enchanter, played by the mayordomo himself. Beside him on the wagon is a nymph, Dulcinea, played by a page. What we see is that Cervantes has imputed to the mayordomo the imaginative *ingenio* or wit which Quixote has shown in the more graphic or imaginative adventures. By means of the mayordomo's wit, he has devised an episode whose meaning is the hero's encounter with the netherworld of enchanters who hold the key to the release of his lady from bondage and as such 'completes' the vision in the cave. In the chivalric originals the sense of such an adventure is that the hero must perform some kind of penitential act as the price for the release of his lady. That Dulcinea is to be disenchanted by some sort of purifying and penitential act is the witty imitation of a chivalric story by the mayordomo and superb manoeuvre on the part of Cervantes as storyteller. By producing one more Dulcinea in the flesh, the mayordomo has also imitated Sancho, to a purpose.

Dulcinea may be said to 'appear' to Quixote on three occasions: the first on the road outside El Toboso, then in the vision of the cave, and now. Since Dulcinea is a 'fiction' rather than a character, Quixote's vision of her in the account of the cave is the one authentic image. At the climax of the twilight procession, Quixote has before him at last a veritable enchanter, clad in the horrible garments of Death, with Dulcinea beside him, a kind of prisoner to be released. Quixote's fantastic world has at last been 'brought to life' (on the stage, that is, and produced as a celebration of itself). Yet his reaction is to remain dumb and pensive. His reaction now was foreshadowed in the consummation of his fiction (and illusion) in the cave. Dulcinea will not be disenchanted, he hears from Merlin, by any heroic or penitential feat of his, but by Sancho's consent to inflict on himself the exorbitant number of *three thousand and three hundred lashes*, on the most sensitive part of his anatomy.

3. Comic Movement

The mayordomo's witty conceit is to entrap both Quixote and Sancho by entangling their separate illusions in one hoax. In the presence of Merlin and Dulcinea they stand duped, overwhelmed by the sensory spectacle, the performance that celebrates their identities as fictional creatures. In Part I we described comic movement as the technique by which the sense of adventure was made to gravitate, as if by physical law, from Quixote's excited mind toward the watery weight of Sancho's body—a movement that swung toward and finally enmeshed Quixote's fantasy and incentive with the inertia and bulk of Sancho's anatomy (see pp. 55–56). Now by means of the mayordomo's hoax the narrator renews this technique as exquisite conceit and wit for the way it imitates and recreates the story from within. Quixote's predicament is that he must accept the fact that his lady has been enchanted into a base form. Merlin tells him she can be redeemed by the most improbable of means, that Sancho should consent to lash himself. For its very wittiness the hoax is a cruel one to inflict on Quixote; not only does it exclude him as the means for redeeming his lady, it attributes to the squire the virtue that will win her release, and declares the squire's vast fleshiness indispensable to the task.

Taking their cue from Part I, the ducal pair and their mayordomo have devised a penitential formula for disenchanting Dulcinea that mimics those techniques the author devised there for enmeshing Quixote's fantasy with Sancho's fleshiness. Recall the balsam of Fierabras, the attack on the sheep, and the fulling-mills on one hand, and Quixote's penance in Sierra Morena on the other. They are playing the role of surrogate authors. So their hoax has had to be a complete performance and spectacle, a sensory experience falsified as adventure. Yet it holds together as a fiction for the conceit that now gives the story a new thrust. The best way to see this is to try to explain the conceit as Cervantes would have understood it: By an act of fate, or more likely by some lapse or failure on Quixote's part, Dulcinea has fallen under the spell of an enchanter. For this a burden of guilt and fault lies heavily on Quixote. She can be released from the spell only by a profound act of purification and penance. But Dulcinea was enchanted into peasant form on the instigation of Sancho. He produced a peasant and Quixote confirmed her as Dulcinea. For this travesty Quixote must expiate his guilt in humiliation and pain. For his part Sancho must pay in physical penitential torture on his buttocks. The formula of disenchantment implies penitential pain where it hurts most and spiritual humiliation of 'the most cutting.' The conceit, we see, works out to an apotheosis of the comic principle and symbiosis of Quixote and his squire.

By prompting his surrogates to this witty hoax, Cervantes has mounted Dulcinea's 'disenchantment' as the structural fiction that will unify his story to the end. Not the hero's but the squire's virtue can disenchant her. The structural idea of the hero's disablement is wittily repeated in the conceit and hoax. By attributing to the squire's "will to lash himself" the power to disenchant Dulcinea the hoax has virtually disabled the hero from the task laid on him by his chivalry. The story is thrust forward now with parody of the most powerful theme in chivalric romance and derived from mythological beliefs. The enchantment of Dulcinea, her 'transformation' in the cave of Montesinos, and now her appearance beside Merlin, are allusions to the abduction-rescue themes of chivalric stories and primitive myths. The most famous and best known is the Arthurian story of Queen Guinevere's abduction by the evil Meleagant and her rescue by the young Lancelot, who replaces King Arthur in this as in other matters.

The abduction-rescue plot of medieval romance is a variation of primitive seasonal or solar myths of the disappearance (abduction by evil forces) of a vegetation goddess through one season and her release at another, Winter and Summer.[70] In the tradition of these myths her rescue or release must be preceded by rites of purgation and a penitential trial for the hero worthy or destined to liberate her.

The duke and duchess have played a cruel joke on Quixote. Their hoax confirms his vision in the cave while rendering him powerless. It is a witty humiliation of him, not just because he must depend on Sancho's will to castigate himself, but because it excludes him. The humiliation and the exclusion, then, are the ordeal of penitential castigation he must bear. Sancho has to accept three thousand three hundred lashes to his buttocks as the price for his chance at governing. So the ducal pair have wittily enmeshed (to their supreme amusement) Quixote's illusion and his lady's predicament with Sancho's fleshy bottom. They will devise one witty hoax after another on this comic principle until they hit on the most 'diabolical' torment. The worst turn to the hero's humiliation will not take place until they quit the palace. On the road (Ch 60), despairing of his lady's plight and Sancho's lack of will, Quixote attempts a remedy by laying hands on Sancho. The 'disenchantment' conceit also meshes Quixote's private concern with Sancho's public role as governor: the story is poised to bring off the hoax of apotheosis for all these themes.

4. Countess Trifaldi

Since so much depends on the mayordomo's wit to bring the story off, one may ask what his motives are, or what he is meant to be like as a character. His motives are complex, to be sure, but can be discussed as both immediate and ulterior. His immediate motive is to provide comical and artful entertainment to his employers. But are the duke and duchess capable of following and appreciating the subtleties of his conceits? Yes, of course, because they catch the intended effect and perform in his hoaxes. Like any entrepreneur or performer, the mayordomo likes to indulge his inventive wit, and his ulterior motive may be said to be to outrival Quixote himself in the invention and execution of his fiction. In order to do this he must display a wit, an *ingenio*, at least equal to Quixote's and, moreover, with a difference: since he cannot produce a spontaneous one, produce a superfiction, one that for its stylized conceits as for its relation of form to substance, and of pretense to life, is both a derision and a celebration of the mythical Quixote. In his role as inventor or actor-producer of satirical burlesque he performs as an authorial surrogate, because the fiction he invents, while retracing the Quixotic fiction inwardly, is directed outward as a satirical exposure of conventions inherent in human society and inevitably of the social function of fiction itself.

It is on the scale of the preposterous that he means to make his point. Quixote's credulity is to be stretched in the proportion that his image is magnified. The mayordomo and his cast of males have exploited a number of dramatic, iconographic and rhetorical devices, the Countess's three-cornered train, the names, *Trifaldín, Trifaldi, Antonomasia, Clavijo* (which in English might be rendered for its sexual allusion, obvious to all but Quixote who is innocent of such insights, 'Mr. Penetrate') and of course *Clavileño*. The stylization and mimicry, then, retraces the Quixotic fiction, and patently as a fraudulent one, as farce and burlesque. Unlike Quixote's invention about the cave of Montesinos, this one is explicit in the design of cause-effect relationships. It makes its point by overstatement.

The mayordomo played the part of Merlin and now in his new production invents and plays the part of Countess Trifaldi. The impersonation of a female by him is the mocking conceit on which the outrageous whole hangs. His fiction is about the moral transgression of a female which has brought ruin on an entire kingdom and its impending deliverance by the feat of a chosen knight. It is a vulgar if not farcical reworking of the biblical fable (and theological doctrine) of 'original sin' but herein lies its supreme wittiness. From the first it is meant to be applicable 'by antonomasia,' by analogy, that is, to the entire human race dependent on Quixote's redemptive act. Since it addresses the question of the original sexual failing of man and woman, it is appropriate that the two sexes should be embodied in the central figure, Countess Trifaldi. It is, thereby, an eminently social fiction, because the nature of original sin is the central issue in the relations between the sexes. The central conceit depends on, or results from, the unexpected relationship brought off by the underlying and contrary ideas, one of which is sex or sexual differentiation. In the conceit this differentiation is anatomically expressed by the social sanction and taboos assigned to facial hair. The two social attributes of sex are designated respectively by 'beards' and 'skirts.'

So Trifaldi's hoax concocted with visual and musical effects before Quixote and Sancho might well be given the title *"Hair,"* like a recent popular musical.

When the Countess's squire, "Trifaldín of the White Beard," enters the hall accompanied by mournful music and robed in mourning and addresses the duke, inquiring the whereabouts of the knight Don Quixote, while stroking his outrageously long beard, his bearing introduces the major theme of "beards" and his name alludes to the other, "three-pointed" or "go-between skirts." Countess Trifaldi (the Countess of the three skirts) then appears, her face veiled, and accompanied by exactly twelve ladies in waiting or *dueñas*, their faces also veiled. Her account, like Quixote's about the cave, is in the form of dialogue and a parody of chivalric romance that mimics the grotesque distortions of Quixote's *ingenio*. In Spanish chivalric romances, the *dueña* (French *dame*, Italian *donna*) is a lady of high social standing, a queen, princess or countess, usually widowed, who in her distress seeks out and requests the aid of a famed and powerful knight to defend her land, property or family.[71] Countess Trifaldi is a '*dueña*-in-distress' ('*dueña menesterosa*'), but unlike her models in Spanish romances, the cause of her plight lies in her moral laxity, in her 'fatal' lascivious inclination.

The mayordomo's wit has imputed to chivalric *dueñas* a moral fault ascribed in popular opinion and literary satire of Cervantes's time to women of a social group with little esteem or prestige. Only Quixote for his illusion and madness is oblivious to the satire and malice intended in the ambiguity. In the chivalric originals, a *dueña* for her dignity and moral authority is never involved in affairs of sex or love and never requests, like damsels-in-distress, a knight's help in thwarting or avenging a seducer. As Quixote should know, they are noble and honorable ladies, never engage in erotic affairs, and never serve as go-betweens, the role reserved exclusively for damsels. By Cervantes time, however, the term *dueña* in this sense was archaic. It designated what Sancho understands a *dueña* to be, the lady-in-waiting of a servant class, like Doña Rodríquez. This servant class of older, unmarried or widowed females, was particularly vulnerable to satirical detractors for the enforced idleness of their parasitic existence. They were thought of as vain gossipers, tricksters, sharp-tongued, big eaters, and worst, denounced for venality and hypocrisy because they concealed, supposedly, beneath their dignified robes of moral authority, a lascivious indulgence in illicit affairs (Sp. '*tercerías*') and the seduction of chaste younger women. The *dueña* as go-between is part of this satirical portrait created or preserved by authors like Cervantes, Mateo Alemán and Quevedo.[72]

Because of her fateful inclination, Trifaldi allowed Don Clavijo's music and erotic charm to seduce her moral authority. Her fault was especially grievous because she was tempted and then consented to the role of go-between in the seduction of her charge, the princess heir Antonomasia. Because of her venality and hypocrisy, the very moral integrity of the kingdom of Candaya has been grievously compromised, for Clavijo is not of royal blood, but something of an up-start noble out to exploit his sexual and social attraction by seducing the heiress of the realm. The moral scandal of an unwed heiress about to give birth became the kingdom's downfall when by the hypocrisy of legal trickery Clavijo was designated Antonomasia's legal husband, a scandal so enormous the shock killed her mother, the Queen Doña Maguncia. At her burial, her cousin the giant and enchanter Malambruno appeared, mounted on his wooden horse, to avenge his relative and punish the culprits. He castigated the lovers by transforming them, on the spot, her into a brass monkey, him into "a hideous crocodile of unknown metal," and declared the condition—and the champion—by which they might recover their form. He would have punished the Countess with death, had she not pleaded movingly for her life. He spared her but inflicted on her and all the *dueñas* of the palace 'a living death.' At the climactic moment of her near farcical performance, Trifaldi and her *dueñas* uncover their faces and reveal them "all bushy with beards—some fair, some black, some white, some grizzled." At this sight the duke and duchess pretend to be wonderstruck. Sancho and Quixote, and anyone else not in on the hoax, really are struck dumb.

Behind the farcical effect and sight of bearded women is the mayordomo's supreme wit and Cervantes's superb art as novelist and satirist. Malambruno is an enlightened enchanter, for all his malice and perversity. He has castigated Trifaldi and *dueñas* with a sign adequate to their guilt. The hair on their faces denounces their lascivious indulgence in illicit affairs of the flesh. It is an eminently social punishment for the ugly reprobation and ostracism inflicted. In the male dominated society of Cervantes time, it would seem to be a joke of outrageous chauvinism, and it may well be the most comical if not thickest slice of male chauvinism on record. A particularly odious sexual failing is attributed by males to women already reputed to be the least attractive and least esteemed. Where indeed will a bearded *dueña* find any pity or a champion?

Malambruno has inflicted on women the facial hair that imputes their femininity, but that on male faces is a sign of virility and honor. Is the mayordomo aware that his conceit and impersonation point both ways, and implicate not just both sexes but the very idea of sexual differentiation, in nature and society? The great lengths to which he has gone to stage and stylize his hoax would seem to indicate that he does. But certainly Cervantes is superbly aware of the predicament that his mimetic art implies for the male-mentality of his contemporaries for whom beards were nearly sacrosanct. This is the sense of the mock-encomium the narrator addresses to himself on beginning chapter 40.

Facial hair on a woman is a sign of (self-inflicted) dishonor, but a male beard is a sign of (self-complacent) honor. The mayordomo's hoax takes delight in the discomfiture the sight of bearded ladies causes to all onlookers, but particularly the serious male reader who like Unamuno would prefer to look the other way and denounce it all as the worst possible taste. The hoax is directed to the serious male sensibility that would attach to facial hair an unequivocal and even transcendental importance. In the pathetic picture of bearded *dueñas* Cervantes' wit brings to a head two concepts of nature and society and proposes mockingly the transcendence of both in Quixote's redemptive virtue. The serious sense of his travesty suggests that the very essence of fiction, and of the highest fiction as of the highest wit, is to perform and provide for precisely this redeeming human necessity.

5. Clavileño

At nightfall the mournful plight of bearded *dueñas* is promised relief by arrival of the magical horse, the vehicle of their redemption. The scene shifts to the garden in the courtyard where a wooden prop is brought, so to speak, on stage. For their grotesque details, wit and linguistic distortions these scenes are probably the funniest in the book; they are in fact its climax in terms of technique and structure. Quixote, backed up by his fat squire, is about to undertake a heroic feat of transcendental proportions and thereby consummate his fictional efficacy. Malambruno's script calls for the *dueñas* to be redeemed by a champion, pure in heart, astride a vehicle replete with mystical and magical meanings as it flies through the cosmos. The illusion of flight is to be furnished by the wooden prop "*Clavileño.*"[73] It is brought on stage by four hoary savages or "wild men," to impress on all the legendary aspect of this flying machine. The mayordomo has been keen on minor as on major details; the design of the whole 'fiction' must obey and embody a singular conceit, and so his staging counts for more than Quixote's and Sancho's thoughts and sensations. His art has become sensory adventure elevated to artifice, with Quixote and Sancho as star performers. It must be spectacle, performance and mimetic fiction, the consummate Quixotic fiction, staged and directed by the mayordomo in the style of Quixotry.

Compare his linguistic invention "*Clavileño*" with others by Quixote—"*Rocinante,*" "*Dulcinea.*" It is a style that identifies the thing named immediately as make-believe. The difference is that the mayordomo's conceits are self-conscious in the artistic sense, whereas Quixote thinks his apply directly to life. The prop on stage is named Clavileño. But is the prop the fiction, the illusion of fantastical flight, the wish fulfilment?

The pattern of adventure that emerged from the cave episode was a ritual descent to the underworld, and now the pattern to be imposed on the hoax of the wooden horse is that of an ascent through the heavens. The cave fiction began and ended in insoluble enigma but this one is mockingly explicit as to its meaning. Quixote and Sancho are to ride on the magical horse through the heavens to effect the liberation of a 'fallen humanity' and redeem the kingdom of Candaya. Malambruno has furnished not only the means but the meaning as well. In so many words: the transgression of lovers and *dueñas* is to be (could only be) atoned for by the selfless act of the purest of knights, chaste, valorous, generous. The least attractive and perhaps the least deserving of mortals—*dueñas*—are to be redeemed by the noblest of champions. To this end he provides the machine on which knight and squire can fly through the pre-Copernican heavens to Candaya, on the other side of the planet. His script ensures nothing less than the apotheosis of the Quixotic fiction. It is wish fulfillment, hoax, fairy tale. It endows him with the semblance of mythical hero. For what is a mythical hero if not a semblance? The satirical meaning is that Quixote performs quite literally like the fictional hero he is.

As sensory experience the ride on the horse prop must simulate the mythical and mystical meaning of ascent, beginning with the hard seat. So why must Sancho go along . . . ? In no other detail of his book has Cervantes been more witty nor more comical. By literary tradition Clavileño descends from the magical vehicle or flying animal of fantastical transport to the far reaches of outer space (a tradition that includes flying carpets and flying elephant), or the vast expanse of inner space. But the transport he provides is specifically for two persons, the romantic couple, knight and 'abducted bride,' because his fast and easy ride is precisely the fantasy getaway of erotic flight. His twentieth-century counterpart would be a high speed motorcycle. Hence the exquisite conceit insisted on by the mayordomo: Sancho is to accompany his master and ride on the horse's crupper "like a woman," sidesaddle, in the place literary tradition has reserved for the 'abducted maiden,' thereby displacing her with his huge buttocks and his squeamishness. And in the style of Quixotry and the very apotheosis of sensory experience they are to ride blindfolded, to intensify the sensation (or illusion) of flight. A pictorial illustration would best convey the structural conceit behind the hoax, the sensory illusion of flight, and the real situation.

They sit on the prop transfixed, immobile in the most ridiculous way. The mayordomo's wit has tricked them into this farce in order to produce the by now irrepressible image of their comical apotheosis. Or of their comical symbiosis. The picture simulates flight, yet their awkward position on the 'horse' is the very idea of chivalric adventure made immobile. Since no stirrups are necessary, Quixote's legs hang loose, "no parecía sino figura de tapiz flamenco, pintada o tejida en algún romano triunfo" [he looked like nothing so much as a figure in a Flemish tapestry, painted or woven, riding in some Roman triumph] II.41, 348. "Slowly and reluctantly Sancho managed to get on the crupper . . ." but he finds it painful and hard and asks for a pillow, is refused, and has to ride sidesaddle ("*a mujeriegas*"). They are blindfolded so that without the visual evidence the adventure can prove to be totally sensory. Of course the blindfold is the means of deceiving them outrageously, but it ensures that the onlooker's or reader's mind recognizes it as a condition inevitably imposed on such journeys in fiction, or that it mimics the idea of a test imposed on the hero's *élan*. Some commentators compare this nocturnal hoax to the adventure of the fulling-hammers in Part I: both involve a stationary mount, enforced togetherness of master and squire, a folkish fabrication by Sancho, and an immobilized Quixote. In terms of story, however, the connection I see is that here Cervantes has managed to transfix comic movement into an image of apotheosis and mythical ascent. The episode in Part I parallel to Clavileño is the scene of turmoil in the inn over the barber's basin and the mock prophecy that followed. In both the ridicule of Quixote's illusion is elevated to a celebration of it.

Quixote rides with complete self-confidence (he is deceived more easily), Sancho in fear, apprehension and trembling. The mayordomo's wit has at last accomplished physically what Cervantes could only attempt up to now figuratively: mount his characters on a single or the same carrier, locked in mutual dependency; the fat one shaking with fear and hanging astutely onto the lanky, emaciated master for dear life. Blindfolded, they ride into the wind blowing first cold, then hot on their faces, their sensory illusion transfixed into unforgettable image.

Clavileño is "that very same wooden horse on which the valiant Pierres carried off the fair Magalona (not exactly; it was *Clamades* and *Clarmonda* who escaped on a magical horse in chivalric story) guided by a peg in his forehead that serves as bridle, and he flies through the air with such great speed that the devils themselves seem to bear him" II.40, 340. The magical horse is meant to be the apotheosis of the hero's steed in the chivalric tradition, and of the animal participant in Quixotic adventure. In the zoology of fiction Clavileño would be not so much a necromancer's as a child's idea of the magical horse at the disposal of the hero. Since he represents as well the *reductio ad absurdum* of a literary pedigree, it seems logical that the rockets stuffed through his tail should blast him to smithers at the end of his flight. Hereafter the idea could live on only as Uncle Toby's hobbyhorse.

Behind the wit of his surrogate, we can detect the author immanent in the social world in which his fictions revolve in 'orders.' After Sancho protested about going along on the hard wood "to shave *dueñas* of their beards," Quixote took him aside and told him this was a good time, before setting off, to make a start on the lashes to his bare behind. "¡Par Dios! . . ." "are you crazy," he answers. "Esto es como aquello que dicen: '¡en priesa me vees y doncellez me demandas!'" II.41, 347. [This is like saying: 'You see I'm practically in labor and you ask if I'm virgin.'] He blurts out a proverb (unconsciously) aimed at the mayordomo's conceit. He's not 'virgin' nor female, but his fat presence on the horse prop displaces the 'abducted bride' of the chivalric getaway. And his proverb alludes to the sexual 'cause' of the 'fall' of Candaya as well as to the transposition of sexes. It is a subtle reminder that Dulcinea's fate depends on the punishment his buttocks can take.

Malambruno's scheme for Candaya's redemption is the mythical 'order' of fiction contained within another, the mayordomo's staged hoax, and the hoax in turn is contained within the social reality of the ducal household, the whole making up a series of fictions receding from the onlooker. Unlike the 'orders' of fiction in Part I extended, so to speak, horizontally, here as in the puppet play the 'orders' are contained one within the other as if in a revolving motion. The 'order' of the inner fiction is mythical (or mock mythical) because the deliverance of Candaya by Quixote amounts to a mythical feat by the "savior of society" and the 'order' of the second, the staged hoax, is the mimetic representation of it.

The mayordomo has depended for success not just on Quixote's credulity and Sancho's fear, but on another factor beyond even Quixote's imagination. When Sancho protests that he can hear voices when they are supposed to be far above the earth, Quixote replies with complete aplomb that this time one should not believe one's ears. For him the sensation of flight is complete. When the bellows blow cold and then hot, he interprets the blasts as evidence they have passed first through the region of hail, thunder and ice then through the region of fire of pre-Copernican skies. When its all over, Sancho gives his version of the flight, a folkish and rustic account of the view of earth from heaven (Scipio's dream of the classical tradition) and his romp with the gaudy constellation of seven she-goats, providing a sexual allusion aimed strategically (and again unconsciously) at the mayordomo's conceit.

The firecrackers in the horse are set off, explode, and Quixote and Sancho are hurled to the ground. Removing the blindfold, they are amazed to be back in the same garden, among witnesses, and before a parchment whose lettering says:

> El ínclito caballero don Quijote de la Mancha feneció y acabó la aventura de la condesa Trifaldi, por otro nombre llamada la dueña Dolorida, y compañía, con sólo intentarla.
> Malambruno se da por contento y satisfecho a toda su voluntad, y las barbas de las dueñas ya quedan lisas y mondas, y los reyes don Clavijo y Antonomsia, en su prístino estado. Y cuando se cumpliere el escuderil vápulo, la blanca paloma se verá libre de los pestíferos girifaltes que la persiguen, y en brazos de su querido arrullador; que así está ordenado por el sabio Merlín, protoencantador de los encantadores. II.41, 352

> The illustrious knight Don Quixote of La Mancha has ended and achieved the adventure of Countess Trifaldi, otherwise called the Doleful Duenna, and her company, by merely attempting it. Malambruno is content and satisfied, and the chins of the duennas are now smooth and clean, and their Majesties Don Clavijo and Antonomasia, restored to their former state. And once the squirely whipping is completed, the white dove will see herself free from pestiferous gerifalcons who persecute her and in the arms of her loving mate; for thus it is ordained by the sage Merlin, proto-enchanter of enchanters.

Malambruno's script has ensured the consummation of Quixote's fame. The satirical meaning is that he performs the feat with the efficacy of a hero in fiction "by simply attempting it."

In the mythical-satirical fiction Quixote performs according to his illusion because he is also the knight innocent of guile and acting from the purest of motives. Nothing less than his virtue qualified him for the task. This is implicit in the encompassing fiction and public image of a knight (in the mayordomo's hoax) entrusted with the feat of a mythical deliverance. Their ordering mimics with satirical overtones the heroic and Christian conception of the hero who qualifies for the task by vitue of his innocence and invincible faith in himself. Quixote's innocence, a fool's purity of heart, is the quality that now confers on him a social efficacy. The mayordomo's hoax mimics his *ingenio* and heroic pretense: the meaning conveyed is that Quixote is derided for his illusion that he is valorous, invincible. This is satire aimed at his imitation of chivalry. He is anything but effective in the real sense. But for what he so comically represents, the manly virtue of a chaste knight, and for the genuine way in which he represents it, innocent, sincere, child-like, he is efficacious in a fictional sense. To this end he has been subjected to the 'trial of purification.' His child-like faith, or a fool's purity of heart, is what ensures success to the mayordomo's hoax. His illusion and credulity are sustained as satire, ridicule, but this effect ensures the other: for his purity and innocence a mythical efficacy may be imputed to him by the immanent author. One must make some effort to catch the author's comical design. Story and technique ensure that the three 'orders' of fiction, social and realistic, satirical, mythical, the first two revolving around the nuclear third, bring into focus the meaning of a trial of purification from which the comical hero, victim of his own pride, presumption and credulity, and thus vulnerable to the cruel mockery and derision of his hosts and their household, emerges with mythical efficacy in social life. His treatment at the hands of the 'perverse' ducal pair and their servants, the arrogant ecclesiastic, implied what now is consummated in the mayordomo's hoax: his sincerity of purpose and his purity of motives. The redemptive image of Quixotic innocence, instrumental for the later versions of the character in Parson Adams and the Romantic interpretation, has emerged from the hoax of the wooden horse. "*Alma de cántaro*" ["numskull"], II.31, 282, the priest called him in the dining room, intending insult and cruel derision.

The derision and its social cruelty are to be understood in at least two respects: Quixote's fictional efficacy, epitomized in the hoax of the wooden horse, and his moral stature as object of derision at the hands of the ducal pair and their household. The point to be made here is not why but how a mythical Quixote emerges incarnate from the representation of fiction and society. In the second 'order' readers of Quixote's story (i.e., Part I)—the ducal pair, their servants—have become not only instigators and performers in adventures, their mock but cruel adulation and their mimetic performance dramatize a mock apotheosis and celebration of the hero and squire for their 'entertainment value.' The hoax depicts the hero at his redemptive task in society (the mythical 'order'), so that it illustrates or exemplifies the meaning of the garden scene, the social reality of the ducal household revolving around the figures of hidalgo and squire, their frivolous entertainment and seemingly empty lives 'redeemed' by the fascination Quixote and Sancho exude as literary creatures. The social satire directed at them is the validation of Quixote's cause.

The subtleties of this well-devised turn in the process of Quixote's ficitonalization are hardly ever taken into account by critics and interpreters.[74] The techniques of satire and story and the very structure of the book have endowed Quixote with the outlines of a mock mythical paragon, not despite the satirical design but because of it. The hardline critics are right in insisting that the meaning to be inferred from the scenes in the palace is satirical, but they fail to see that this meaning cannot both illustrate and invalidate the figure as drawn in the story now elevated to a new plane. The title of this *Second Part* (1615) has mockingly supplanted the social satire intended in "ingenioso *hidalgo*" with the literary satire directed at his mock mythical celebrity: "ingenioso *caballero*."

6. Governor Sancho of Barataria

Having effected the image of their inseparability, Cervantes will now separate his characters. Nowhere in the story are the workings of the author immanent in his creation more enlightening than in the purpose to which he has directed their separation. The duke's new strategy is to separate his guests, to send Sancho off to the "island," a village on his estates, while Quixote stays in the palace, in the expectation of the greater amusement their isolation from one another will provide. He and his accomplices suppose the pair will be more vulnerable to trickery and deception, and they are right. They have just brought off a hoax that implicates Quixote's heroic illusion with Sancho's fleshy presence; now from their separation will surge the hoaxes and deceptions that subject them to the penitential trials of moral purification in a social setting devised to their illusion. The perpetrators are shown controlling the design of cause and effect by which the two fools of fiction are permitted the illusion of their efficacy in social life, to be fooled in turn by the child-like innocence of one and the native, folkish or foolish wisdom of the other. Quixote's ordeal becomes a trial of mortification in public leading to inner purification. In the cause-effect unfolding of the plot of wiles and feminine intrigue in the palace Cervantes has given a grand comico-moralistic purpose to these traditional Christian themes. Sancho's experience on Barataria, the ordeal of the public official, unfolds as an accompanying subplot whose design of cause and effect subjects him to a parallel ordeal. The outcome of the subplot is by comparison conclusive and definitive, illustrating as if from below the conflict between private and social virtue that is the heroic burden of the elect or the great and powerful. In this way their separate experiences carry out the theme of fiction and society on the new plane introduced by the hoax of the wooden horse.

Barataria is of course the consummation of Sancho's illusion and ambition. An "island" to govern has figured as the nerve center of his motives since the first day. Its utopian nature was also evident from the start because he has always believed he was entitled to it, with or without the necessary qualifications or merits. From the moment Quixote promised it to him he expected it, in the way of a magical prize or reward. The name *"Barataria"* that the duke and mayordomo have coined for it patently describes a "joke," a "cheap fraud," a meaning evident to anyone not infatuated with his self-importance. So Sancho's experience as governor may be said to bring into conflict two notions, by thematic design: the 'art of governing' as a public or political question and the moral and personal qualifications of one who governs, with instructions and counsels on how best to do the job. Because these questions had had a long and rich development in political and moral literature down to Cervantes' day, we can assume that he meant to draw on it for various satirical meanings applicable to both Sancho's case and the performance and record of real officials of his time and society.

Quixote and Sancho will be separated in the story from chapters 44 to 56, to be reunited under very different circumstances. His send-off is preceded by the thematic introduction that is Quixote's discourse to him, two sets of maxims for governing well (the procedure we saw in discourses on the "Golden Age," I.11, "Arms and Letters," I.37, and "Poetry as Science," II.18). The first set of instructions apply to "the soul," the second to "the body." They ostensibly pertain to the 'art of governing' but evade politics (or questions of political power in the Machiavelian sense, all of which Quixote would know little or nothing), to concentrate on the personal and moral qualities of an idealized Governor. They are aptly those of a Christian believer: faith and fear in God, humility, prudence, moderation in food and dress, compassion for the weak, no favors to the rich and no ear to bribes and self-enrichment. The general sense is that because too easily its exercise invites vanity, ostentation, indulgence in vice, food and wine, for one who holds political power the cardinal virtue is self-denial. We have been prepared for the inversion of roles to follow: on Barataria the fool will govern the unknowing.

The contrast between the relevance of all this advice to the practice and ambition of real governors among his contemporaries and its application to Sancho, who is illiterate, untrained, "a sack of proverbs," forms a composite satire on government appointees whom Cervantes, one may suppose, observed first hand. Sancho has neither the education nor experience to catch more than a few phrases; he forgets almost all of this advice as soon as he hears it. But, to his credit, in a vague way the idea that in order to govern well an official must 'know himself' (know or face his limitations) has sunk in.

On the eve of his departure he is riding the crest of his popularity with the duchess for his clownish wit (*donaires*) and boastful self-infatuation. So much so he appeared to lose his common sense. In her presence he shows the strangest combination of traits, to his detriment it would seem, though he does not lose his integrity, as when he says that he follows his crazy master out of love and loyalty. Nor his fear, because we have seen him hide under her skirts. The experience on Barataria will be a purgation of misplaced pride and ambition, but in the process Sancho displays an unsuspected native ability for 'governing' and a moral example to the duke's real shortcomings.

We are moving into the area of his creativity where interpreters have argued that in Sancho Cervantes endowed the Spanish peasant with the moral virtue to compensate for and redeem a depraved aristocracy. A popularizing and democratic bent to the outcome of the episode is undeniable, yet an interpretation of Sancho as a tribute to popular values must deal with the whole of his personality, with the limitations that define his virtues. Only in the satirical or comical sense of the story does he qualify to be a 'Governor.' The office is given to him 'gratuitously,' without his deserving or qualifying for it. In this the duke's intentions retrace Cervantes' conception of him in Part One. On Barataria the duke and his mayordomo devise and carry out a series of hoaxes which put to the test some attribute of Sancho seen previously. The outcome, unforeseen by them, will reveal a simpleton easily duped in the same body as a shrewd, honest and even wise peasant with hidden moral resources. When they send him off dressed (II.42, 356) partly as "clerk" and partly as "captain," with Dapple following close behind, they reveal their strategem.

On arrival he is put through the installation ritual and judicial cases to solve; then follows the test of his will for gastronomic penance at the banquet spread, then the nightwatch to test his skill for handling chance encounters. To try his patience or "discretion" (or his peasant's stupidity) a number of importunate money seekers and riddlers, not all improvised or stage managed, are brought before him. A scribe is present on all these occasions to take down a record of what he says and does, whether for the duke's information or amusement we never know, nor do we know whether the clerk's account is objective or satirical.

The action on Barataria is reported by the narrator; the motives and incentive of the hoaxers account for the tests imposed on Sancho, yet the real situation is beyond their control. The majority of the inhabitants of the village (including the priest at the church) assume the duke has sent a genuine governor to rule them; quite a few, however, are in on the secret. The ritual at the Court of Justice consists of three cases to be solved by providing "answers to some intricate questions." The narrator, it seems, cannot be precise about whether the three judicial cases brought before Sancho are real, improvised or stage-managed. Why? Because the ambiguity is inherent in the theme/structure, "fiction and society"; not only are the boundaries between them blurred, they are made to interact on various levels. The three cases are not so much questions of legal right or wrong, or of violations, as of unmasking fraud and deception. They are hardly original with Cervantes, but belong to a long tradition in European folklore.[75] They are really about astute ingenuity unmasking deception, malice and fraud. Each represents on a mini scale an imposition of fraud as apparent truth, fraud in the guise of truth. All of this is very much Sancho's element and his fool's wisdom and shrewd cunning cut through, denounce and expose fraud. The case of the tailor's caps appears to be a trick devised by the mayordomo; of the three it appears to be the one stage-managed by him. Sancho's decision, that the five small caps be given to jail inmates, draws laughter from the spectators and is wittily appropriate to the absurdity of the case (for what are the inmates to do with them?), so Sancho in the first instance has outwitted the mayordomo on the latter's own grounds. The second and third cases appear to be genuine, and permit a 'fictional' governor to pass judgment on persons who assume he is for real. Cervantes' point is that Sancho is as good and no worse a governor than the real thing. ". . . los presentes quedaron admirados, y el que escribía las palabras, hechos y movimientos de Sancho no acababa de determinarse si le tendría y pondría por tonto, o por discreto" II.45, 379–380. [. . . the spectators were amazed, and the man who recorded Sancho's words, deeds and gestures could not make up his mind whether to consider him a fool or a wise man.] The third case, the dishonest woman, has every attribute of a real case, for the gravity of its social and moral implications, and Sancho's fulmination of her is equally serious. The three cases are 'structured' from the levity of the first to the gravity of the third. Sancho's wit and discretion have outwitted the mayordomo and the duke's intentions. They could not have expected him to dispatch these cases so effectively. Fiction, it would seem, has been legitimized as good government, at least with respect to cracking 'hard nut' cases of deception.

The banquet scene is a truly outrageous deception, a sensory experience on the lavish scale of Sancho's well-known gluttony, yet he is unable to see through it and is victimized in the most tortuous way. Why? We would need to retrace the main lines of his characterization for reply. Sancho is most vulnerable to deceit where his illusions about the island promise him material gain and physical comfort, an easy life, food, drink, leisure, sensory satisfaction. His expectations of power and privilege have led him to believe that as Governor he could satiate his appetite and complacently indulge his slothful side. It could not have occurred to him that to be Governor he should continue to go hungry or to abstain from feasting for the sake of his office or that it would demand of him a penitential sacrifice. The scene in the dining hall has been stage-managed by the mayordomo who remains out of sight. In line with the duke's scheme, he has ordered a table spread with savory dishes certain to arouse Sancho's appetite for their visual and olfactory stimulus. Like any reader of Part I, he knows all about Sancho's sensory expectations. The mayordomo has placed another character in charge, one so well suited to the task, it is nearly impossible to decide whether he is pretense or real, a satirical genius or a blockhead, Doctor Pedro Recio. With his wand and gestures he subjects Sancho to a torture of gastronomic expectations aroused and then denied, much like a Tantalus of the stomach. Sancho cannot see through the farcical deception because he cannot separate his illusions from his ravenous hunger. His ordeal is a cruel one, for all its carnavalesque comedy.[76] The duke and the mayordomo would like nothing better than to break his illusion and humiliate him. Eventually he gets to eat something, but it is his old fare, a bunch of grapes and bread. The experience shows him that despite the pomp and power of office he gets to eat no better than a peasant.

The banquet scene brings together the themes of carnavalesque indulgence and penitential trial, of make-believe and fiction, directed toward an inner moral conflict and correction, in a 'Governor' sorely tried. These themes are carried over to the scenes of the night rounds, where Sancho's wit is able to cope with the vagaries of 'civil' cases of personal illusion, where he can envision moral reforms for life on the streets and gambling houses, but lacks the understanding of human nature to make them effective. His ambition and self-interest become implicated in the case of adolescent brother and sister whose only transgression is to be curious about the world and to want a little freedom.

The climax comes on the seventh night when a military attack puts his ability to 'captain' the defense of the island to the cruelest of tests. The outcome was foreseeable to the perpetrators, of course. What they did not foresee are Sancho's moral resources to face up to the reality of himself. The duke knows that Sancho understands nothing of military matters or preparations and could suppose that he would fail as governor in this respect spectacularly even without the cruel joke of the false attack. So the awful punishment Sancho takes is both gratuitous and penitential. The mayordomo and his cohorts know that Sancho's illusion, or ambition, will not survive the mortal fear and physical punishment they have in mind; they mean to 'teach him a lesson.' He is about to fall asleep when he hears an uproar, of cries and alarms in the dark. The jokers rush to their 'captain,' describing a fierce attack on the island, and urge him to lead them against the invaders. He submits, bewildered, allowing them to put on him, or, rather, put him into his armor, two large shields tied together tightly around his short fat body, his head hardly protruding. He cannot see nor move. They have jokingly and cruelly disabled, immobilized him; they put a lance in his hand, urging him to lead. He falls flat on the floor, where he lies like "a tortoise in its shell or a flitch of bacon between two boards." There in the dark they play their war game on top of him, trampling him mercilessly. Encased and helpless, Sancho suffers through the pain, fear and anxiety of the darkest hour of his life. In this 'moment of truth' a dire choice overtakes him from within.

The joker's motives are to disport themselves at his expense and to teach him that as 'captain' the governor should prove he can take the physical dangers and punishment of combat or else he cannot make strategy nor lead, but of course their cruelty and mockery are evident when they release him, shouting victory and acclaiming him victor. The indignity inflicted on his person compels him to see through their mockery. The fear and pain force the truth of the joke, the deception and the 'lesson' on him, yet he cannot grasp the scale of the conspiracy devised and carried out for his demise. Their 'lesson' has been driven home in the only way his mentality could have grasped it. The pain, fear and humiliation have shocked him out of his illusion and ambition. When freed he dresses himself silently and goes to the stable to saddle Dapple, mounts with difficulty because of his pained body, and addresses his mockers:

> —Abrid camino, señores míos, y dejadme volver a mi antigua libertad; dejadme que vaya a buscar la vida pasada, para que me resucite de esta muerte presente. Yo no nací para ser gobernador, ni para defender ínsulas ni ciudades de los enemigos que quisieren acometerlas. Mejor se me entiende a mi de arar y cavar . . . que de dar leyes ni de defender provincias ni reinos . . . digan al duque mi señor que, desnudo nací, desnudo me hallo: ni pierdo ni gano; quiero

decir, que sin blanca entré en este gobierno, y sin ella salgo, bien al revés de como suelen salir los gobernadores de otras insulas. II.53, 444-445.

—Make way, gentlemen, and let me return to my former liberty. Let me go in search of the life I left, and rise again from this present death. I was not born to be a governor, or to defend islands or cities from enemies who wish to attack them. . . . I know more about plowing and digging . . . than about making laws or defending provinces or kingdoms. . . . Tell my lord the duke that naked was I born and naked I am now. I neither lose nor win; I mean that I came to this government without a penny, and without a penny I leave it, quite the opposite to what other governors of other islands are wont to do when they leave them.

Sancho is as unaware that he has frustrated the duke's intentions as he is unaware that his illusion, vanity and ambition have victimized him. Yet he is aware that the experience has taught him a punishing if not penitential lesson that is also a purifier of his inner self. Thus his disillusionment with governing is also the reintegration of his true self at a higher moral level. He renounces his island because at last he sees and judges himself from within, discerning his limitations and 'true self.' He recovers his self-respect and dignity and acquires the humility and insight of the peasant sage which by implication is the equal of the king sage. And almost like a king or saint he renounces the vanity of ambition, riches and power, to accommodate himself to the humble status of Dapple's owner. The animal has been kept nearby on the duke's orders but not in anticipation of this turn in events. Sancho surprises everyone by his decision to abandon the island and return to the palace by himself. His departure must be the bleak act of a penitential desolation imposed on himself in order to round out Cervantes' meaning: it is preferable, however painful, to assert the moral qualities that round out self-knowledge than to live in the self-deception that are power and ambition. He loses his island but regains his equanimity and with it his dignity and freedom. He eventually finds (is forced to find) the level of self-effacement that by confirming 'his true self' does in fact enlarge his public image and esteem. If as 'wise fool' he has grown wiser, it is only with respect to himself, and only in this sense with respect to the world of his experience.

How plausible in terms of the story is this revelation, this change in Sancho? The Sancho who can feel and articulate his disillusionment in these new terms is the opposite of the prevaricator and fabricator of lies, wiles and deceptions we saw previously in all his moods. Has

Cervantes been so intent on making a thematic statement here, he has foregone not only the satirical purpose (the exposure of corrupt and incompetent public officials) but the basis of his realistic art as well, the verisimilitude of psychological character? Rather, no. Sancho has undergone an unexpected but not unlikely change. He has not changed with respect to putting physical self-preservation and material self-interest above all other considerations. It is the punishment his body has taken that compels him to renounce his ambition. And in terms of the story his character has been purified of those clownish elements that made him so ridiculous in the presence of the duchess. The Sancho who rides away from Barataria is a sober, penitent peasant. The experience has released him to his freedom.

For all his shrewdness and common sense, Sancho on Barataria is out of his element and in no way prepared to deal with the realities of governing. Yet to the onlooker or reader he has taught the duke not one but several lessons, though it is problematical whether the duke could see the point. At his best Sancho shows that he has the native shrewdness, discretion, sense of justice and good conscience to promulgate laws and reforms without previous experiences for it, to be a governor genuinely attentive to the public good. The mayordomo no less is amazed that an illiterate peasant should show good natural wit and disposition. Sancho even achieves a measure of permanent success in the laws he leaves behind to the inhabitants of the duke's lands. If the duke and mayordomo were capable of admitting as much, they would see that he has furnished a good example of an efficient and conscientious public official who because he places public good above self-interest, and his humble self-respect above privilege, ambition and power, he redeems for public service and the social order what the duke in his infatuation with pleasure, lineage, and wealth is incapable of. What we perceive as senseful here is the hoax and fiction of Sancho as Governor imparting to social reality a meaning it could not otherwise lay claim to, precisely for the gratuitous nature of the fiction. Thus, if self-abnegation is the indispensable prerequisite for governors, then Sancho in his failure has learned a lesson of incalculable value. Yet ultimately it is of as little value for him as for the duke, for neither is really capable of turning it to account in real life. So the gratuity of its meaning as fiction or as political and moral satire is left in suspension, to be remarked on as an exemplary instance of the redeeming action of fiction on society.

7. Altisidora

She does not make her appearance until the right moment. Unlike the *dueña* Doña Rodríguez, who was made conspicuous from the moment Quixote and Sancho arrived at the palace, she has been indistinguishable up to now among the maid servants or *doncellas*. With her appearance the theme of *'dueñas y doncellas'* (*'dames et damoisels'*) or *'ladies and maids'*) becomes explicit. In the absence of his squire, Quixote is faced with the choice of accepting the duchess' offer of a number of serving maids "as lovely as flowers" to look to his personal needs or to depend on himself. Sancho's absence has also aggravated his melancholy and brought on a deep sense of loneliness. Quixote's isolation in the midst of social life in the palace is a result of his loneliness and melancholy but for this reason also it becomes the structural condition that invites, first, the duchess' importunities about chaste maids to wait on him, and then Altisidora's. The importunities of *doncella* and then *dueña* are a new thematic development of a hero subjected to a trial of mortification.

The insinuations the duchess makes about *doncellas* are meant to remind us of the scene in the loft in Part I when, laid out like a convalescent, Quixote fantasized about a chaste maiden who approached his bed. Concern for his chastity (or, rather, his timidity) compels him to reject the duchess' offer. The narrator intends that we should have in mind that hallucinatory scene in which he invited temptation and seduction because that scene is now the instigation for a real *doncella* to come forth and act out a new version of that fantasy. Quixote's concern for his chastity and integrity is made to conflict with his public obligation to live up to the image of the knight who redeemed the kingdom of Candaya.

The guest in the palace compounds his isolation and melancholy by withdrawing to the privacy of his room, expecting to preserve his virtue and integrity. But it is here that two females seek him out, the younger one to importune him maliciously, the older one, the simple-minded duenna Doña Rodríguez, to ask for his help. They seek him out, maliciously or naively, for his 'heroic' qualities, his manliness, social benevolence and virtue. Their demands turn out to be, for the assault on his vanity and pride, the purifying trial through mortification of heroic fiction. His relationship to the two women begins under the guise of a chivalric motif (they are for him primarily *dueña* and *doncella*) and develop into an experience of the intricate personal dependencies of social life, servant to master, master to servant, men to women and women to men, a heroic world encapsuled in domestic intrigue. The encounter of two servant women with Quixote's most intimate resources provide a narrative at once epical and novelistic for its self-conscious mimetic techniques. Palace life imitates heroic fiction on the one hand; on the other, the minutiae of social life are magnified to epical scale.

Confined and lonely, beset by his ripped hose, Quixote's spirits are at a low ebb when he hears female voices in the garden below his window. An 'aggrieved damsel' reveals to her companion the passion aroused in her by the handsome stranger in the palace. "—No me porfíes, ¡oh Emerencia!, que cante, pues sabes que desde el punto que este forastero entró en este castillo y mis ojos le miraron, yo no sé cantar, sino llorar. . . ." II.44, 372. [Do not press me to sing . . . for you know that ever since the stranger came to our castle and my eyes beheld him, I cannot sing, but only weep. . . .] From the first moment Altisidora knows the right combination of story elements to catch Quixote's attention and cast herself in the role of demure seductress and victim. Apparently she did not need the prompting of either the mayordomo or the duchess to throw herself into this role. This distinction she confers on herself is unique, because in the ducal household she is just another serving maid. Altisidora is motivated by a feminine instinct deep in her character. Unlike the mayordomo whose wit fabricated a more or less impersonal deception, since his personality was not involved, she will invent and act out an entire hoax fiction of a passion aroused in her by Quixote. Her hoax appears to be entirely her own doing, she is both relentless and frivolous at it, calculating and coy. Although she depicts herself as the chaste damsel, she is in fact a version of the diabolical female, for the torture and mortification she inflicts on him. She has both the wit and malice to conceive the role and play it out as make-believe, but the role is really an expression of her own pathological feelings of inadequacy. Hence the grotesque but still comical sense of the siege laid by her to Quixote's virtue, to his love and loyalty for Dulcinea.

The role she makes up is an ingenious parody and combination of several from chivalric romance, classical myth and poetry and legend. She is first of all the innocent daughter-damsel of the lord of the castle who falls hopelessly in love with her father's guest; she is also Queen Dido at Carthage who, having welcomed the stranger Aeneas fatefully to her lands, is overwhelmed by a passion for him. In the first scene she has already cast her companion Emerencia in the role of her confidant and Dido's sister, Anna. Later, when Quixote's resistance to her becomes entrenched she compares herself to other heroines of myth and legend who were betrayed, seduced and abandoned by their lovers.

Knowing he overhears at the window above, she introduces herself as a damsel and as Queen Dido who expects to be betrayed and abandoned by Aeneas. ". . . este nuevo Eneas, que ha llegado a mis regiones para dejarme escarnida" II.44, 372 [. . . this new Aeneas who has come into my kingdom to mock and then abandon me.] Her tactic is to convey her erotic message in the suppliant guise of a ballad set to music, a sensory temptation. Her ballads are absurd lyrical confessions designed to absolve her of any blame and heap remonstration on remonstration on Quixote for his obduracy. Hence her role is also a grotesque inversion of the usual relationship where the female is cold and chaste and the aroused male vehement, pleading and driven to lyrical despair. For his innocence and vulnerability to guile, Quixote is put in the role of offender, insinuating thereby into his trial of mortification the Aeneas theme of the hero who out of loyalty to a higher calling spurns the devotion of a love-mad queen.

Enforced idleness makes him particularly vulnerable to her importunities. She is lying in wait for him the next morning in a gallery and pretends to faint at the sight of him into her companion's arms. His reaction, bloated with vanity and pride, is to observe her paternally and indifferently. The sensory temptation Altisidora offers is not erotic (Quixote's melancholy makes him impervious to her charms) but to an indulgence in the idle life of sensuous pleasure in a courtly, aristocratic milieu, out of his class and out of his calling. For his age as for his courtesy, he lectures down to her on the modesty required of good girls. The conventions of court and poetry require that he reply in kind, so he asks for an instrument to be placed in his room. Provoked to reply, he becomes the victim of another trick, this one devised by the duchess.

A female and thus a feline trick. The duke and duchess order a sack of cats prepared, to be dropped from a balcony above his window that night on a rope to which are also attached many loud-sounding bells. The perpetrators mean to frighten and humiliate him by dropping on him this horde of cats, with small bells tied to their tails, in the midst of his singing, to torment and castigate the old fool who likens himself to a troubadour lover. The feminine perpetrators are perhaps only thinking of a particularly howlish and scary trick and the spare cats in the palace serve their purpose. But for other reasons well known to the author behind their deceits (and to the reader), cats have been associated for centuries with female wiles, concupiscence and witchery.[77] So the sense of this misadventure is that Quixote is tormented for his obduracy to Altisidora, castigated for his old fool's illusion of his attraction to females and for his pride and vanity, which rendered him vulnerable. Two or three panic-maddened cats get loose and jump into the room. Quixote draws his sword to attack this legion of enchanters (again an animal adversary). One of them gets to his face and sinks its claws into his nose. Is the allusion evident? His shrieks bring the duke and duchess to his rescue. Altisidora is available for applying ointment and bandages to his face and murmurs he has been rightly punished for his cruelty to her and his vain attachment to Dulcinea. He is confined to bed and now disabled fears he is more vulnerable than ever to the aggressive 'damsel.'

Altisidora is the prime case of a female character who intrudes into Quixote's illusion under the guise of make-believe to thrust the full force of her neurotic personality on his. Is the connection between them reducible to sadistic attraction on her part, defense and repulsion on his? In her Quixote has at last met a *'doncella'* cut psychologically to real life. Her intrusion is not only mockery of him and perverse deception, but an intimidation as cruel for its make-believe as for its psychological reality. If the enchanters he supposes are out to revile and persecute him were to devise a temptress to carry out their perverse and evil ends, that female would be feline Altisidora. We do not overstate her intentions if we say she would like to accomplish something like the figurative castration of Quixote.

She 'throws herself' at him out of a psychological compulsion that is gratuitous with respect to her parody. In this her motives and character are novelistic in our modern sense. Her need to see herself vicariously as victim of an uncontrollable passion (for an older man) has at least masochistic overtones as well as sadistic ones. Her ego is undoubtedly served by embarrassing and tormenting an older, timid man, by feigning that he produces in her an irresistible attraction. All this gives release and satisfies the frivolous, flirtish, aggressive flair of her character. Perhaps Quixote is not the first older man whom she has singled out for intimidation. She is described by others as *"desenvuelta"*—bold, flirtish, forward—and as an aggressive flirt she shows unmistakable traits of a nymphomaniac. Nor is she as attractive as she would like to believe. The gossiper Doña Rodríguez lets the cat out of the bag when she tells on her bad mouth odor. Her congenital halitosis would seem to be a symptom of a sickly constitution, or of any one of various diseases. She appropriates to herself the role of temptress in epic narrative who seeks to thwart or delay the hero from accomplishing his mission. But her behavior suggests she needs to compensate for some deep psychosomatic inadequacy by casting herself in the role of chaste maiden overcome by love against her will. Her make believe is not simply to ridicule and humiliate Quixote, but an expression of her need to feel desired or loved, of emotional inadequacy and even of her malice and perversity. Her malicious wit foists on Quixote the role of deceiver and ungrateful Aeneas. In her parody a motif from epic literature and chivalric romance is turned inside out, into novelistic exposure: a clinical case of female sexuality.

8. Doña Rodríguez

His face bandaged, Quixote is confined forcibly to his room and his bed. The hero is immobilized and from this very circumstance sensory experience as mock adventure is made to reveal and transform itself into the reality of social relationships. The nocturnal scene in Quixote's chamber is the climax to which Cervantes has pressed his representational techniques to assume the stance of parody. The multiple contrasts between what Quixote is and his illusion of himself (or the duenna's), between the facts of reality and chivalric fiction, or semblance and reality, are pressed to sustain to the maximum our expectations according to the narrator's pattern of arousing then denying or satisfying them. In the silence and darkness Quixote hears a key turn in the lock to the door and fears that Altisidora has chosen this secretive hour to accost him. Again the scene is an obvious parody of the secretive and nocturnal encounter in romances of chivalry. But the figure in the doorway turns out to be not a 'damsel' but a 'duenna.'

Doña Rodríguez has chosen this hour not for malice nor for any 'fictitious' intent but because she comes in earnest. She has unwittingly or stupidly chosen an hour that coincides with a literary motif. By now a nocturnal visit by a female can have for Quixote only one meaning; he does not suppose that a duenna from chivalry would come to his room at this time of night, as indeed she wouldn't (in the originals). From this semblance to chivalric fiction Cervantes goes on to develop a delightful play between the illusion and alarm of two middle-aged characters who fear in each other's presence for their private and moral purity with the scruples of their age and social class. The illusion of their desirability to the other (not the narrator's representational techniques, it would seem) impart to the scene the attributes of a magical, other worldly temptation by night. On recognizing her as the duchess' duenna, Quixote understands that another servant of the household (and not a great lady like Countess Trifaldi) has come to accost him with an erotic proposal. He sees a grotesque figure in the long gown and glasses of a duenna and supposes she has come in her role as go-between. None of this penetrates the duenna's mind, for in her simple-mindedness she has chosen an hour and place to confide her anxiety and problems to Quixote and ask for his help. Her motives are real and sincere, but unwittingly she has assumed a fictional role only vaguely, misleadingly connected to her position as duenna in the household. This is Cervantes' telling stroke of wit. This simple-minded woman has been present at the scenes in which the duke and duchess and their servants have performed or played hoaxes and tricks on Quixote and Sancho, but had not the wit or intelligence to understand the mockery. She took in the entire scene with Trifaldi and bearded *dueñas* and ride on Clavileño and believed it was all real. The supposition that Countess Trifaldi was a real *dueña* and noble lady with a real grievance has instigated her to imitate that fiction. She not only believes naively and foolishly in Quixote's efficacy, for her witless simplicity she is the antithesis of both the mayordomo and Altisidora.

This naive and almost stupid woman believes in Quixote and takes his chivalric mission seriously. Is she a character with a childlike faith in Quixote? Her case is almost unique in the entire book. From the outset she is ready to unburden herself to him, confident in his valor and his compassion for the afflicted and dispossessed, or just as well she perceives they are of the same social class and nearly the same age. Before she reveals her problem and her plight she tells her life story. In the process she reveals her astounding simplicity, her simple-mindedness. In Trifaldi's account the reader is treated to an ingeniously comical invention; in Doña Rodríguez's Cervantes discloses a vain and foolish yet good and simple woman whose plight (in literary terms) is to find herself dispossessed of her honor and dignity by the very social forces which formed her character. She is by nature talkative, but she lacks vivacity or wit to express herself. Her speech is a tissue of commonplaces, the style of boredom itself, as it were, except when she becomes gossipy.

She claims illustrious parentage from Asturias (a family of hidalgos), which feeds her vanity. Yet without wealth as a girl she was consigned to a position of waiting maid—*doncella*—to a wealthy noble lady in Madrid. She was trained in needle work, no doubt her value to her mistress. Separated from her parents, then orphaned, she grew up dependent on her mistress's goodwill to treat her well and provide for her according to her parentage and class status. Then a squire and hidalgo, an older if not elderly man (probably taking advantage of her youth) sought her out and compromised her virtue so her mistress married her off to him. She bore him a daughter. The account of her husband's death is a minute picture of court and city life in Madrid transparent with a meaning that would be impossible to convey without her ingenuousness, her stupid naïveté. We conclude that her husband was even more simple-minded than she, or so bound to ritual and custom he could not use his meager native intelligence to any but self-defeating ends. He insisted on giving precedence over himself and his mistress to two court judges on a narrow street, when in fact her title, wealth and rank required they defer to her. In her simple-mindedness Doña Rodríguez still believes her husband was correct in deferring to the two officials and a model of courtesy. One may ask what purpose Cervantes has pursued in depicting two such devital-ized characters as the duenna and her husband. They represent a degree of social conformity so mindless as to reduce to the minimal their value as individuals. They appear to be creatures routinely produced and as routinely and mindlessly overcome by the social order. Does the fact that this duenna and mother resorts to Quixote for a solution to her problem represent a spark of life, of intelligent initiative in her?

Her plight turns out to be similar to those of noble *dueñas* in chivalric romance who seek out a champion to defend their rights of family and property. The coincidence, however, is none of her doing. Her daughter has been seduced by the son of a wealthy farmer who promised to marry her but failed to keep his word. Her daughter is dishonored and the duke whose obligation it is to rectify this wrong refuses to intervene in the matter. Oblivious to Quixote's disablement by a mawing cat she pleads with him to take up her cause and force the farmer's son to marry her daughter. (As if to underscore the bleakness of the case, the daughter's name is never mentioned.) If we are to believe the duenna, the duke will take no action against the boy because he has borrowed from his father to pay off gambling debts. But another reason would be that the duke feels no compulsion to aid so unpleasant a woman. She pleads her case by goading Quixote's pride and praising her daughter's good qualities, then, incapable of avoiding comparisons and gossip, she reveals the private, unwholesome secrets of Altisidora and the duchess, the two phantoms who burst into the room and in the dark exact vengeance by beating her and pinching him to the point of torment. Accosted and now victimized by three females, Quixote finds himself entangled in the web of feminine wiles, intrigues and vanity of the household. The reality of social experience is a stultifying encounter with the intimacy of others.

The duenna's story turns out to be a vulgar variation of Trifaldi's fiction: a girl seduced, deceived and dishonored and her mother who comes to plead for aid. When she reappears days later with her daughter, dressed in mourning and moaning and sobbing, mindlessly repeating the formality and ritual of such scenes in chivalry, her desperation is real and it shocks the entire household, particularly the duke, not only because her disclosures implicate him, but because the foolish woman has been unable to distinguish between mockery and fiction and her grim despair. But precisely because she breaks the fictional illusion, her instigation and her case are paradigmatic of Cervantes' ends.

In her witless folly she has placed before Quixote a social grievance that cuts through the fabric of obligations and relationships between persons and classes. A girl's honor and that of her family are at stake. Quixote, however, is himself not free to intervene directly; he too must respect the rule of hospitality and his obligations to the duke. Yet what we are made to perceive is that a humble, even foolish, appeal is placed before Quixote, instigated by a genuine faith in his efficacy. Are the foolish as well, like the meek and the defenseless of the Christian admonition, to have access to justice through the redemptive powers of a champion? But fiction is one thing, real life another. A women victimized by the social order to which she so mindlessly conforms appeals, out of foolish innocence, to Quixote the nonconformist, the pure in heart, expecting him out of compassion and righteousness to redress the social order. Is the fictional hero to be allowed to effect a solution to a problem of real life? Cervantes himself at this point would seem to be most distant from his story, yet his mind and artistic control are fully evident. His meaning will come across in the manner he deflects the situation.

Doña Rodríguez has of course been mindless to the predicament in which she puts Quixote, who is bound to respect the rules of courtesy and hospitality to his host the duke. For all his madness and self-illusion, Quixote is aware of the delicate nature of his predicament and of the moral and social dilemma closing in on him. Pressed by both the crafty and devious Altisidora and the duenna, he is disposed to take his leave from the palace and evade the matter, forgetting that he would leave without his squire who is tied up with affairs on the island. But when the duenna and her daughter formally request his aid before the duke and duchess and the entire household, he has no recourse but to agree to defend her cause and to challenge the farmer's son to chivalric combat. The duenna in her foolish and witless manner assumed the fictional stance of a duenna-in-distress (as she had seen Trifaldi do), and this is the clue the duke seizes to redirect her real need and request back into farce and fraud, claiming that the challenge is in effect and taking upon himself the responsibility for summoning the culprit. He is genuinely surprised and taken aback by the duenna's action but still treats it as one more entertaining nonfeat to be attempted by Quixote. He is ready to convert the matter into another diverting spectacle. The duke's vanity and weakness, and his ill will toward the duenna and her daughter, are motives that now perpetrate his fraud and false condescension.

9. Interlace

The arc of narrative between chapter 44, when Sancho departs for the island, and 55, when Quixote rescues him literally from the pit of darkness, spans an interval of about two weeks in which they undergo the most telling experiences of their story. The impression that this period has been much longer is attributable to the relaxed pace at which each episode develops as well as to the ease with which the narrator combines their unfolding. In order to keep an equal focus on his protagonists, the narrator transports the reader back and forth alternately between Quixote at the palace and Sancho on the island.

Between these major threads he develops the minor one that shifts the scene to the village in La Mancha with the visit there of the page entrusted by the duchess with the delivery of letters and gifts for Sancho's wife. A scheme of this parallel and alternate unfolding of incidents and their effects is given on Chart IV. The narrator shifts from palace to island sustaining a parallel development of time and place. For instance, one may assume that the night Quixote is visited by the duenna is approximately the same night Sancho has been on his rounds, so that one may view their separate experiences as having reached at this point a similar level of development. Cervantes' strategy was to separate his characters, at first drastically, then develop the two threads of narrative, interlacing them back toward their reunion, but developing as well a third thread that connects their stay in the palace and on the island with relatives and acquaintances in their native village. By weaving or interlacing—interrupting and then realigning—these threads across time and space he achieves not just the illusion of an extended interval but that the interval is the prolonged consummation of his story. Interlace, then, becomes the technique for the consummation of illusion.

Just after Sancho agreed to whip himself in order to disenchant Dulcinea and was assured for it a governorship, he dictated a letter to his wife (Ch 36), which the duchess took from him, read and promised to deliver with presents. The very idea that Sancho should communicate in writing with his wife is a new development brought about by his self-importance as a public figure. His letters (dictated to a scribe) confirm his public image. They provide a means for looking into his mind, motives and ambitions unavailable by any other narrative technique. This side of Sancho was introduced back in chapter 5 in the scene of leave-taking from his wife Teresa. The technique there is dialogue. The letters, for the strictures epistolary conventions impose on a rustic's outpouring of pride and ambition, are the consummate form for his rise to public importance. The central topic in all of the letters exchanged—there are seven—is his new importance as Governor and the materialization of his illusion. To such an extent does his new importance occupy the attention of the narrator that a critical argument has arisen about whether Sancho doesn't displace Quixote at this point. Admittedly, Quixote's social ordeal seems secondary, beset as he is by females back in the palace, while Sancho is up to his head in public matters, instituting reforms and running a government. The theme and conflict in Quixote's case

The Mythical Don Quixote 217

CHART IV

INTERLACE—Chs 44-57

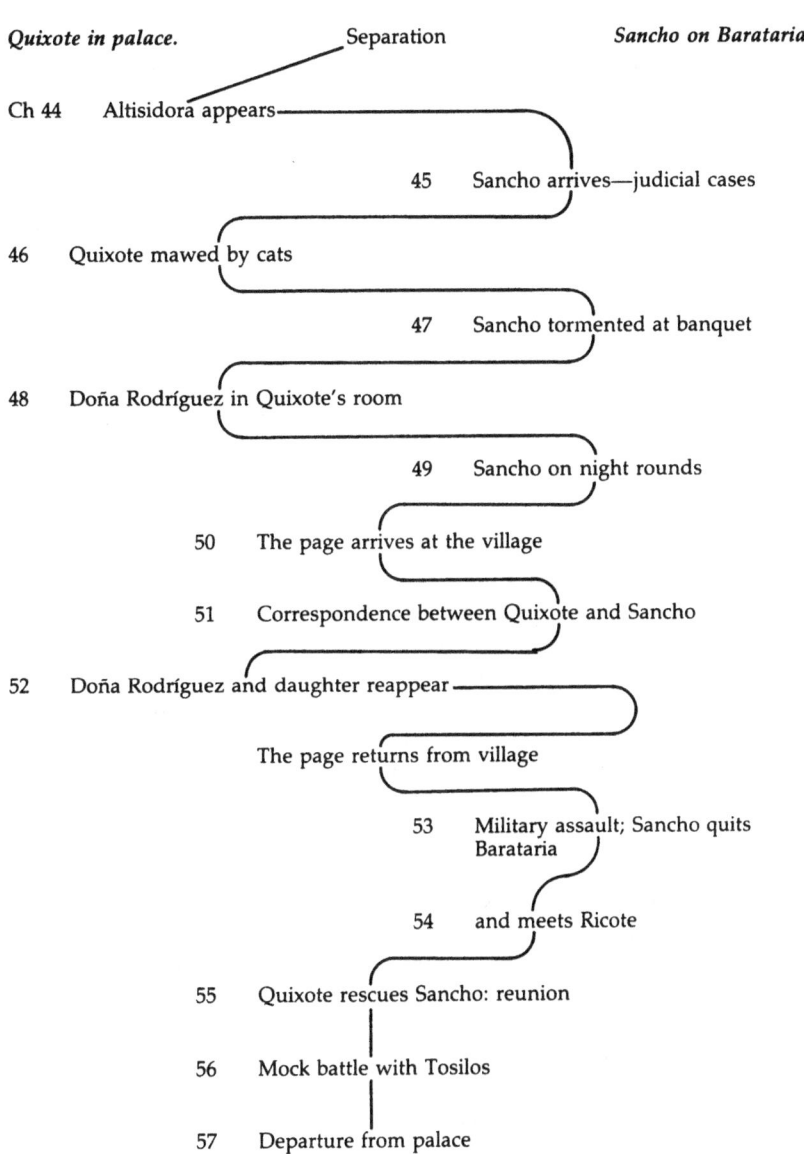

is, however, the major one and Sancho's the minor. The demands on the hero's public image are in conflict with his private and personal needs. The basis of his public image is his virtue, and that virtue is laid siege to by the importunate Altisidora and the witless duenna. His trial of mortification is on the high and subtle level of pride and vanity purified through moral vexation and humiliation. Sancho's is parallel, but on a lower level of immediate, often brutal, violent physical mortification. Because it is secondary and less complicated Sancho's social ordeal is more clearly defined, as seen in his letters, and more conclusive in its outcome.

The exchange of letters is clearly a device for attaining a breadth of social meaning from the perspective of personal illusion and feeling. Through the exchange of letters the story assumes the scale of communication between the highest and lowest classes of society, where peasants gain in dignity and respect. Our suspension of disbelief at this point will make the connection to the idea of a totalizing encyclopedic breadth of social experience aimed for by the epic poets of the classical tradition. The letters to Teresa and the page's visit to the village provide an anchor to Sancho's former life, while they undergo the radically different experiences of palace and island. The letters are of course also a handy vehicle for social satire, not the least what we perceive directed at the duchess and her condescending way of communicating with a villager, offering gifts and requesting a supply of acorns in return.

Chapter 50 relates the page's visit to the village and it is interesting to see that his presence there is the only thread the narrator wishes to draw between Sancho's family and the situation seen in chapter 5, and Quixote's acquaintances and the ducal palace. Otherwise life in the village is closed off to us. The point being that only where fiction (Sancho's island) disrupts the routine of social existence in La Mancha is there any novelty. The page brings the great news of Sancho's rise to the governorship and the good account of himself that servants in the palace know about. He tells it all with tongue-in-cheek. He is the page who played the role of Dulcinea on the wagon and chided Sancho to whip himself. He is as much a jester as messenger and his encounter with the priest and Samson leaves little room for doubt that he belongs among the mockers of Quixote. Samson and the priest are not quite taken in by what amounts to a hoax, despite the evidence and value of the gifts from the duchess.

The page arrives at the village just as the narrative of events at both palace and island reaches a plateau, indicated by the letters exchanged between Quixote and Sancho, while the letters from Teresa to the duchess and to Sancho may be likened to the calm before the storm. Teresa's letter to Sancho provides a delightful view onto trifling details of village life and it must have tickled Cervantes immeasurably to compose it. The duke's letter to Sancho prepares the way for the attack that brings his stay on Barataria to a violent close. Back in the palace Doña Rodríguez and her daughter make their formal appeal to Quixote. In his letter to Sancho we learn of his reluctance about the matter as well as his intention to proceed with it. The letters serve not only for delving into motives and reactions, or to tie loose threads of the plot, they are not only the paradigmatic form of social intercourse, they are the cleverest instance of interlacing.

They have also been seen as evidence that Cervantes treats characters from different social classes alike. Even to the point of variation in the technique of disclosing their contents, or when they are composed, or opened and their contents read by the recipient. Members of the nobility condescend to correspond with rustics on a common level, of course with the advantages of their class on their side. The situation is not typical but anomalous and not to be thought of as democratic or social realism, but again an instance where the Quixotic fiction is inflicted as jest and hoax on an unsuspecting and impoverished reality. The plausibility of the ducal pair's treatment of Quixote and Sancho, even to the point of entrusting the government of one of their villages to an illiterate peasant, whose qualifications for the job come straight out of a book of fiction, is no more and no less than the round of diversions which make up their life of ease, ceremony and ostentation. The duke cannot allow Quixote to intervene in the real affairs of his servants and dependents where his authority is at stake (though he allows Sancho to decide cases and make reforms), but he can divert himself and his household by entertaining the idea.

The inner meaning of their separate ordeal is both mortification that purifies and renews their self-respect, integrity and honor, and the social experience that consummates their personal illusion. Yet the story's frame of reference has been magnified outwardly onto the scale of social relations brought to a minute crisis within the palace and, in the case of Sancho, the art of political survival. We are at the opposite extreme of those adventures like the attack on the windmills, lions, or the enchanted bark, where the outcome was restricted to purely personal and fanciful consequences. Here, through the technique of surrogate inventors and hoaxers, adventure has become social experience on the scale of the epic with particular consequences for the lives of real persons, while projecting Quixote's fictional efficacy against an increasingly discernible historical scene in a manner both complex and naive. Quixote's efficacy on historical and social reality can be only imaginative or 'fictional' (some readers would prefer 'spiritual'), but this has become the prerequisite by which as madman or fool a redemptive virtue may be attributed to him. His mythical efficacy is what we are persuaded to accept as the plausibility and crux of the story. Whatever moral or social censure one may suppose Cervantes directs at the ducal pair for their sport at the expense of Quixote must be looked at in the light of what he, Cervantes himself, as author or creative artist, has inflicted on his character in the way of refined satire, ridicule and humiliation.

10. Sancho and Ricote

The aftermath of Sancho's experience on Barataria introduces the thematic anticlimax to 'fiction and society'; social, moral and political considerations prepare a historical stage, so to speak, for the departure from the palace of master and squire. On Barataria the duke's and mayordomo's deceptions provide a situation where Sancho is permitted to pursue his illusion, not to the realization of his native potential, but of course toward their own ends of diversion. The outcome nonetheless illustrates the theme of *desengaño* (disenchantment, disillusionment) with the exercise of political power and the materialistic values its pursuit entails. Sancho's experience permitted a treatment of political themes within a pretext of make-believe. Now Cervantes will expand his political theme with an oblique treatment of a controversial issue or question of historical significance in 1609–1613.

Sancho makes his way back to the palace alone, mounted on Dapple. His return and reunion with Quixote must complete the analogy to a penitential mortification and purgation of his individual conscience, locked in combat between worldly ambition and the desire for freedom and self-respect. On the road he meets up with a group of alms-begging pilgrims, recognizable as foreigners by their appearance. In their company Sancho finds his way back to a life of companionship, laughter, release from cares, and the satisfaction of basic desires, food and wine, sleep and rest. The alms-beggers turn out to be deceptive (their appearance suggests need and abstinence; but stripped of their garb, their feasting becomes a carnivalesque indulgence); they are young Germans who have taken up this way of wandering about Spain under the pretense of visiting religious shrines to exploit materialistic gain without work or social obligations. In the company of these deceivers and hedonistic nonconformists, Sancho puts behind him his anxieties and faces a political and moral question of an entirely different dimension. One of the pilgrims is neither German nor young; he is Ricote, a Morisco and an old friend of Sancho's, a former shopkeeper in the village, who has disobeyed and defied the King's order of banishment and returned clandestinely to Spain. His appearance introduces the historical dimension (the year is 1614) to the theme of freedom and social conformity. In Sancho's relationship to Ricote Cervantes has cut through to a question affecting personal conscience and the social order.

In the century and more since the fall of Granada in 1492, the Moorish population of the Spanish kingdoms had been subjected to many measures, civil, military, and ecclesiastical, to force their assimilation into Christian, that is, Spanish society, without success. The great majority of Moriscos (and no longer Moros or Moors), remained loyal to their customs, language and Islamic religion, so much so they were considered a dangerous element within the nation for their contacts with the Turks, Spain's formidable enemy in the Mediterranean. In 1609 Philip III, acknowledging the failure of the policy of forced baptism and assimilation, decreed their expulsion and named the Count of Salazar to carry it out. The Morisco population had been concentrated in the kingdoms of Granada, Valencia, Murcia and Aragon, regions peripheral to Castile. The Moriscos living in La Mancha (in Castile), like Ricote, had been resettled there in the course of the sixteenth century. The policy of expulsion was a harsh recourse that furthered the political aims of Castile to impose a centralist order and hegemony over the peripheral kingdoms where Moriscos were essential to the economy. For economic, social and religious reasons the policy of explusion was more or less controversial from the point of view of Castilian policy or the social order and economies of the peripheral regions. Cervantes gives us a personalized view of the issue, not necessarily impartial, in the figure of an idealized Morisco whose plea for tolerance and acceptance is essentially an appeal to conscience.[78]

Ricote has the spirit, verve and intelligence to foresee and accept banishment from Spain on rational terms, and to attempt to build a new life on them. Unlike the great majority of Moriscos, he did not go to North Africa, but (like a significant minority) to France, then Italy and finally Germany where he expects to settle, in a town in Catholic Bavaria. His experience in Germany opened his eyes to life in a nation with fewer social constraints and greater religious tolerance, "where there is liberty of conscience." He has searched, it seems, not for the "liberty of conscience" of the reformists but for the political and social liberty to live by conscience rather than conformity. His story is one that pits the individual against the power of the state, even now when he has returned to Spain. Yet one of his idealized traits is the heated justification he makes of the King's policy of expulsion which has victimized him and driven his people to the despair of exile. More remarkable, however, is the fact he did not choose to rely on cohesion and solidarity with his fellow Moriscos and their Islamic customs and faith, but set out on a trajectory of his own (this is how he depicts it) that took him to other European countries with customs equally if not more inhospitable to the uprooted. And he is something of an opportunist to have joined up with a group of Germans disguised as pilgrims, deceiving authorities and risking detection. He is a rare nonconformist who attempts to reshape his life according to his preferences, desire and illusion as well as his conscience.

He represents not just a member of a group on whom the Spanish state has brought to bear its power first to compel religious and social conformity and then, failing in this, to expatriate them, but an individual of that group for whom, the group notwithstanding, personal liberty and conformity are a matter of conscience. A sincere man, he would not have feigned conversion to Catholicism to be able to remain in Spain. His wife and daughter are believing Catholics and for their sake as well he has sought refuge in a nation like France and then found a home in Bavaria. He has not returned to Spain simply for love of homeland, but to recover the hoard of riches he left hidden outside the village in La Mancha.

Like Sancho, Ricote is an idealized individual, or, rather, an idealized Spaniard. His name would indicate that he represents but does not typify the Morisco cause. In him and his story Cervantes has crossed or combined certain historical elements, like the Moriscos' reputation for hoarding, with traditional elements of story. His appearance now is only the first portion of a story of separation of family members, a story of forced separation and reunion (he will reappear in Barcelona and be reunited there with his daughter); at its center is the traditional motif of a treasure whose recovery poses risks which must be undertaken if the resolution is to be a happy one.

When he asks Sancho to return with him to the village to help him recover his wealth, promising to pay him well, Ricote's presence becomes a question of conscience for Sancho, who must decide between personal gain and compliance with the law, between loyalty to an old friend or to his King and nation. In any case Sancho will not denounce Ricote to the authorities. The choice is not really difficult, even when Ricote insists he can enrich him. But Sancho's decision brings out the contrast between the intelligent, crafty and risk-taking Morisco and his experience of the world and the old-Christian peasant, who as shrewd and nonsensical as he is about his self-survival, has little or no experience of the world, even to the point of not knowing what islands are. Ricote has felt the full force of political power to compel conformity and obedience and he shows no patience with Sancho's talk of governing. Sancho has just lived through the illusion and disillusion (the fiction) of having held political power for a brief spell. Freedom from those anxieties has meaning for him in moral, not political terms.

11. Departure

The means by which Cervantes reunites his characters illustrate the theme of moral purification and provide another turn to Quixote's redemptive role. Their reunion is the indispensable preliminary to departure from the palace. The final scene of leave-taking will complete the process by which Quixote's fictional efficacy is endowed with mythical significance. It has been a complex process of elevation through mortification and a trial of purification and humiliation bringing about those conditions that assure he can exercise his full fictional efficacy . . . by virtue of his disablement. Cervantes' grand strategy is to elevate his protagonist to mythical status by denying him the real or historical efficacy of his pretension and illusion (or the reader's unconscious expectations). The outcome of both the duenna's and Altisidora's demands disclose the structural paradigm.

Night has overtaken Sancho, when, disoriented, he falls into a cavern or pit with Dapple, and escaping serious injury, is unable to climb out. Lost, helpless, bereft of means or power to save himself, he passes the night in mournful lamentation, and works his way into another part of the grotto the next morning. The fear of death, trapped and forsaken in the pit, is the final stage of his trial. The underground experience recalls but is not parallel to Quixote's cave adventure. That episode (the epitome of adventure) was inconclusive in form and meaning. Sancho's 'fall into the cave' is conclusive both as event and as meaning. Its meaning is that of a penitential ordeal leading to inner illumination. "¡Desdichado de mí, y en qué han parado mis locuras y fantasías! . . ." II.55, 455 [What an unlucky wretch I am! Where have my ravings and follies brought me!] His lamentations are a new version of his monologues, conveying the sense that he has found a new awareness of his humble humanity in the ordeal that purifies his soul of vanity, ambition and worldly illusion. In the accounting of his government told to the duke he also shows that he has undergone purification of those boorish traits he displayed on arrival at the palace. At the depths of his gravest despair the narrator takes up Quixote's experience: on that very morning Quixote is out on a training exercise for the forthcoming joust and finds Sancho. He rescues his squire literally from the pit of death because he is the only agent feasible; this is the final turn to interlace. Quixote himself just missed falling into the pit, mounted on Rocinante. The point is that he was in the right place to redeem his squire from a hellish death. For all his prominence in the foregoing episodes, Sancho is without the means to save himself in his hour of gravest peril, and his master is efficacious at least to the extent of redeeming him fortuitously. They call to one another as if from one world to the next, as strangers, in order to re-establish—on a new basis?—the relationship of their mutual dependence.

The combat with the boy supposed to be the farmer's son is planned as another public ceremony and spectacle. A large audience gathers in the courtyard to witness a battle that is plausible only as Quixotic fiction imposed on social reality. The duke consented to go along with Doña Rodríguez's request that Quixote challenge and fight the young man who deceived her daughter because he intends to thwart such a solution by disguising his lackey Tosilos as the culprit, expecting to deceive those most concerned. His plot goes awry. He expects Tosilos to follow instructions; the lackey, encased in armor and his identity concealed, is to unhorse Quixote with as little violence as possible, will be declared the winner and freed of any obligation to the girl.

Cervantes' formula up to now (in similar situations) has been to let some antic of one of the animals decide the battle. The situation here, however, is unique. It is not Quixote's prowess nor Dulcinea's beauty which are at stake, but the contender's word and the girl's honor. Nor is the contender anything like a real or false knight anyway. A lackey is a whimsical creature who behaves like a lackey, so he can be made to substitute for the animal's antic.

When Tosilos approaches the girl and sees her face, he falls in love with her (wounded by Cupid) and decides he doesn't want to fight. Indeed, she is a much better match than he could hope to get in a normal way. He spoils the duke's plot by committing the vulgarity of falling in love with Doña Rodríguez's daughter and offering to marry her. The duke is incensed and exasperated to see his plan go awry, his expectations of amusement defrauded. The little people—duenna's daughter and his lackey—with Quixote's intervention—are apparently to decide things for themselves. To all appearances Quixote's intervention has been providential. The girl's honor will be restored through the social sanction of marriage, to the satisfaction of mother and daughter. For the moment the duke has no recourse but to twist the notion of a magical transformation to his use. Of course Quixote cannot suspect him of guile or deception. His naive innocence places him above the level of deception and intrigue. So his madness does not prevent him from accepting the expediency of any husband for a girl desperate to marry. Quixote's presence in the palace alone has proved him adequate to furnishing a solution, apparently. He departs supposing the matter settled. It remains to be seen how the duke (or Cervantes immanent in the cause and effect of his characters' motivations) prevents this solution. Quixote must be depicted as inadequate to the reality of social intrigue as a condition to his mythical efficacy.

Quixote and Sancho take their leave in the same courtyard where they were welcomed clamorously. The setting again confirms their public image as celebrities. Yet the most cutting humiliation that vindicates, as it were, the personal virtue behind that image and completes the process of phase two is heaped on Quixote in this final moment. From among the crowd of servants Altisidora raises her voice and in four stanzas of a grotesque ballad sings out a brazen accusation. She feigns the role of the injured, seduced and then betrayed damsel-heroine, in a sadistic version of this poetic motif—encased in another. She does not accuse him of having stolen her heart. That would not be in character. She accuses him of taking three of her kerchiefs and a pair of garters. In her wit and malice she conceives no crueler mortification than to accuse him of a vulgar fetish for her intimate items of wear. Then mimicking Vergil's vengeful, despairing Dido, she heaps maledictions on him: may Sancho not whip himself and Dulcinea remain disenchanted, may Quixote pay heavily for his cruelty to her.

His mortification and humiliation are all the greater for being exposed to public ridicule. Even the duchess is aghast at Altisidora's effrontery. But the duke, sensing the moment is right for avenging his own person and dignity, cruelly takes up Altisidora's accusation: ". . . habiendo recebido en este mi castillo el buen acogimiento . . . os hayáis atrevido a llevaros tres tocadores . . . [y] las ligas de mi doncella . . . Volvedle las ligas; si no, yo os desafío a mortal batalla." II.57, 469 [. . . after all the hospitable treatment you have received in this castle . . . you should make off with three kerchiefs and a pair of garters belonging to my maid. Return the garters to her, or else I challenge you to mortal combat.]

Quixote answers this gravest of charges with superb courtesy and respect, professing his innocence. And indeed his innocence before the duke's ignoble joke and malicious falsehood is what testifies to his moral superiority over his hosts. His innocence, the innocence of a fool or child falsely accused by one guilty of malice and wile, together with his personal dignity and social courtesy, vindicates his public image and certifies his mythical efficacy. The characters of the ducal household have engaged in diversions and mock rituals that celebrate his chivalric identity and mock his social mission, but the efficacy of his person among them vindicates even their ridicule . . . in the form of fiction. At the close of the trial or process of purification within and mortification in public, Quixote's moral qualities have endowed him with a mythical (that is, a 'fictional') efficacy.

12. "The Knight of Faith"   Chs 58–60

The final phase begins with a pivotal scene. Out in the countryside again, Quixote releases his pent-up frustration in a paean to liberty (leaving little doubt that Cervantes' theme is the liberty of personal choice). The course of adventure prepares to swing from the social scene in the palace forward to a new course of fortuitous encounters on the road. The first is a strategic stroke of narrative, one of the most enigmatical situations devised by Cervantes. Beside the road about a dozen workers are resting and eating on the grass. Nearby, under some linen covers, are four figures or images carved in relief on wood (and colored, as one worker explains). Quixote politely asks to see them. The worker uncovers, in this order, four religious images, destined for an altarpiece in a village church: Saint George, Saint Martin, Saint James (Santiago) and Saint Paul; they are handsomely, though conventionally done. The grouping is probably a traditional one: each saint, in Christian hagiography, embodies legendary and doctrinal significance. (The order above is incidental in the scene, but its significance as narrative is not.) As each figure is uncovered, Quixote delivers a brief 'doctrinal' explanation of his own of it. His remarks single out the Christian, redemptive act of each saint.

Saint George and Saint Martin belong to the venerable medieval tradition of pious legend; George is a young warrior (and patron saint of various peoples) who embodies both valor and chastity, shown delivering a maiden from a hellish serpent. Martin embodies charity and valor. Santiago is the patron saint of Spain, shown in his role as fierce redeemer of Spain from Islam, the warrior of the bloody but holy sword. Paul is entirely different. By tradition he is the great intellect, the Saint, not of the 'sword' but of the 'word' (evidencing his Semitic origin). The significance of the scene rests on the inclusion of Paul with the other three who are knights in the medieval tradition. The instance in Paul's life depicted is the moment of his conversion, his 'fall' from the horse on the road to Damascus. He would seem to be "The Knight of Faith"—is he depicted with a sword?—redeemed by the force of his new faith and by which he redeemed the gentile masses. His efficacy was spiritual because intellectual. Quixote's comments justify the inclusion of Paul among the other three saints 'on horseback'—*caballeros*. In their presence he is moved to meditate, first on the grouping then on a comparison with himself and on his mission. Does he feel a greater affinity to Paul, the intellectual "Knight of Faith?"

The significance of the encounter is evidently religious. The figures are holy images made and destined for an altarpiece. Some modern translators have not understood this, supposing the worker's explanation to refer to a 'show' or 'play,' i.e., a secular performance. The scene is therefore exceptional in the book. Cervantes has consistently evaded confronting Quixote with one of the inescapable realities of life in Spain: the ecclesiastical presence, churches, priests, convents, monasteries, images or icons, and doctrines. Various priests appear in the book, but engaged in secular activities, like the village priest and Samson Carrasco. Only once are these two shown at prayer, in a field. And Quixote never enters a church or any ecclesiastical structure in the course of the entire narrative. Only once, and by mistake, does he ever approach a church. Cervantes' conception of his story is overtly secular throughout. It would seem at the very least irreverent to depict Quixote, a madman and fool, in churches or attempting acts of devotion (not the case in Sierra Morena, where he improvised a rosary). His nonconformity and 'illuminated ingenio' is not concerned except marginally with Church practices, dogma, ritual or holy images. And to portray him taking up questions of religious doctrine or the use of holy images would seem gross and entirely alien to Cervantes' artistic sensibility. Nowhere else in the book does Quixote take notice of and comment on a religious image (cf. I.52, 598). Yet he does here, on four, and in his element, the countryside.

> Por buen agüero he tenido, hermanos, haber visto lo que he visto, porque estos santos y caballeros profesaron lo que yo profeso, que es el ejercicio de las armas; sino que la diferencia que hay entre mí y ellos es que ellos fueron santos y pelearon a lo divino, y yo soy pecador y peleo a lo humano. Ellos conquistaron el cielo a fuerza de brazos, porque el cielo padece fuerza, y yo hasta agora no sé lo que conquisto a fuerza de mis trabajos; pero si mi Dulcinea del Toboso saliese de los que padece, mejorándose mi ventura y adobándoseme el juicio, podría ser que encaminase mis pasos por mejor camino del que llevo. II.58, 473

> I consider it a good omen, brothers, to have seen what I have seen, because these saints and knights professed what I profess, which is the calling of arms; except that the difference between me and them is that they were saints and fought in a heavenly manner, and I am a sinner and fight in the human way. They conquered Heaven by force of arms, because Heaven suffers violence, but as for me up to now I do not know what I conquer by force of my labors; yet if my Dulcinea del Toboso could be released from the pain she suffers, my fortunes being improved and my mind set aright, it might be that I could direct my steps along a better road than that which I am now following.

"They conquered Heaven . . . because Heaven suffers force . . . and I up to now do not know what I conquer by force of my labors. . . ." Has the effect of the images been like a flash, divinely inspired, illuminating his mind and conscience? Nowhere else does Quixote quote from Holy Scripture to explain or justify his chivalry. Nowhere else has Cervantes taken recourse to the same to characterize, depict or 'analyze' his abnormal state. It would seem that his madness has turned inward, to wrestle with his conscience, so to speak. The scene and Quixote's introspection is provokingly enigmatic because it suggests so much more than it depicts, as story, as psychological, or pathological, characterization.

Is the effect the images produce on him religious? Precisely what Cervantes has evaded up to now? Evidently, despite what the character says about "omens," an allusion to their importance in the classical epic. Quixote has been incited to introspection, to reflect on his actions and his words, concepts . . . on his efficacy. Or his monomania, others would say. In any case, he conceives his chivalry in intellectual or spiritual terms, and for this reason the image of Saint Paul has been decisive.

Has the image of Dulcinea now become identified unconsciously with a cure? With return to sanity? Were we to interpret, like Unamuno, his admission of doubt as an expiatory assertion of his faith in himself (faith superior to doubt) we should have an analog to the divine passion of Christ on the Cross. The scene with the images, the initial scene of the final phase, announces the closing of the book. There the hidalgo will recover his sanity and with it the spiritual illumination and peace that restores his Catholic belief. But that sane man *renounces* his chivalry. Here it is his madness—or is it approaching sanity?—that inspires him to compare himself with pride or humility to the four saints.

Up to now Quixote has voiced few doubts about his chivalric mission and his experience in the palace has confirmed it. The characteristic stance throughout Part I was a choleric declaration of the kind we saw inverted in the cave of Montesinos. Here, taking a cue from the image of Saint Paul, he endows his chivalry with the dignity not only of the comparison, but with the intelligence or the sanity of the comparison, and he voices self-doubts about his mission, about his present condition and about the outcome of his adventures. Has the exemplary story devised a schism and a conflict within Quixote? A self-conscious hero at the center of the self-conscious narrative?

The scene with the images is obviously a turning point in the story, for it anticipates the final resolution of the exemplary idea behind it.

So it is no mere coincidence that this scene has served as the basis for the best known of the existentialist interpretations of the story, Miguel de Unamuno's, developed in his book *Life of Don Quixote and Sancho* (in Spanish 1905) and other essays, which in turn derives in many respects from the philosophical and symbolical or Romantic interpretations of the last century. Of this scene and the passage quoted above Unamuno wrote: ". . . perhaps there is no more profoundly sad passage in all of the melancholy epic of Don Quijote's life."[79] In his book we find the phrase "Knight of Faith" applied to the hidalgo. The scene and the passage cited are decisive in Unamuno's view of Quixote as a surrogate Christ: "Our Lord Don Quixote," a cultural hero and redeemer of the Hispanic peoples in the modern world of scientific materialism. For Unamuno, Quixote's self doubts about his mission have become a spiritual ordeal. Not only does he accept Quixote's view of himself as definitive, he redirects the mockery aimed at the hero and even the objective stance observed by the narrator or Cervantes as the derision that confirms his divine and expiatory mission. Unamuno's interpretation is subjective, philosophical and epistemological, psychological and moral. It is not and should not be thought of as literary criticism in the technical, professional or precise sense. Or, rather, it should be seen as a different and 'uncritical' approach to fiction in the modern era, and from a point of view totally opposite to the Aristotelian tradition. Unamuno is not interested nor concerned with establishing an objective, critical approach, but a subjective and empassioned one, hence his declared affinity to Quixote's illusion and Quixote's 'idealism.' Most Cervantean critics never bother or fail to see this distinction, and for this reason it is important to make here a critical accounting of Unamuno's interpretation, and others like it, to explain it in terms of the book's structure.

Unamuno's sensibility and philosophy did not so much create a Christ-like Quixote as intuit the scale of the process of humiliation/ elevation as an approximation to the hero's trial of purification in the epical tradition and as an analogue to the divine passion of Christ seen along existentialist lines. In other words, Unamuno read or intuited correctly the structural schema of the hero's trial of purification through mortification and comical humiliation and its issue in a mythical Quixote, for that is what the schema of the Quixotic fiction implies, but then he proceeded to erect on it an interpretation to suit his religious impulse. He was, moreover, unwilling to recognize

The Mythical Don Quixote

Cervantes' artistic originality. For it is the story no less which at this point shows a hero disposed to explain his trial in terms of saints who served Christ as knights and who ponders, between wisdom and foolishness, his efficacy.

In the final phase of the story Quixote's pathological condition reoccupies the center. But also Cervantes will now undertake to give his hero's madness a greater moral spiritual refinement while at the same time pressing to fix his mythical attributes within a historical or contemporary frame. In the aftermath of the palace sojourn, his hero's actions are drawn even more problematical and disparate under subtly new circumstances. His discretion and wisdom are more pointedly 'sane,' as in dialogues with Sancho, while his actions are drawn more discernably foolish and 'mad' and in flat contradiction to his 'sane' social attributes of courtesy and eloquence.

After they leave the workmen, in a wood they come across some nets stretched between trees to catch small birds, an Arcadian pastime of the wealthy and beautiful youths of the region, and meet two of them, dressed as shepherdesses, who explain the nets' purpose. When Quixote courteously greets them and introduces himself, the two young ladies recognize him as the famous knight of the book in print. Again his fame has preceded him, this time to an adventure of "feigned Arcadia." Or, rather, to a frustrated adventure of the same. The group of youths invite him to their festival and performance. They lay out a sumptuous meal and at its close Quixote raises his voice to express his gratitude, as if to give another of his discourses. His speech is, to a point, an exquisite and eloquent expression of his social courtesy and of his mind and person. Until he describes the action he will take to show his gratitude. In the style of his chivalry, he will maintain against all comers (on a nearby road) for two days that the two shepherdesses are the most beautiful and courteous ladies in the world, a gratuitous, lavish act, apparently sane (so long as its execution remains purely verbal). But at this point, Sancho, overcome by the verbal show, interrupts to give a vulgar, declamatory praise of his master, insinuating that he cannot be mad. For this tactless humiliation Quixote breaks out furiously at his squire; his behavior turns violent. In a rage he goes out to the highway, to put his challenge into effect. In the middle of the road he utters it and repeats it twice (in the formulaic style the narrator repeats in describing the outcome). Then a group of herdsmen on horseback driving bulls and cattle come down the road. Quixote, Sancho beside him, ignoring all warnings, stand in the road with their mounts and are trampled in the dust horribly by animal hooves. His shouts at the "fleeing rabble" underscore the mad foolishness of what he attempted.

One aspect of the new strategy emerges: the disparity between his vain manner and mad action is drawn in finer terms. Sancho's interruption frustrated a conceivably positive outcome that would confirm Quixote's illusion. Instead Quixote is driven to a mad act that brings on physical abuse and abject humiliation, before spectators whose horror or dumbfoundness is not elaborated. The reversal and mortification are all the more humiliating for the assumption that, displaying the social attributes of eloquence and courtesy before an admiring audience, Quixote had somehow gained or was regaining sanity. In the aftermath, unable to eat for the affront to his dignity, he reflects on the very process of elevation/humiliation, as if he were at odds with his mission and its demands, or seeking a way out of his predicament.

> —Come, Sancho amigo . . . sustenta la vida, que más que a mí te importa, y déjame morir a mí a manos de mis pensamientos y a fuerzas de mis desgracias. Yo, Sancho, nací para vivir muriendo, y tú para morir comiendo; y porque veas que te digo verdad en esto, considérame impreso en historias, famoso en las armas, comedido en mis acciones, respetado de príncipes, solicitado de doncellas; al cabo al cabo, cuando esperaba palmas, triunfos y coronas, granjeadas y merecidas por mis valerosas hazañas, me he visto esta mañana pisado y acoceado y molido, de los pies de animales inmundos y soeces. II.59, 482

> Eat, friend Sancho . . . sustain life, for you have more need of it than I, and let me die at the hands of my thoughts and the force of my misfortunes. I, Sancho, was born to live dying, and you to die eating, and to prove the truth of my words, look at me: here am I, printed in histories, famous in arms, courteous in my actions, respected by princes, courted by maidens, yet, after all, when I expected palms, triumphs, and crowns, won and deserved by my valorous exploits, I have seen myself this morning trampled, kicked and trodden on, by hooves of unclean and filthy animals.

In his dejection he asks Sancho to lighten his present misery by using the occasion (he will sleep) to lash himself and so further along Dulcinea's disenchantment. This concern now more than any other will become symptomatic of his predicament. His request foreshadows the incident that follows the episode in the inn, where they take shelter from risks of travel on the road.

There the next disclosure is introduced without comment, preliminary or preparation; it arises from the flux of the action. Yet it is the disclosure that completes the turning point, and we must attribute it directly to the strategy of Cervantes the author who on this occasion makes no pretense of Cide Hamete. In the inn Quixote and Sancho overhear two men who are discussing a book in their possession, called *The Second Part of Don Quixote de la Mancha*. That book is a fraud; Quixote himself hears that it tells how he has "fallen out of love," has forgotten his love for Dulcinea. He raises his voice to challenge such an assertion, the two men hear him, and rush into the room and immediately recognize him as the authentic, the one-and-only Don Quixote. In this way Cervantes introduces into his story the imitation and "apocryphal *Quixote*," published in 1614, by a Spaniard using the pseudonym "Avellaneda" and otherwise unknown. This is the work Cervantes refers to in the Prologue to Part II. There he replies to the insults directed at him by the contemptible unknown in his prologue. Now, at this point in the story, he incorporates the "fraudulent book" into the flow of the Quixotic fiction, as a travesty and imposture.

What did he wish to accomplish by thus allowing the intruder entry into his book? Obviously to show up and censure its defects by having his 'genuine' characters castigate the bad imitator and vent their anger at his execrable product. And accomplished in the line of the fiction-within-fiction. For by reducing the imitation to a 'fact' in the existence of his fictional creatures, Cervantes definitively situates his creation into the contemporary world of 1614. In this year Quixote becomes historically real and alive, while the imitator's book with its false characters is reduced to a travesty. Quixote leafs through a copy of the false version and makes a definitive judgment on it. In this apparently improvised manner, the autonomous character reasserts his mythical status, thus propelling his fiction onto the historical stage of literary rivalries and political factions. He preempts whatever might have been according to the original plan for him to show up in Zaragoza in time for the jousts on the feast day of Saint George. The decision to bypass and omit Zaragoza and set out for Barcelona (discrediting the false book) is one made by Quixote himself and it completes the recasting of the narrative, now pointed to bring off his final apotheosis and disablement on the historical stage of 1614.

13. Barcelona: The Summer of Myth   Chs 60–64

The road to Barcelona takes Quixote and Sancho from the social experiences of the palace to the historical experience of a teeming city on the shores of the Mediterranean, one of Spain's imperial seas. The climax of the story will take place, so to speak, on the historical stage facing the sea. As they move north and east, the story advances, incident by incident, toward the final time-frame that, while fixing the historical moment of the exemplary or realistic plot around the year 1614, prepares the way for the emergence, out of the book itself, of the mythical Quixote. So, in fact, two narrative movements will converge in the climactic episode. The upward trajectory is the course of Quixote's mock fame and the depiction of his mythical celebrity. The downward is the course traced by his pathological depiction to the truth of his inefficacy and disablement. The tension between these two movements support the Quixote fiction to its final resolution in the story. But, as we shall see, the very effect of this resolution is to launch the hero and his fiction 'out of the book' and beyond.

In the closing episodes of the second phase of Part II the story moved onto a historical setting (the Morisco question, the apocryphal version) in proportion to Quixote's mythical depiction. In the final or third phase, the story is poised to depict Quixote as a 'historical' character. But he is such of course by virtue of his mythical fame, his notoriety in the contemporary world of 1614. For this reason his arrival and welcome in Barcelona is contrived to take place exactly at Midsummer, on the feast day (June 24) of the Nativity of St. John the Baptist, the solar feast day that celebrates the summer solstice. I have dealt with this matter at length in my book *The Golden Dial*, a study of the temporal configurations of the story. There I compare temporal movement in Cervantes' book with the time pattern in chivalric romances where events, reunions and celebrations follow the seasonal course of the Christian liturgical calendar, from one feast day to another, retracing the cyclical movement of old solar mythologies. The action of Part II is grouped around the spring festivals of the Christian calendar (Carnival and Lent, Corpus Christi, etc.). The adventures leading up to the stay in the palace take place in spring (Quixote expects to arrive in Zaragoza for jousts on Saint George's day, April 23). The palace sojourn lasts through the months of summer, July and August. But now, when Quixote decides to set out for Barcelona, the story and its time-frame are recast to conform to a new purpose. Quite literally, the season reverts to Midsummer, as if on a cyclical reordering, and, again, so that the time and duration of adventures is a constant summer, in a parody of the conventions of chivalric romance. The dynamics of story are aligned to bring the convergence of the two narrative movements, the upward and the downward, in a time and setting that places Quixote's fleeting triumph and then disablement in line with the triumph and eclipse of solar heroes and divinities in solar mythologies, in the perpetual "summer of myth."

The two movements are of course identical with the process of elevation/humiliation and the submission of the hero to a trial of purification. All this now moves to its final variation: the Quixotic hero is martyr to his own fiction. On the road to Barcelona the "Knight of Faith" suffers a 'falling' that foreshadows his demise. After six days of their journey north and east, Quixote and Sancho prepare to spend the night beside the road under some trees. It is here Quixote attempts, or, rather, commits the one unequivocally rash, mad and irrational act of his career. Foolishly, he attempts to apply violent punishment to Sancho's body, in order to disenchant Dulcinea. The depiction of a pathological state now meshes with comic movement. The fiction of Dulcinea's enchantment and the hoax of her disenchantment conspire to entrap the hero in his own ineffectualness. These lines of theme, plot and deception not only cross one another, they are veritably tied and bound into a "gordian knot," the very metaphor Quixote uses to describe his predicament.

Contrary to all his usual impulses of restraint and respect for the person and dignity of others, he attempts to strip Sancho while he sleeps and to lash at his buttocks with Rocinante's reins, in a mad and vain attempt to speed up or bring about his lady's disenchantment according to the formula of the ducal hoax. The act is not only mad and foolish in the extreme, not only 'out of character,' is it not also at war with a hero of mythical attributes? Of course. A deep schism within the hero, a crisis of his insanity, now pits his ineffectuality against his mock-heroic image. He has been driven to this predicament and dilemma by the cruel hoax that put Dulcinea's release in Sancho's hands. Given his obligation to his lady, given his deranged sense, the predicament has overtaken his 'noble, humane and Quixotic' impulses. The hero for his inner fault must fall to a depth of utter humiliation, as to seem to sacrifice his integrity. The self, the dignity of the man, is laid low in the cause of Dulcinea to disenchant. The ends to which Cervantes has pressed a depiction of an abnormal, pathological state compels Quixote to fall a victim to his own cause, to his fiction. It may be the ultimate cruelty to which he subjects his hero.

Note how the theme of food and eating is brought forward from Quixote's outburst and dejection in chapter 59, then the scenes at the inn where the bad imitation is discussed, as preparatory to the scene here. Sancho has eaten well and sleeps. Quixote's insomnia is aggravated by the thought that his lady's release is at the mercy of the fat slob sleeping away so complacently. Then the narrator describes Quixote's mind and its dilemma by retracing the story. It is a supreme artistic moment for the depiction of a pathological state as fiction. Finally, in a monolog, Quixote justifies his move, "si yo azotase a Sancho a pesar suyo . . ." II.60, 491. [If I were to lash Sancho against his will. . . .] Unable to accept his own ineffectuality, driven by frustration, in a kind of delirium he tries to untie the laces to Sancho's breeches. But no sooner does he touch him than Sancho wakes up, in full control of his senses. "Who touches me?" "It is I, come to make up for your negligence and to remedy my torment: I come to whip you. . . ." The story plunges to the gravest crisis between master and squire. Quixote madly persists in unlacing Sancho's breeches; Sancho protests, resists, gets up, and lunging at his master, gives him a back trip and sends him sprawling to the ground face upwards. Restraining the deranged man, he answers Quixote's cry "How, traitor, you dare to raise a hand against your natural lord?" with the reply, "I neither depose king nor make king, but defend myself who am my own lord" II.60, 492. He forces him with threats to promise not to try the same again. Quixote's worst "fall" is at the hands of Sancho. Is the scene comical? Laid low, forced to a humiliating reversal, the hero's ineffectuality is complete at the hands of his squire. In the next incident he is made prisoner by a captain of brigands, to complete the picture.

14. Roque Guinart and Don Antonio

The attempt to whip Sancho becomes the lapse, failing or disregard of duty that delivers the hero into the hands of a rival. On foot, without reins, lance or sword, Quixote can put up no resistance to the bandits who surround and take them prisoners. Or, rather, Quixote is powerless to defend himself because his illusion is in eclipse. Melancholy and dejection have already overtaken him and now events do. The meeting with Roque Guinart is another turning point. The stature and efficacy of a real bandit captain and historical hero looms over a disabled and dejected 'knight.' Quixote's illusion and fortunes are renewed, yes, but not his incentive. The attempt to whip Sancho was, one may say, an abdication of his will to adventure as well as a gamble with the illusion of his effectualness. Roque Guinart takes over the direction of the story because he is an efficacious hero in real life, and the fictional hero will enter Barcelona under his protection.

In what follows the lines of story are recast to show Quixote effective in a historical sense and against a scene of violence and power struggle in the age of gunpowder. The initial theme is violence, conflict, bloodshed and killing. Two deaths, one by gunfire, occur in rapid succession. Roque carries and depends on pistols as well as his sword to impose his will on others. Quixote's arms, by contrast, are a pathetic anachronism. The bandit captain is the only character in the story drawn from or according to the historical reality known and lived in by Cervantes. It is interesting to note that the idealized features of the fictional Roque—his dynamic personality, pride and arrogance, acute intelligence and chivalric generosity—make him a counterpart to Quixote's mythical attributes.

Roque Guinard, or (in Catalan) Perot Rocaguinarda, is known to have lived from 1582 to about 1630.[80] He has come down in history and legend as one of the most dashing figures of Catalan banditry in the years 1600–1615, a period in which civil disorder in rural areas of Catalonia was perpetuated by the infighting and rebellion of factions or bands ("*bandos*," hence "*bandoleros*," bandits). The two most important bands were the *niarros* and *cadells*. They controlled the countryside and villages, had allies and protectors in the cities and among the rural nobility and even clergy. Their chieftains controlled the roads to Barcelona, terrorized and extorted travellers, and defied the viceregal authority, threatening the capital itself. In December of 1613 one of these bands raided the royal caravan transporting a quantity of silver to Barcelona for shipment to Italy. In 1610 Rocaguinarda had led an attack up to the very gates of Barcelona. Moreover, their followers included many *Gascones* from across the border with links to the Huguenots who supported their rebellion against the Spanish crown. In 1614 Rocaguinarda's age would have been roughly 32 years. In that year, however, he would not have been a bandit leader in Catalonia. In that year he was already in Italy having agreed to give up his life of banditry for a pardon and service in the Spanish army based in Naples. The fact that he was no longer a menace to civil order and viceregal authority in Catalonia may explain why Cervantes could draw so favorable a picture of an outlaw. He was a popular or folk hero who had become legendary for his exploits.

When Quixote and Sancho find themselves prisoners of Roque Guinart, their story moves into the framework of historical experience. In Roque's company they learn of the outcome to a love story set in the violence and passion of the historical moment. The story of Claudia Jerónima and Don Vicente retraces the theme of separated lovers. In their story, the historical circumstance 'decides' the tragic outcome. They end up becoming lovers separated by death. In life they were separated by the hostility between their families, for they belonged to rival factions. Despite the enmity, he courted her and she, behind her father's back, agreed to be his wife. Yet their affair could not be normalized because of the warring between factions, and in this situation the false rumor that Vicente was to be married to another woman was enough to enflame Claudia with jealousy. In a burst of passion she put on a man's outfit complete with two pistols and a carbine and on horseback sought out Vicente and on the spot fired two or three bullets into him, to avenge her honor. Now she seeks out Roque for protection and aid to cross the border into France. Instead, Roque sets out with her to look for the wounded Don Vicente and they find him dying in his servant's arms. From him Claudia learns that the rumor of his infidelity was false; she has murdered her lover unjustly. He forgives her and with his dying breath takes her as his wife. Their love has become the victim of passion set to violence. Unlike Dorotea, who in Part I sought out Fernando under similar circumstances, Claudia eschewed reason and rushed to avenge herself violently. In a word, the historical situation of recourse to violence destroyed their love, his life and her future happiness. She will seek solace and penance for her guilt and grief in a convent. She expects her father to be threatened by avengers of Vicente and Roque promises to protect her family.

This story has taken place mostly out of sight, so to speak. Quixote and Sancho see almost none of it. They do not see the weeping scene, where the tragic edge of the outcome is driven home: Claudia bemoaning her rashness and Roque moved to tears. The reader does see it. The narrator discloses the full story so that we will get the full picture of Roque's and Claudia's character. When Roque returns to his men and Quixote pleads with him to give up such a risky and violent way of life, we recognize a variation of the technique in Part

I where he meets various and younger counterparts of himself (Chrysostom, Cardenio). But Roque is a complete contrast to Quixote. He is a man of action whose motives are dominance over others and vengeance. The only point of similarity between them insinuated is that providence may yet grant to both release from a way of life disruptive to the soul. Roque's greeting to Quixote seems to allude to a future cure, while Quixote's statement to the bandit captain seems to allude to the more honorable life the historical Roque found in Italy.

Quixote and Sancho look on with alarm, wonder and terror as Roque displays his traits as leader of a robber band. He has an instinct for leading and controlling violent men; his sense of justice plays off their greed and fear. When in a position to strip the group of travellers of all their money, he shows a calculated restraint and generosity. His victims' fear of losing all their money to him makes them grateful to submit merely to extortion. When Roque takes out his sword and with one blow splits the head of one of his men who grumbled in protest, and Quixote and Sancho witness bloodshed for the first time in the book, we ascertain that no fictional illusion, no literary device like hoax or deception, or comical irony, can detract from the stark brutality of a historical scene. No other plot is woven around Roque because none is necessary to depict his effectiveness in real life. He writes out a letter to his friend in Barcelona announcing Quixote's and Sancho's arrival there within four days and then himself conducts them through dangerous territory to a spot on the beach facing the city. Note that this letter to Don Antonio Moreno includes an endorsement of Quixote's mythical status and efficacy. On his authority as a real hero, and with no literary pretensions, Roque may claim that, for what Quixote represents, the spirit of Spanish chivalry incarnate in comical form, he is a mythical personage who may conciliate between the rival bands of Niarros and Cadells.

Quixote's decision to come to Barcelona (in Ch 59) was a display of his autonomy, like so many of his previous acts. But now Roque contrives to make his arrival there coincide with the festival of Saint John's day (June 24th), the midsummer festival that is in one sense a celebration of the summer solstice and in another a fertility ritual. With perfect timing he brings Quixote and Sancho to the beach at Barcelona and departs. The historical hero has conducted the fictional hero onto the time and space, the historical stage that will consummate his mythical depiction.

The image of Quixote and Sancho awaiting the sunrise over the sea is a counterpart to the image of their ride on Clavileño. The elements that fix the image of a mythical Quixote against the historical scene now appear one by one: the sunrise, the sea, the city, the fleet in the harbor, martial music, drums, trumpets and clarions, and volleys of artillery. The inhabitants of Barcelona have celebrated this feast day in a similar manner for centuries, but this day is special. At this point our illusion becomes Quixote's because, for once, there is no deception on the part of the narrator or surrogate authors. The sights and sounds of joyous celebration, display of flags and pennants, the mock artillery war, just happen to coincide with Quixote's arrival and welcome. Roque's friend and ally, Don Antonio Moreno, leading a group of horsemen in splendid outfits, rides up and greets him:

> —Bien sea venido a nuestra ciudad el espejo, el farol, la estrella y el norte de toda la caballería andante. . . . Bien sea venido, digo, el valeroso don Quijote de la Mancha: no el falso . . . sino el verdadero, el legal y fiel que nos describió Cide Hamete Benengeli, flor de los historiadores. II.61, 507

> —Welcome to our city, O mirror, beacon, and north star of all knight errantry. . . . Welcome, I say, the valorous Don Quixote de la Mancha: not the false one . . . but the true, legitimate and faithful one described to us by Cide Hamete Benengeli, flower of historians.

The formality, the refined ridicule concealed in exquisite courtesy, is a celebration of Quixote's own civility and his public image. The mock encomium identifies him as the 'historical' personage whose arrival the city of Barcelona celebrates. These scenes of arrival and welcome are the consummation of sensory illusion; the real or realistic festivities become a mock celebration. What Quixote perceives is a mock ovation but one confirmed by the senses, so his ride into the city must resemble a *via crucis*. The boys who shove briars under Rocinante's and Dapple's tails, so that they plunge violently and throw their riders to the ground, carry out the indispensable act of humiliation and derision amidst acclaim.

In Barcelona the demented hidalgo has stepped out of the pages of fiction in print into the historical life of his depiction, and of his readers. Disabled as a hero of action, he functions as a celebrity and laughingstock. The renown this exposure provides becomes a new expiatory trial. Readers of his book see him in shops, on balconies and on the street. He has lost the incentive for action, for adventure. What he sees and hears is depicted as experience in a historical setting. The experience confirms his illusion of course, but without the incentive to snatch (or, rather, imagine to snatch) a self-glorifying outcome from circumstance or fortune, experience cannot be translated into adventure. He is the victim of his illusion, yes, but his child-like innocence as much as his pride or vanity sustains him in his hour of public attention, triumph and derision.

And here again the narrator's techniques and strategy are pointed to the scale and objectivity of epic narrative. A balance is to be sustained between the subjectivity of Quixote's illusion and feelings and the breadth of the action that now swirls around him. In other words, Quixote's incentive must be borne forward by the actions of others, in order to produce the literary effect of objectivity commensurate with epic narrative. Roque entrusts him to his friend Don Antonio Moreno, a wealthy nobleman and representative of Barcelona's ruling class, who installs him and Sancho in his splendid house on one of the city's principal streets. Don Antonio is a model of civility, a refined aristocrat whose idea of amusement, nonetheless, is to put Quixote on display to throngs in the street. Under his auspices Quixote and Sancho now gain access to the higher circles of social life and move among noblemen and ladies who have, one may presume, both aristocratic connections and commercial interests. Don Antonio's motives are the "cause" behind the literary effect of objectivity, while Quixote's illusion, sustained through devices (rather than deeds), is the 'effect' that now bears the story out on a new mock epical and social scale.

Don Antonio's intentions seem honest and even humane. The amusement he wants is apparently not at the expense of Quixote's mortification. He intends no insult, no disrespect. His intention is to amuse himself and his friends "without prejudice or injury" (p. 509). Yet his first act is to put Quixote on display on a balcony. . . . So he, too, acts like a surrogate author. . . . The narrator's effect, the cold objectivity, is not to expose malice or cruelty (as in the case of the duke and duchess), but to point to the expiatory sense this treatment confers on Quixote. By putting him on public display in a manner that is both derision and acclaim, Don Antonio accomplishes explicitly and exquisitely a consummation of the narrator's various techniques. Or has the narrator seen fit to turn Quixote over to a kind of Pontius Pilate whose hands are washed clean? The impression is inescapable that to be mythical on the historical scene is a kind of expiatory trial, or that the mythical Quixote is a martyr (comically, we don't forget) to his own fiction.

The next day Don Antonio reveals to his guests and acquaintances a 'secret' plaything, an oracular or talking 'machine' (a head cast in bronze resembling a Roman bust) installed in a separate room of his home. His necromancer's secret works out to be his own version of hoax become (not adventure, Quixote attempts no action, but) experience. Is Don Antonio a kind of craftsman? Did he make the "oracular head," or did he have his servants make it? In any case, his technological artefact is meant to ridicule (like Cervantes' book) any notion of magic or 'black science' as cause and effect. But even a mock magician's artefact in 1614 is subject to the scrutiny of the Inquisition and this is the point of the outcome to the hoax, its historical point, so to speak, and why Don Antonio must dispose of it in the way he does. The head represents the 'state of the art,' or of technology, in contriving mechanical tricks. In this respect it is also quite revealing of Don Antonio's character. The "enchanted head" is a mock recreation of the epic hero's consultation with oracles, but what is truly epical about the episode is the picture of social and family life in a Barcelona household. Quixote and Sancho turn out to be the only ones deceived and victimized by the trick, for this is the point of the story. They must react as characters in it, while all others react to the talking head as characters out of a historical setting. Quixote's question to the head about Dulcinea's disenchantment reveals that his incentive for adventure has been reduced to this obsession.

Don Antonio's social life is typical of aristocratic society in the city and for its urbanity may be said to represent a level on the social scale where the bourgeoisie and the nobility coincide in their manner of life. At his residence Quixote and Sancho are treated to a round of social gatherings and from there venture out into the streets. Hidalgo and squire, their wants and illusion confirmed, put on their best social behavior. At a dinner with gentlemen friends, Quixote is treated as an honored guest and 'true' knight. The experience renders him "so puffed up and self-satisfied he could not contain himself" ("hueco y pomposo, no cabía en sí de contento," p. 509). What this treatment confirms is that the literary personage provides amusement so long as he performs like himself. One feels no consternation at this so long as one thinks only of the literary personage. Do these fine gentlemen have any sensibility for the real personality of their mad guest? That afternoon Don Antonio leads him out to the street with a party of horsemen. Quixote rides on a large mule, oblivious to the placard his host has ordered sewed to the back of his coat with the lettering: "This is Don Quixote de la Mancha," and is led through crowds on the street. The scene is like a flash back to the declaration before the four images of saints. How serious is the narrator's suggestion that Quixote is put on display, an object of ridicule and derision like a mock Christ, with an *Ecce homo* on his back, a Christ-like figure in a fool and madman? There are probably many precedents for this treatment in folk diversions and rituals with fools, scapegoats and even madmen. The narrator's comical objectivity is gained now much less at the expense of his character than of the fiction his character now incarnates. That evening the ladies of the group subject Quixote to the social ordeal of dancing, achieving a slightly different result in the hero's exhaustion.

Don Antonio prepares two more diversions, a tilting at the ring and the visit for Quixote and Sancho to the galleys anchored off the beach in the harbor. The first fails to materialize, the second develops into a full episode of action at sea. As the central episode of Quixote's visit to Barcelona, it is paradigmatic of adventure turned historical experience.

Hidalgo and squire are welcomed on board the general's flagship with ceremony and mock adulation. This and the sight of activity on board fills them with wonder and apprehension. Quixote is overwhelmed by the reception given his person by the general and the whole crew and Sancho marvels at the mass of men in rows, the galley slaves stripped to the waist. Suddenly, Sancho is seized by the head oarsman and is sent flying over their heads from bench to bench, down one side and up another. Two instances out of Part I are recalled. Quixote is confronted with galley slaves, like the ones he freed in chapter 22. Sancho is subjected to a scary prank like the blanketing he got on leaving the inn in chapter 16, while Quixote looked on. In Part I incidents unfolded according to an exemplary purpose of narrative. Here they serve to confirm the mythical status of the personage on board with his squire. Along the way the course of narrative mounted a Quixotic fiction on the exemplary story and the result is the mythical personage we witness now 'live' on a historical scene and epic scale. Quixote lacks initiative, but what initiative does a 'star' performer need? It is sufficient that he perform as himself. The flagship puts out to sea, powered by the straining oarsmen, who are lashed to fury by the boatswain. The sight provokes Quixote to think that lashes like these applied as effectively to Sancho could disenchant Dulcinea. At this point the action (the thread of story) veers.

15. Ricote and Ana Félix

An alarm from land rings out with the threat of a raid by Algerian corsairs. The lookout on land has sighted an enemy brigantine. The galleys give chase and when two Turks fire muskets and kill two soldiers on board the flagship they run down the intruder with vengeance. When the galleys return to port with their prize, the viceroy comes on board the flagship as the general is preparing to avenge the death of his two soldiers by hanging the brigantine's youthful, handsome captain. The youth, downcast, reveals that he is neither Muslim nor male but a Christian woman—a Morisca, exotic and beautiful. She pleads to be allowed to tell her 'story,' in a nearly hopeless plea for her life. Her presence—a woman in male disguise, an exotic heroine—now converts the episode of realistic action at sea into a contemporary (or historical) variation of Byzantine romance with its idealized figures, rare if not bizarre occurrences, concealed identities and marvels, and its own inner consistency of cause and effect. How can we explain Cervantes' purpose in developing this historico-romantic story within the central episode of Quixote's visit to Barcelona? Most tellingly in the structural relationship between the idealized figures in the story and a mythical Quixote.

No sooner does the woman end her story, with the plea to be allowed to die like a Catholic and Christian, than an aged pilgrim rushes forward from among the townspeople who came aboard with the viceroy and falls at her feet with sobs and sighs, having recognized her as his daughter: the heroine in male attire is Ana Félix; the old man in the pilgrim's dress who recognizes his daughter is Ricote, the Morisco; he turns to the viceroy and general to plead for her life. The scene is the dramatic recognition that reunites father and daughter.

What artistic instinct has guided Cervantes to retrace the narrative of a separation of a Muslim (Morisco) father and Christian daughter, the situation, we recall, at the center of the captive's narrative in Part I? There the exotic Moorish girl named Zoraida abandoned her father for the sake of a new life and faith in Christianity and escaped across the sea to Spain with the captive she liberated. Recall the moving, tragic scene where the father Agi Morato cries out his desolation to the waves. The two episodes are clearly and strategically paralleled, with as many points of contrast as of similarity. The scene of recognition is the point exactly opposite to that scene of separation. Like Zoraida, Ana Félix possesses a spiritual beauty and delicate femininity which in no way contradict her dominance over her lover, Don Gaspar Gregorio, a Christian and adolescent heir to an aristocratic title, who nonetheless is subject to her will and incentive. And like Zoraida (and all of Cervantes' idealized females), her virtue and chastity are all-but-inviolate. To her beauty and sexual attraction are added a superior intelligence to sustain her vitality. She is the idealized female who functions as effectively as a male in the perilous world of adventure. Her lover and betrothed is so completely dependent on her (his beauty so nearly feminine and she so protective of him as to shield him from the barbarous homosexuality of the Algerian king), the inversion of sexual roles is nearly complete. Yet having been taken prisoner, her plan to return to Spain and recover her father's treasure in order to rescue and ransom her lover has been frustrated and she faces death. But then, by providential design (the meaning of the otherwise implausible coincidences), she has been reunited with her father, who will now generously contribute from a nearly fabulous treasure an amount sufficient to ransom Don Gaspar. Their situation is also that of separated lovers, to be reunited now not exactly by her efficacious deed but by a more appropriate agent. Once Ana Félix is reunited with her father, the way is cleared (the design of providential cause and effect) for her life to be spared and for the rescue and liberation of her lover by the skill and courage of the renegade accompanying her. Ana Félix and Don Gaspar are the final pair of lovers grouped around Quixote's love for Dulcinea. They are a pair of 'separated lovers' happily reunited (recalling the pattern of stories in Part I), while Quixote's separation from Dulcinea is inevitable to the end of his fiction as knight. Since the full cast of paired lovers in the book has now emerged, we can conveniently plot it on Chart V, with a notation of their relationship to Quixote/Dulcinea. Also like the captive's narrative, Ana Félix's story is triangular (heroine, lover, father), because it combines the two principal structures of Byzantine romance: the separation (and reunion) of lovers and of offspring and parent. Finally, like Zoraida and Ruy Pérez, Ana

CHART V PAIRS OF LOVERS IN PART II

	Type of Narrative	Separated by...
Quixote—Dulcinea	ironical romance	her abduction
Knight of the Mirrors—Casildea de Vandalia	satire	her cruelty
Basilio—Quiteria	serious romance	her parents *reunited by his astuteness
Durandarte—Belerma	legend	his death
Gaiferos—Melisendra	myth and legend	her abduction *reunited by his valor and skill
Pierres—Magalona	myth and legend	*escape on magical horse
Clavijo—Antonomasia	mock legend	*redeemed by Quixote
Altisidora—Quixote	satire	his rejection hoax on her part
Claudia Jerónima—Don Vicente Torrellas	sentimental story	his death
Ana Félix—Don Gaspar Gregorio	serious romance	separated by exile *reunited by Providence

Félix and Don Gaspar move from the idealized plane of myth, romance and legend onto the problematic plane of contemporary life where their love becomes subject to the political barriers of class and race.

The whole then is a retracing in serious and idealistic narrative of a mythical and legendary pattern, alongside the comical and ironical depiction of Quixote as a 'historical' character, and with an ending that proposes or projects the reintegration of father and daughter into Spanish society on strictly historical terms. The pattern is exemplaristic in the way we find typical of Cervantes in the final years of his career as novelist or storyteller.[81] The movement in the pattern spells out the reintegration and redemption of expelled or renegade members by virtue of an expiatory act or agent. The feelings of benevolence and charity Ana Félix inspires in the viceroy and general who pardon and spare her any punishment promote the spirit of reconciliation between a people expelled from Spain and the established power of the Spanish monarchy. It is Ana Félix's good fortune to have come within the orbit of Quixote's experience, for it is his presence—his Quixotic benevolence and generosity—that promotes the spirit of political and civil concord, as Roque insinuated on announcing his arrival in Barcelona. Yet Ana Félix is deserving of compassion because her cause is more than just in political terms. She is one of perhaps many of her people who have been wronged most cruelly and unfairly by the order of expulsion because she feels and sees herself to be a loyal, believing and conforming Catholic. She pleads for herself as the innocent and dispossessed victim of a political decision. The law of expulsion disinherits her from both her homeland and her faith. Moreover, her Catholic belief is in her a triumph of conscience over race or blood. Her individual cause and plight arouse compassion and charity in representatives of the Christian majority like the viceroy and Don Antonio because her faith and innocence are the equal of her idealized beauty and discretion. On this basis, then, she may stand figuratively before a tribunal that dispenses not political but poetic justice. It is on the level of poetic justice then that we may assume Cervantes motivates the viceroy and Don Antonio to intervene with authorities in Madrid on her and her father's behalf for permission to remain in Spain, despite the implacable order against this laid down by the Count of Salazar. In this way Cervantes the author reconciles his (or Quixote's) fiction to the inexorable realities of political power.

Meanwhile preparations are made to rescue Don Gaspar from the harem in Algiers where at the risk of his life he is concealed as a beautiful girl. Quixote has gallantly and generously offered to go to Barbary and free him, but no one is disposed to even humor him in this illusion. The rescue operation led by the renegade sets out for Algiers. The historico-romantic episode is left in suspension. In the interval Quixote—the agent of reconciliation—meets head on an implacable adversary straight out of his fiction.

16. Knight of the White Moon

The shoreline where the city faces the sea is the precarious meeting ground of experience and myth, history and adventure, of commerce and conflict, of earth and the tides of war and peace. The narrator contrives that about the year 1614 two combatants in full chivalric armor, their lances lowered and pointed, charge at one another for real on the strand at Barcelona, in a scene archaic by at least a century. The scene would be implausible to contemporary witnesses except as a mock revival of chivalry in the spirit of the season, the festival of Midsummer.

Quixote rides out to the beach with Sancho, wearing his battered armor, and sights another knight, also in full armor, ride out of the city. The stranger approaches and brazenly cries out an arrogant challenge (in insolent tones and with the familiar *tú* as if he held a grudge against him). The stranger calls himself the "Knight of the White Moon," for the insignia on his shield.

The time and place, the how and why, of this encounter are a stroke of strategic staging on the part of the narrator, for now the climax of his story is staged to be *anti-*climactic. His story was consummated many episodes back in Quixote's illusion, in the ducal palace. Now in the Midsummer of his mythical depiction the narrator brings off the one scene rendered inevitable all along by his theme and yet consistently evaded by his techniques. By now in the story Quixote has become a 'historical' personage whose movements about Barcelona are public knowledge and diversion. On the strand, in full view of a 'reading public' and leading citizens of the city the literary and 'living' personage is unhorsed by the enigmatic stranger and disabled from further adventures. The timing is perfect (whatever our feelings) in every way. The hero, depressed by melancholy and made vulnerable by vainglorious pride (the epic hero's *hybris*), is ready and riding for a fall.

The reader, only half aware of this, is almost always shocked by the appearance of this knight, just as the inhabitants of Barcelona would have been. Who is he in disguise? Because his outfit must be a disguise, surely, or a costume. And how calculated, how arrogant, peremptory the challenge he hurls: —Take up your lance and fight me or confess that your Dulcinea is inferior to my mistress, whoever she may be . . . if I defeat you, I shall ask no other satisfaction than that you withdraw to your village for the period of one year and abstain from seeking any more chivalric adventures, . . . for this will contribute to the increase of your estate and assure the salvation of your soul. . . . A humiliating challenge under any conditions, more so because couched in terms to allay the fears of an old man who could not really put up a fight. Isn't it right out of the mouth of another surrogate author? Indeed, but one who looks toward the exemplary end beyond the hidalgo's demise.

Quixote overcomes his shock to reply in courteous terms to the gratuitous provocation. The image of Dulcinea is the soul of his illusion as knight, and of his fiction. He agrees to fight on the challenger's terms where they concern the supremacy of his lady. The challenger counted on this reaction, though he seems unaware the lady is enchanted. The viceroy is alerted and arrives to intervene and wants to stop the fight, either because it is illegal or because, if it is not a hoax, Quixote's chances don't look good. Concluding that the fight has to be a hoax, he allows the combat to take place. With no time to waste, the author's surrogate charges, collides with such force against horse and rider he brings both to the ground. He dismounts and stands over the fallen body:

> —Vencido sois, caballero, y aun muerto, si no confesáis las condiciones de nuestro desafío.
> Don Quijote, molido y aturdido, sin alzarse la visera, como si hablara dentro de una tumba, con voz debilitada y enferma, dijo:
> —Dulcinea del Toboso es la más hermosa mujer del mundo, y yo el más desdichado caballero de la tierra, y no es bien que mi flaqueza defraude esta verdad. Aprieta, caballero, la lanza, y quítame la vida, pues me has quitado la honra. II.64, 534

> —You are vanquished, knight, and a dead man, if you don't confess in accordance with the conditions of our challenge.
> Don Quixote, bruised and stunned, without lifting his visor and as though speaking from a tomb, said in a faint low voice:
> —Dulcinea is the fairest lady in the world, and I am the most unfortunate knight on earth, and it is not just that my weakness should discredit this truth. Drive, knight, your lance, and take my life since you have taken my honor.

The combat has been a no-contest and everything about it except the outcome as accepted by Quixote is a hoax perpetrated on the fiction of his chivalry. True to his word, the challenger demands only that Quixote withdraw to his village for the period of a year. Though the humiliation does not seem final, the hero's disablement is complete, for he gives his word not to attempt any more adventures. He has surrendered his freedom, if not his autonomy. The stranger provoked him to combat at an hour and place of his own devising, according to a formula we had come to expect from the narrator in the final phase: contrive appearances to conform to Quixote's illusion, he will respond accordingly, and the fiction of his chivalry will ride on. But in this case the surrogate acts to break Quixote's illusion by inflicting a physical defeat. So the hero is not only disabled from further adventures but defeated spiritually as well. This is the sense of those words he utters "as though speaking from a tomb." The deed was done in public, with the elite of Barcelona looking on. What then is the sense of the timing and the shattering of the viable formula?

Time and place have conspired to bring about the hero's defeat as an all-but-ritualistic act, performed on a historical stage, in full view of the public, at the moment or time of the festival of Midsummer. The two lines of narrative movement, the ascending line of his mythical depiction and the downward course of his fortunes, depression and pathological illusion, have converged. Now, precisely for this conspiracy and convergence certain effects and consequences are set in motion and confer on Quixote his final configuration. The narrator's strategy has accomplished something entirely unique and yet of course intrinsic to his story.

The strange knight disappeared into the city and the viceroy ordered Don Antonio to follow him and find out who he is. It could only be Samson Carrasco, the only adversary Quixote has faced or could face in the story. Having recovered from his first attempt and determined to avenge that failure and humiliation, Samson arrived on the scene with vengeance uppermost on his mind and carried out the deed with dispatch. This time he succeeds by brute force where before he relied on whim and neat strategy. So the hero is defeated and disabled by the false friend just when he and we least expected it, in the moment of illusory fulfilment of his self-image, and to our consternation. Will the hero's cure and return to sanity really follow, as expected by Carrasco?

The illusion that he submitted to chivalric combat and lost is sufficient to produce an indubious result on both the character and the fiction of his knighthood. The narrator's strategy has been to disable the hero by means that ensure he will fall a victim to his own illusion, to his fiction. His defeat is the next-to-last step in the process of his fictionalization. When he is knocked off Rocinante and falls to earth, Quixote brings down with him the weight of his 'mythical fame.' He falls, so to speak, as a sacrificial victim. But to what end? The ritualistic and sacrificial overtones are neatly insinuated by his challenger's enigmatic stance and outfit, this executioner directly out of the fiction itself.

Don Antonio's reaction, when he learns the truth of the hoax, discloses the new framework whereby the hero's defeat is reconciled implicitly to his mythical and pathological depiction: "—Dios os perdone el agravio que habéis hecho a todo el mundo en querer volver cuerdo al más gracioso loco que hay en él. No veis . . . que no podrá llegar el provecho que cause la cordura de don Quixote a lo que llega el gusto que da con sus desvaríos?" II.65, 536–7. [May God pardon you the injury you have done the whole world in your attempt to restore the most amusing madman to his senses. Don't you see . . . that no benefit to be derived from Don Quixote's recovery could outweigh the pleasure afforded by his extravagances?] The mythical figure of the mock knight survives in defeat; or, rather, from his defeat Quixote emerges a martyr to his fiction. Beatings, humiliations and derision have doubled as an expiatory trial to produce the paragon (not of chivalry, of course, but) of the process by which fiction conspires to bring into existence its most original creations, purifying them while conferring on them its own distinction. If there is one moment when the Quixotic hero can be said to emerge for the first time in the reader's mind as the autonomous and unique creature of universal literature, it is very likely this, the moment of his disablement and defeat. Let each reader answer for himself the question: does his defeat ennoble Quixote? The answer implies the narrator's formula and his timing were on target.

In the interval of his defeat and confinement to bed for six days the renegade and his band of rescuers have gotten to Algiers, rescued Don Gaspar and returned to Barcelona. The historical fiction has been the backdrop to Quixote's demise. A secondary character like the renegade is endowed with the skill, courage and efficacy to carry out an heroic feat over the sea, as an expiatory act that restores him to the true faith. His individual act of daring is not adventure but an act of historical meaning. Quixote's defeat is likewise a 'historical' act by virtue of its staging. Which is to say that now the mythical depiction of him is explicity 'historical'; his incentive no longer provokes or precipitates 'adventures.' Experience of historical events is what now overtakes him. This is the sense of the impending decision on whether Ana Félix and Ricote can remain in Spain. It is a political decision, of course, and looked at realistically the chances for them of a favorable decision from bureaucrats in Madrid are not good. But having come within the orbit of Quixote's mythical efficacy, their expectations can be lifted to the plane of idealistic and wishful outcome. One can envision an idealized Spain in which Ricote and his daughter would be permittted to live out their lives happily in their homeland, such is the reconciliatory power of the Quixotic myth.

17. The Winter of History   Chs 66–73

But defeat has disabled the hero from further adventures and true to his word he retires to his village for the period of a year. If at first he thought of his defeat as a temporary setback from which he could recover, it will be his own dejected spirit that will confirm its finality. A deepening gloom overtakes him from within even as the 'winter of history' overtakes the summer of his mythical depiction. The return to the village retraces in frustration and impotence the way to Barcelona; the way back is a penitential ordeal of a devastated illusion. His faith in himself is rapidly dissipating and with it the literary illusion of himself as knight. The final chapters retrace the return phase of the hero's going forth in heroic poetry with a new variation of what we may call the 'structure of separation' in Cervantes' narratives. The hero is to be separated from his illusion as from his fiction. This process and ritual begins when he takes off his armor and loads the pieces on Dapple's back, much to Sancho's consternation. The way back is a 'return to reality,' a ritual of penitential divestiture.

The 'structure of separation' has many variations in Cervantes' works and *Don Quixote* is of course the outstanding example of it, at both its close and its beginning. This structure now completes the cycle of the hidalgo's going forth—the separation from his 'true' or 'real' and sane self—and return by separating a defeated Quixote from his illusion and his fiction and restoring the 'real' man, thereby separating myth and fiction in the story from life and history. The defeated Quixote is divested of his illusion much as a returning hero divests himself, one by one, of his arms in defeat. But the ritual of divestiture is also Quixote's final purification that will end with the return to sanity and an exemplary death, and as such the ritual that invests him with a mythical permanence. The disabled, dejected and defeated hero is the historical figure, the martyr to the fiction. The hero of illusion, the mythical Quixote, will survive, but separated from the historical figure who must die in a time and place.

As the story approaches its ending the exemplary plan moves back to the center. The return to the village is the precondition for return to sanity. Quixote's psychological state is passive, melancholic and dejected. Also note that the main scenes of the action on the way home happen at night. Their effect is to recast the importance of the various nocturnal scenes in Part II (beginning with the scene outside

El Toboso), where Quixote's melancholy is decisive, to the course of the action. The final series of encounters on the road becomes symptomatic of withdrawal, depression and alienation moving to a crisis. He is not disposed to be sociable, not even with Sancho. He turns away from the villagers who request his intervention and can have no real interest in Tosilos who tells him of the outcome of the affair with Doña Rodríguez. Dulcinea's enchantment weighs on his spirit, not as a challenge he must meet, but as one more aggravation to bear. He cannot conceive, in his dejection, that an incentive on his part will liberate her. When they arrive at the site of the "feigned Arcadia" he recalls the pleasant life of shepherds, not the outcome of the frustrated adventure. For one last incident the 'pastoral' and 'chivalric' life styles meet and cross. Disabled from engaging in the latter, he contemplates the former as an alternative; he describes it rightly in terms of personal fulfilment, with hedonistic overtones. To begin with, he would assume a new variation of his name, *"Quijotiz,"* and Sancho, *"Pancino."* The acquisition of some sheep is as far as he goes in a materialistic sense. What he describes or, rather, contemplates is the essential paganism of an Arcadian life; a primitive state of emotion and conscience, without labor or trials, the elimination of any 'test.' They spend the night in this place; Quixote's sleep is cut short by his endemic insomnia and at this juncture the narrator reintroduces the motif of the epic hero's vigil (*'el desvelo del héroe'*);[82] Dulcinea's plight weighs on Quixote's mind as once before (Ch 60); he gazes down on Sancho, who snores away. This time he awakens Sancho to try to talk him into lashing himself. At this point they hear a deafening uproar that shakes the hillsides. A herd of swine driven to market overtakes and tramples them and their mounts, exactly as the herd of bulls had trampled them in the same location (Ch 58). The incident is a 'return to Arcadia.' Then Quixote had stood in the road to challenge the herdsmen and bulls. Now he accepts a swinish castigation for a hero disabled and defeated.

18. Return to the Palace

On the next evening they are intercepted by the horsemen sent out by the duke to seek out and capture them. Once more the duke intervenes to subject master and squire to a hoax of his own devising. The horsemen take them prisoners and return them forcibly to the palace. So, to their surprise, Quixote and Sancho find themselves back in the palace, subjected to a new 'hellish' experience, and deprived of all but their right to complain. What does the duke have in mind? Or, rather, what does the narrator have in mind? Why must the two return to the palace?

The duke's spectacular hoax is a display of funeral pomp with penitential and netherworld attributes. He knows that Dulcinea's enchantment and his defeat are on Quixote's mind, so to distract and exacerbate his hopeless condition, he has his servants prepare a hoax in which Quixote is made to look guilty for Altisidora's death while the power to resurrect her is attributed to his squire's 'virtue.' The hoax is the final twist to the theme of *'doncellas'* and repeats the formula for Dulcinea's disenchantment. The funeral pomp in which Sancho must participate is a restaging of various hoaxes carried out previously with their conceits (see pp. 186–7 above). Quixote's failing or guilt is to be atoned for by pain inflicted on Sancho's body. Quixote's cold disdain has caused Altisidora to die, the kings of the netherworld decree that she can be brought back to life if Sancho will submit to the ordeal of torturous slaps and pinching by duennas. Once more the duke and his cohorts carry out as surrogate authors a playacting that by its witty theme and structure mimics the epic design the narrator (or Cervantes as novelist) imputes to senseful social and psychological reality. The infernal ritual and castigation carry out a hoax version of the vexation and penitential trial that the hero's homeward journey has become. The insistance on Sancho's 'virtue' is a comical but still cruel way of divesting the hero of his role and of his illusion. Sancho submits to grotesque physical punishment but has nothing to gain by it. The disabled hero is subjected to the spiritual castigation of exclusion and impotence. Altisidora is most nearly in character when she turns on him with cruel and cutting insults and reveals her true feelings. The narrator through his surrogates means to convince that the return to the palace was necessary in order to recapitulate the themes of the hero's mortification and divestiture through penitential trials. The palace setting is funereal as if in mourning for the hero's defeat. The hero's *via crucis* is a way back to the village through 'historical' reality, a reality already devoid of the illusion of his invincibility. This helps explain why Altisidora (of all persons) brings up the subject of the 'apocryphal book' published by Avellaneda in 1614. She says she saw the devils in Hell kick apart a copy of this execrable book. The existence of the false version of himself as a 'historical' fact is one more vexation Quixote must endure.

19. Return to Village

Convinced he has witnessed the power of Sancho's 'virtue,' Quixote is now ready to effect Dulcinea's release by offering payment to Sancho for the lashes that should bring it about. The duke's hoax has served to motivate him to this decision, so we may suppose that this has been the purpose behind the forced return to the palace and its funereal and penitential setting. Between the palace and arrival back in the village Quixote is divested of the last shred of his efficacy, his illusion of Dulcinea. Payment for the lashes is the major concession that repeats the outcome of various adventures where payment for damages compromised or replaced Quixote's incentive and illusion. Now payment to Sancho brings the hope of Dulcinea's disenchantment down to the level of a grubby material interest. And of course a deception as outrageous as any Sancho has brought off before. On the first night after leaving the palace Sancho goes off to a clump of trees to thrash himself, while Quixote keeps count on his rosary of over a thousand lashes resounding through the night, until, overcome by what he supposes to be Sancho's unbearable torment, and fearing for his squire's life, he compels him to stop beating himself and goes to his aid; yet he never asks to see evidence of physical marks on Sancho's body even while helping to cover him with his cloak. It is Sancho's final deception and a complete victory on his terms over his master's illusion. One more scene of the same nature after they leave the inn will convince Quixote that sufficient lashes have been applied to disenchant his lady. He expects to come across her at any moment in her 'true' form. The illusion of Dulcinea fades away in his mind when she fails to materialize. Or, rather, with approaching sanity.

One final stop at an inn brings out the hidalgo's defensiveness as well as another side of Cervantes' contempt for the imitation by Avellaneda. Master and squire express a certainty about their literary immortality and originality when they compare themselves to characters in the *Iliad* and *Aeneid* depicted on tapestries hung on walls in their room in the inn, yet confronted with Don Alvaro Tarfe, the character introduced from Avellaneda's book, Quixote requests an affidavit signed by this character to the effect that he and Sancho are genuine, and the paltry characters in the false book a patent falsification. The narrator expects to fix on our minds the importance the two characters place an discrediting the apocryphal version of themselves. Divested of his own initiative, Quixote needs legal testimony to assert not just his mythical identity but his very autonomy as fictional being. The credence he gives to Sancho's hoax about thrashing himself and the insistence on a legal document to discredit the false version are acts of divestiture: material and historical reality have displaced illusion and initiative. The hero seems resigned to accept existence in the historical and material world on its own terms. Could he, we ask, take up the pastoral life with any meaningful aim, as he expects? As they approach the village, the ritual of divestiture portends the final separation of the mythical figure from the character who dies and remains enclosed within the story or book. "Don Quixote" will survive the character who on his death bed declares his true name to be Alonso Quixano.

Their last moments together on the road are the scene on the hilltop and Sancho's apostrophe and the scene with the hare pursued by hunters, two scenes along the thread of epic narrative. In his depression Quixote is disposed to 'read omens.' Structurally, this is the moment of final separation from Dulcinea and all that she means as ideal lady and illusion. He hears one of the boys say, "You'll never see her in all the days of your life," and then takes the hare, muttering to himself "*Malum signum!* . . . ," and concludes that he will never see his lady again. Dulcinea vanishes from the story at this point. He will mention her only once more, when he speaks of her as his future shepherdess, but then he transforms her into something like a nymph of the fields.

On entering the village they separate. They do not converse again until the hidalgo, having recovered his reason, dictates his will and Sancho hears that he will inherit a sum of money.

20. "The Christ of Fiction": Sanity and Death   Ch 74

To complete the pattern of the exemplary story, the narrator brings Quixote back to his village and home as the indispensable to his transformation back into a country hidalgo. Yet the final episode cannot be a simple return to sanity or clinical cure to his madness, but

The Mythical Don Quixote 257

the eventful integration of the character with his 'true' self that brings about the final separation of a fictional and mythical Quixote from the figure of the hidalgo who submits to the trial of an exemplary death. In other words, the close of the book is simultaneously a resolution to the exemplary story along clinical lines and a resolution to the Quixotic fiction brought about by the character's final autonomous and gratuitous act, his death. The character is figuratively crucified on his own fiction; transformed back into the hidalgo Alonso Quixano, his identity as "Don Quixote," the mythical figure, survives at his expense. The narrator concedes to his character both the triumph of his true self over error and madness and the triumph of his fictional self over humiliation and ridicule. The narrator disposes of his hero much as a "Christ of Fiction."[83]

His melancholy and depression at a point of crisis and his illusion expended, once past the threshold of his home (after the conversation on pastoral life with niece and housekeeper) the hero nearly collapses and requests he be put to bed at once. He never gets out of bed again. This time the period of rest and convalescence fails to produce recovery; instead a fever sets in lasting for six days and indicating a depleted body and spirit. The narrator attributes this first to nature and then to divine providence. It is one thing for the exemplary pattern to prescribe the hero's return to sanity, but another that return to sanity and reality should precipitate the character's death. In such a situation we shall have more than one 'cause' for his death. There is a 'clinical cause' and there is a 'literary cause.' The narrator must handle both because his purpose is to conclude with an account of the hidalgo's death as well as how Quixote's fame lives on.

His friends try to rouse him by inciting him to take up the shepherd's life, to no avail. They summon the doctor and his diagnosis confirms their worst fears. He warns the patient to look to the health of his soul because his condition is serious. The doctor's diagnosis points to the 'clinical cause': "Fue el parecer del médico que melancolías y desabrimientos le acababan" (587). [The doctor was of the opinion that melancholy and mortifications were putting an end to his life.] Is the calm resignation shown by the patient on hearing the gloomy diagnosis an indication of lingering madness or of approaching sanity? He wants to be left to sleep again. He requests to be left alone and falls asleep for more than six hours. On awakening he utters (before housekeeper and niece) the declaration that his reason is restored by divine mercy: "¡Bendito sea el poderoso Dios . . . !" [Blessed be almighty God . . . !]

He has recovered his reason and with it his true identity, and the obvious proof of this is that he sees and judges his life as depicted in the two parts of the book as madness. By exemplary design, then, the emergence, or re-emergence, of the 'true' self or character of the hidalgo has come about during the deep, deathlike sleep.

> Yo tengo juicio ya, libre y claro, sin las sombras caliginosas de la ignorancia, que sobre él me pusieron mi amarga y continua leyenda de los detestables libros de las caballerías. Ya conozco sus disparates y sus embelecos, y no me pesa sino que este desengaño ha llegado tan tarde, que no me deja tiempo para hacer alguna recompensa, leyendo otros que sean luz del alma. II.75, 587. [My mind is now clear and unfettered, without the misty shadows of ignorance which my bitter and continual reading of those detestable books of chivalry cast over my understanding. Now I see their folly and fraud, and my sole regret is that the discovery has come too late to amend my ways by reading others that would enlighten my soul.]

From depression and melancholy to an alert state of sanity and moral insight. The first test of how he faces reality is his accusation against books of chivalry. He castigates himself by abjuring them in the most explicit terms. Thus 'transformed' the character now 'takes charge' of the action. Note how he oversees all aspects of his dying. He faces his end as an act of supreme rationality and this becomes his new and final test as hero of the story. He has his friends summoned because he wants to make his confession and will.

> Dadme albricias . . . de que ya yo no soy don Quijote de la Mancha, sino Alonso Quijano, a quien mis costumbres me dieron renombre de *Bueno*. [I have good news for you . . . I am no longer Don Quixote of La Mancha, but Alonso Quixano, called for my way of life *the Good*.]

(The character himself, in an autonomous act, effects the separation of his 'true' self from the fictional Quixote.)

> Ya soy enemigo de Amadís de Gaula y de toda la infinita caterva de su linaje; ya me son odiosas todas las historias profanas del andante caballería; ya conozco mi necedad y el peligro en que me pusieron haberlas leído; ya, por misericordia de Dios, escarmentado en cabeza propia, las abomino. 588. [Now I am the enemy of Amadís of Gaul and all his innumerable progeny; now all histories of chivalry are abhorrent to me. I now realize my folly and deception and the danger of reading them; now, by God's mercy, I have learnt from my bitter experience, and I abominate them.]

The 'autonomous character' launches a bitter attack on books of chivalry, denouncing them with the conviction of reason and experience and in such explicit terms that one must conclude that his outburst is the source of the censure applied to these books by the narrator throughout the story and by the author in the Prologue to Part One. This is an important aspect of his death as both an exemplary and an expiatory act. "Don Quixote," the fictional self, has been committed to the world of illusion and deception. So now it is the hidalgo himself who thus authenticates the author's thesis of censure and attack on "the abominable books of chivalry." And he rejects any plea from his friends to take up the pastoral life because it too is illusion taken from books and a literary deception. The hidalgo, as reintegrated self, now displaying the greatest rationality and inner illumination, completes in this exemplary manner the sense of a penitential trial and inner purification which the story assumed in its final phase at the hands of narrator and surrogates.

He 'takes over' the story in order to end it. And its close must be his death as expiation. But to what end? On the one hand, he 'must die' in order to complete the exemplary story, in order to effect its closure according to clinical and natural cause. On the other, the character must die according to a 'literary cause' in order to effect the separation of Don Quixote the mythical figure from Alonso Quixano who departs from this world. Yet his death is 'without cause,' his final gratuitous act as the book's hero, "No se muera vuestra merced, señor mío, sino tome mi consejo, y viva muchos años"—Sancho's last words to him bear out the gratuitous nature of his dying—"porque la mayor locura que puede hacer un hombre en esta vida es dejarse morir, sin más ni más, sin que nadie le mate, ni otras manos le acaben que las de la melancolía" (589). [Don't die; but take my advice and live on for many a year; the maddest thing a man can do in this life is to let himself die just like that, without anybody killing him, but just finished off by his own melancholy.]

His death is not 'by necessity'; it is not needed to bring about the story's end, even less to underscore the satirical attack on books of chivalry. As the final twist to the exemplary story, Alonso Quixano the Good allows himself to die, ostensibly as an act of penitential mortification for his error. Yet, by this action his fictional self as "Don Quixote" assumes its permanence as literary illusion. He replies to Sancho and Carrasco, who attempt to arouse him back to illusion, to life: "—Señores, . . . vámonos poco a poco, pues ya en los nidos de antaño no hay pájaros hogaño. Yo fui loco, y ya soy cuerdo: fui don Quijote de la Mancha, y soy agora, como he dicho, Alonso Quixano el Bueno." [Go softly, sires, for in last year's nests there are no birds of this year. I was mad, but I am now in my senses; I was once Don Quixote of La Mancha, but I am now, as I said before, Alonso Quixano the Good.]

His will is the prosaic 'text' that closes the story. The notary who takes it down is an outsider among the group at the bedside. His presence is needed for both legal and literary reasons to record the death (Yet he mis-records it!). The first item in the will clears up the question of money unpaid to Sancho, who will be allowed to keep whatever amount he has in his possession. By design and the character's intent, his will is a prosaic antithesis to the poetic illusion released and consumed in Quixote's chivalry. Recall those poetic outbursts with which he apostrophized the sun, his lady Dulcinea, and the historian of his exploits, on beginning his first outing. His will is an expiatory text of self-purification and must include a final denunciation of books of chivalry. So it includes the provision that his niece will lose her inheritance should she choose to marry a man known to have any knowledge of books of chivalry. The condemnation of books of chivalry would seem to exclude any notion that the character (or author) still thought of imitating them. He denounces them in his will and almost with his last breath.

> En fin, llegó el último de don Quijote, después de recebidos todos los sacramentos y después de haber abominado con muchas y eficaces razones de los libros de caballerías. [Death came at last for Don Quixote, after he had received all the sacraments and once more, with forceful arguments, had expressed his abomination of books of chivalry.]

Quixano's death is meant to be exemplary in the Christian sense, since the last sacraments are administered to him by the priest. So why does the notary who is again at the bedside compare his peaceful death to what was never depicted in books of chivalry? And why does he, like the narrator, still call him "Don Quixote"? With the notary's remark the author and narrator compliment themselves through a surrogate on having surpassed in verisimilitude, technique and much else those "detestable" books of chivalry.

Quixano's death gives the supreme lie to books of chivalry. His fictionalization is complete. However exemplary as story or real life, we perceive two sides to this sacrificial death because we are dealing not with real life but with fiction. The fictional and illusory Don Quixote is rejected, sacrificed to the mental and spiritual well-being of Alonso Quixano the Good, who dies a Christian and exemplary death. But this man gives up, sacrifices, his earthly existence as an expiatory act to discredit what his madness perpetrated as illusion and fiction. The death of Alonso Quixano the Good in the time and place of story perpetuates the existence of Don Quixote the mythical entity and celebrity whose fame the narrator apostrophizes to the very close of his book.

> Hallóse el escribano presente, y dijo que nunca había leído en ningún libro de caballerías que algún caballero andante hubiese muerto en su lecho tan sosegadamente y tan cristiano como don Quijote; el cual, entre compasiones y lágrimas de los que allí se hallaron, dio su espíritu, quiero decir que se murió. [The notary who was present said that he had never read in any book of chivalry that any knight-errant had died in bed as peacefully and in so Christian a manner as Don Quixote, who, amid the tears and lamentations of those present, gave up the ghost, that is to say, died.]

The hero expires, in the style of his narrative, at the end of a self-conscious and forced phrase recording the notary's remark. The "final indignity" Cervantes cruelly inflicts on his hero, according to Borges.[84] But no death by 'literary cause' could be otherwise. Quixano dies in this exemplary manner so that the fame of Don Quixote can live on intact in its proper sphere, the world of fiction.

Notes and References

Quotations from the Spanish text of *Don Quijote* are from my version of the first editions, Part I, 1605, Part II, 1615, published by Editorial Castalia, Madrid, 3rd ed., 1983, 3 Vols. References are to Part or Volume, chapter, and page: I. 2, 30. The English translations are my own.

Since my study is meant to serve as a companion to my edition with its annotation and classified bibliography, to 1980, this portion will include only those notes and references I consider indispensable for readers (English or Spanish) who do not have access to my edition and/or, moreover, wish to have a basic guide to criticism to 1986 on Cervantes and his masterpiece. I refer below to materials listed in my Bibliography (Vol. 3) with the number assigned there, e.g., B 039.

My initial listings are divided into sections: A. Of biographies of Cervantes in Spanish the most readable is still the rather dated one by Miguel Santos Oliver, *Vida y semblanza de Cervantes* (Barcelona: Montaner y Simón, 1916; re-edited by J. Givanel Mas, 1947). Likewise, the older scholarly biography by James Fitzmaurice-Kelly is in some respects the most authoritative and convenient, in the Spanish version (Oxford, 1917). The specialist on Cervantes must rely on the rambling one by Luis Astrana Marín, B 039. Three excellent biographies in English are available, by Richard L. Predmore (London: Thames and Hudson, 1973), William Byron (New York: Doubleday, 1978) and Melvenna McKendrick (Boston: Little, Brown, 1980).

B. *Don Quijote* is available currently in several English translations, listed here by translator (and publisher): Samuel Putnam (Modern Library, 1949), J. M. Cohen (Penguin, 1950), Walter Starkie (Signet Classics, 1964). The Motteux translation (1700–3) is probably the best of the 18th-century translations and the Ormsby (1885) the best of the 19th century. The latter has been edited and revised recently by Joseph R. Jones and Kenneth Douglas as a Norton Critical Edition (1981). A discussion of English translations recommended for teachers and students is available in the volume edited by R. Bjornson, cited below.

C. Two studies of a basic, introductory nature appeared recently: Richard Bjornson, ed., *Approaches to Teaching Cervantes' Don Quixote* (hereafter *ATC*), published by the Modern Language Association (New York, 1984) in its series "Approaches to Teaching Masterpieces of World Literature," a survey of primary (texts, translations) and background materials and of contemporary critical and teaching approaches, with short articles by contributors; and the study by E. C. Riley, *Don Quixote* (Unwin Critical Library: Allen & Unwin, 1986), a detailed introduction along the lines of a topical discussion of literary background, characters and structure, rather than a unified analysis of story. Both provide a selective bibliography.

Other book-length studies on a particular theme: John C. Weiger, *The Individuated Self: Cervantes and the Emergence of the Individual* (Ohio UP, 1979); —*The Substances of Cervantes* (New York: Cambridge UP, 1985). Walter Reed, *An Exemplary History of the Novel, The Quixotic Versus the Picaresque* (U of Chicago P, 1981). Alexander Welsh, *Reflections on the Hero as Quixote* (Princeton UP, 1981). Ruth El Saffar, *Beyond Fiction; The Recovery of the Feminine in the Novels of Cervantes* (U of California P, 1984). Edwin Williamson, *The Halfway House of Fiction: Don Quixote and Arthurian Romance* (Oxford: Clarendon, 1984), a doctoral dissertation expanded to an "intertextual" study.

D. Anthologies of critical articles. Some of the best criticism on *Don Quixote* is available in collections or anthologies. The following list is limited to standard items or recent publications not listed by Riley or Bjornson (*ATC*, 17-20). I have assigned an acronym to those I refer to in my Notes.

Lecciones Cervantinas, ed. Aurora Egido. Zaragoza: Caja de Ahorros y Monte de Piedad, 1985.

El Quijote *de Cervantes*, ed. George Haley. Madrid: Taurus, 1980 [1984]. Serie el Escritor y la Crítica. QC

Cervantes: su obra y su mundo. Actas del I Congreso Internacional sobre Cervantes, Madrid, 1978, ed. Manuel Criado de Val. Madrid: Edi-6, 1981. COM. The contents of this volume (more than 100 papers) have not been classified in any standard bibliography.

Cervantes and the Renaissance. Papers of the Pomona College Cervantes Symposium, 1978, ed. Michael D. McGaha. Easton, PA: Juan de la Cuesta Monographs, 1980. CR

Suma Cervantina, ed. Juan Bautista Avalle-Arce and E. C. Riley. London: Tamesis, 1973. SC

Cervantes, A Critical Trajectory, ed. Raymond E. Barbera. Boston: Mirage, 1971.

Cervantes, A Collection of Critical Essays, ed. Lowry Nelson, Jr. Englewood Cliffs: Prentice-Hall, 1969. CEN

Cervantes Across the Centuries, ed. Angel Flores and M. J. Benardete, New York: Dryden, 1947; Repr. Gordian, 1969. CAC

Cervantes, Bulletin of the Cervantes Society of America. 1981–. Published twice yearly. CB

Notes

[1] It is usual to translate *hidalgo* as "gentleman," i.e., a member of the gentry or landowning class. But the word is listed in Webster ("a Spanish nobleman of the lower class," —as is *Morisco*, see p. 221 above), so I consider that its use in English is acceptable. The *h* in Spanish, however, is never pronounced.

[2] "He had reached the zenith of his skill as an exemplary novelist when he sat down to write *Don Quixote*, and what he had in mind to write was, in the first instance, an exemplary novel," the British scholar William J. Entwistle on "Cervantes the exemplary novelist," *Cervantes* (Oxford: Clarendon, 1940), p. 101.

[3] In his *Die Theorie des Romans* [1920] (*The Theory of the Novel*, B 146) the Hungarian writer Georg Lukács enshrined *Don Quixote* as the archetypal work of its kind, and alongside the great epic poems of antiquity. For a more recent presentation see Frederick R. Karl, "Don Quixote as archetypal artist and *Don Quixote* as archetypal novel," ch 1, *The Adversary Literature* (New York: Farrar, Straus and Giroux, 1974), and materials listed under B 301.

[4] Cervantes' own presumed 'theory' has been studied by E. C. Riley whose earlier book (*Cervantes's Theory of the Novel*, B 108) has been replaced by his new study as well as by his "Cervantes: a Question of Genre" in *Medieval and Renaissance Studies on Spain and Portugal in Honour of P. E. Russell* (Oxford, 1981), 69–85; in Spanish, QC, 37–51.

[5] A good introduction to *romance* is Northrop Frye, *The Secular Scripture, A Study of the Structure of Romance* (Harvard UP, 1976); also Ben Edwin Perry, *The Ancient Romances, A Literary-historical Account of Their Origins* (U of California P, 1967).

[6] See my Bibliography, entries 150–159.

[7] Scholarship on the Arthurian materials is extensive. For one unfamiliar with them a good introduction is Roger Sherman Loomis, *The Development of Arthurian Romance* (London: Hutchison Univ Library, 1963). Loomis is also the editor of the standard reference work: *Arthurian Literature in the Middle Ages: A Collaborative History* (Oxford: Clarendon, 1959), with separate articles on Arthurian influence in Italy and Spain. The older study by W. P. Ker is also important, *Epic and Romance, Essays on Medieval Literature* (New York: Dover, 1957). More recently: Norris J. Lacy, ed., *The Arthurian Encyclopedia* (New York & London: Garland, 1985).

[8] See the article on Chrétien de Troyes by Jean Frappier in the volume edited by R. S. Loomis and the study by Loomis *Arthurian Tradition and Chrétien de Troyes* (Columbia UP, 1949).

[9] Consult the article by Jean Frappier in the volume edited by Loomis or the *Encyclopedia* edited by Lacy.

[10] See Daniel Eisenberg, *Romances of Chivalry in the Spanish Golden Age* (Newark, Del.: Hispanic Monographs, 1982), chs 1 and 5.

[11] See my article, "*Lanzarote* and *Don Quijote*," *Folio, Papers on Foreign Languages and Literatures*, n. 10, September 1977, 55–68.

[12] Also missing conspicuously are works of moralistic and devotional content which formed the mass of output from Spanish presses in the 16th century.

[13] The Spanish scholar Ramón Menéndez Pidal mistakenly attributed the 'genesis' of *Don Quixote* to influence of an anonymous theatrical piece called "*El entremés de los romances*" ("Interlude of Ballads," see Entwistle, *Cervantes*, pp. 104–5) in which a peasant named Bartolo goes mad from reading ballads. The similarities between this piece whose character 'reads' verse and Cervantes' story (I. 5) lead one to conclude that the anonymous author imitated Cervantes. See my article "Cervantes y *El entremés de los romances*", *Actas del VIII Congreso de la Asociación Internacional de Hispanistas* [1983], ed. A. David Kossoff et al. (Madrid: 1986), II, 353–7.

[14] The strategic importance of this ballad as of other Arthurian motifs was pointed out by Wm. J. Entwistle in the pioneering study, *The Arthurian Legend in the Literatures of the Spanish Peninsula* ([1925] Repr., New York: Phaeton, 1975), 250–52.

[15] This is the title on the title-page and the title used by Cervantes in his dedication to the Duke of Béjar and elsewhere. In the first edition of 1605 a shortened title "*El ingenioso hidalgo de la Mancha*" appears in the *Tasa* and Royal Privilege and is explicable as an erroneous or unconscious omission on the part of officials who perhaps found it offensive to their tastes to include such a comical name as "Don Quixote" in their official documents.

[16] On the "extrafictional structures, title(s), prologue," etc., see James A. Parr, "Extrafictional point of view in *DQ*," *Studies on* Don Quixote *and Other Cervantine Works*, ed. Donald W. Bleznick (York, South Carolina, 1984), 20–30.

[17] The importance of these theories for Cervantes was laid down by the Spanish priest and scholar Mauricio de Iriarte in the 1930's, B 401. They formed no part of the arguments of either Américo Castro (*El pensamiento de Cervantes*, 1925) or Ramón Menendez Pidal ("The genesis of *DQ*", 1920), and were made current in contemporary criticism by the American scholar Otis H. Green, "El *Ingenioso* hidalgo," *Hispanic Review*, 25 (1957): 175–193. My discussion is based on Iriarte and Green; the description quoted is from Iriarte's book, p. 321, cited below.

[18] See George M. Foster, "Humoral pathology in Spain and Spanish America," *Homenaje a Julio Caro Baroja* (Madrid, 1978), 357–378.

[19] See Iriarte's book in its definitive form: *El doctor Huarte de San Juan y su* Examen de ingenios; *contribución a la historia de la psicología diferencial*, (3rd ed., Madrid, 1948), pp. 311–332. A parallel discussion is available in Lawrence Babb, *The Elizabethan Malady, A Study of Melancholia in English Literature from 1580 to 1642* (Michigan-State UP, 1965).

[20] The 'clinical' interpretation of Quixote and other Cervantine characters began in the 19th century. The earlier theories and interpretations as well as more recent ones were summarized by Antonio Vallejo Nágera, *Apología de las patografías cervantinas* (Madrid, 1958). See B 405–408. Two recent studies have expanded on psychoanalytical theory: Louis Combet, *Cervantès; ou, les incertitudes du désir, une approache psychostructurale de l'oeuvre de Cervantès* (Lyon: Presses Universitaires, 1980) and Carroll B. Johnson, *Madness and Lust, A Psychoanalytical Approach to* DQ (U California P, 1983). See also Johnson's "Psychoanalysis and *Don Quixote*," *ATC*, 104–112.

[21] B. J. Logre, "La folie de Don Quichotte," *Ouest-Medical* (Paris), 9 (1956): 761–7.

[22] The *converso* question has figured largely in Américo Castro's writings on Spanish social and intellectual history and his interpretation of *Don Quixote*, see B 183. Castro's concepts have been refined and brilliantly applied by Francisco Márquez Villanueva, e.g., "Jewish 'fools' of the Spanish fifteenth century," *Hispanic Review*, 50 (1982): 385–409.

[23] See my article "La espada de don Quijote," *COM*, 667–680.

[24] Martín de Riquer, "Don Quijote, caballero por escarnio," *Clavileño*, 7, n. 41: 47–50

(1956); "Introducción a la lectura del *Quijote,"* v. I, ed. Labor (Barcelona, 1967). On Cide Hamete see B 420–424.

25 Chrysostom-Marcela is a 'case' of unrequited love of the kind treated by Cervantes in his pastoral romance *First Part of Galatea* (1585), but reduced to its novelistic essentials, including elegiac, funereal and nocturnal aspects. See also A. Solé Leris, *The Spanish Pastoral Novel* (Boston: Twayne, 1980), ch 4.

26 A segment of contemporary criticism has made much of the comic and "funny book" aspect, attempting to explain a many-sided work by the application of a single critical idea. Cervantes' book is of course a burlesque and a "funny book" but one that challenges the critic to fathom, if not its 'codes', its 'structures', whether the approach is historical, pragmatic or anything else. Moreover, the "funny book" approach is discernible, within the European scene, as a peculiarly British approach to *DQ* in line with a pragmatic tradition skeptical of Continental ideas and theories, e.g., Anthony J. Close, *The Romantic Approach to* Don Quixote (Cambridge UP, 1978).

27 As Sancho's role becomes more prominent his personal characteristics begin to develop with a comical force of their own. He has just uttered his first proverb, at the close of the preceding episode. His linguistic characteristics are probably the most original feature about him. See B 410–419 and R. M. Flores, *Sancho Panza through Three Hundred Seventy-five Years of Continuations, Imitations and Criticism, 1605–1980* (Newark, Del.: Hispanic Monographs, 1982); Monique Joly, "Le discours métaparémique dans *DQ" Richesse du proverb*, Vol. 2, eds., F. Suard & C. Buridant (Lille , 1984), 245–260.

28 See Peter N. Dunn, *The Spanish Picaresque Novel* (Boston: Twayne, 1979) chs. 3 and 5; "Cervantes de/reconstructs the picaresque," *CB*, 2 (1982): 109–31. 'Cervantes and the picaresque' is a subject not yet fully treated in contemporary criticism. Cervantes depicted or created more picaresque characters and types than all other authors of his time combined, yet eschewed for any but one (a dog) the autobiographical form considered indispensable to the genre.

29 See Karl-Ludwig Selig, *"Don Quixote* and the exploration of (literary) geography," *Revista Canadiense de Estudios Hispánicos*, 6 (1982): 341–357.

30 See my study, *The Golden Dial, Temporal Configuration in* DQ, (Oxford: Dolphin, 1975), 131–9 and notes, and Richard Bernheimer, *Wild Men in the Middle Ages* (New York: Octagon Books, 1970).

31 See notes to my ed. (I. 23, 278–80) and R. M. Flores, "The loss and recovery of Sancho's ass. . . ," *Modern Language Review*, 75 (1980): 301–310.

32 The immediate precedent was his own *Galatea*; now, for the comical presentation of an exemplary subject (Quixote's madness), the strategy becomes self-conscious in the artistic sense.

33 The 'interpolated' narratives have been best studied from the comprehensive approach: Raymond L. Immerwahr, "Structural symmetry in the episodic narratives of *DQ I" Comparative Literature*, 10 (1958): 121–35; Américo Castro, "Incarnation in *DQ,"* *CAC*, 146–188.

34 Francisco Márquez Villanueva, "Amantes en Sierra Morena," *Personajes y temas del Quijote* (Madrid: Taurus, 1975), 40–41.

35 John J. Allen, "The providential world of Cervantes' fiction," *Thought*, 55 (1980): 184–195. Javier Herrero, "Sierra Morena as labyrinth: from wildness to Christian knighthood," *Forum for Modern Language Studies*, 17 (1981): 55–67.

36 The concept of 'Carnival' was introduced into contemporary Cervantean criticism by way of the theories of Mikhail Bakhtin in the 1970's, but the concept had been studied before in folklore and anthropology by various Spanish specialists, e.g., Julio Caro Baroja, *El Carnaval* (Madrid, 1965) and applied to *Don Quixote* by Arturo Marasso (see Note 51 below); Manuel Durán, "El *Quijote* a través del prisma de Mikhail Bakhtin: carnaval, disfraces, escatología y locura," *CR*, 71–86; Augustin Redondo, "El personaje

de don Quijote: tradiciones folklórico-literarias, contexto histórico y elaboración cervantina," *Nueva Revista de Filología Hispánica* 29 (1980): 36–59.

37 See Eduardo Urbina, "Sancho Panza y Gandalín, escuderos," *CR* 113–124.

38 The immediate precedent and counterpart is an episode in Jorge de Montemayor's pastoral romance *La Diana* (1559), i.e., "palacio de la sabia Felicia". See Juan Bautista Avalle-Arce, "The *Diana* of Montemayor: tradition and innovation," *PMLA*, 74 (1959): 1–6. In this episode pagan and Christian doctrines and the medieval motif of a pilgrimage to a magical and paradisiacal place are combined with the motifs and figure of the priestess, fay or goddess of Love and her palace, garden or isle (*Venusberg*), the 'Temple of Diana', and others. Cervantes has called attention to this episode in the curate's reference to Felicia's magical philter, I. 6, 118.

39 On these sources see Juan Bautista Avalle-Arce, "El cuento de los dos amigos," *Deslindes cervantinos* (Madrid: Edhigar, 1961), 163–235.

40 The two *novelas* have been edited by Frank Pierce with introd. and notes, *Two Cervantes Short Novels* (Oxford: Pergamon, 1970).

41 The captive's tale has sources in legend, folklore and history. J. M. D. Ford pointed out Italian accounts by Christians taken captive by corsairs, "Plot, tale, and episode in *DQ*" *Mélanges . . . offerts à M. Alfred Jeanroy* (Paris: Droz, 1928), 311–323; 317. Francisco Márquez Villanueva has uncovered and analyzed the most important sources in legend and history, *Personajes y temas*, 92–115.

42 See my article "Cervantes' *Tale* of the captive captain," *Florilegium Hispanicum, Medieval and Golden Age Studies presented to Dorothy Clotelle Clark*, ed. John S. Geary (Madison, 1983), 299–343, and B 472.

43 *Los baños de Argel* ("The Bagnios of Algiers"), see Entwistle, *Cervantes*, pp. 22–5; Jean Canavaggio, *Cervantès dramaturge* (Paris: Presses Universitaries de France, 1977), 73–6.

44 The 'perspectivist' view of Zoraida and her motives taken by Leo Spitzer (and others) is flawed because not based on an assessment of the historical/legendary sources behind the plot and characters, *Linguistics and Literary History* (Princeton UP, 1948), 67–8.

45 See my article, "El *Ur-Quijote*, nueva hipótesis," *CB*, 1 (1981): 43–50.

46 On this aspect of Renaissance poetic theory see Alban K. Forcione, *Cervantes, Aristotle and the Persiles* (Princeton UP, 1970), ch 3; also E. C. Riley, *Don Quixote*, ch 6.

47 See my introd. to Part II for a fuller discussion.

48 No one has stated this better than Thomas Mann in his famous essay "Voyage with *Don Quixote*:" "I know nowhere else in literature where the hero of a novel lives on his own fame, as it were upon the reputation of his reputation," *CEN*, p. 55.

49 Raymond R. MacCurdy and Alfred Rodríguez, "An archetypal factor in the enchantment of Dulcinea," *Revista de Estudios Hispánicos*, 14 (1980): 73–80; Carroll B. Johnson, "A second look at Dulcinea's ass," *Hispanic Review*, 43 (1975): 191–8.

50 The essay by Erich Auerbach on this episode in *Mimesis, The Representation of Reality in Western Literature* (Princeton UP, 1953), is one of the more overrated pieces of Cervantean criticism. It was, moreover, an afterthought added to his book. More relevant on the relationship of story to structure is Cesare Segre, "Rectilinear and spiral constructions in *DQ*," *Structures and Time* (U of Chicago Press, 1979), 161–196.

51 Noted by Arturo Marasso in one of the most original scholarly-artistic works on *DQ*: *Cervantes, La invención del* Quijote (Buenos Aires: Hachette, 1954), pp. 111–114.

52 Don Diego has been analyzed as closely as any character in fiction, B 480. Márquez Villanueva has done a brilliant scholarly analysis of him from which I have drawn several ideas, "El Caballero del Verde Gabán y su reino de paradoja," *Temas y personajes*, 147–227. For another opinion see John Weiger, *Cervantes and the Individuated Self*.

⁵³ See Marcel Bataillon, *Erasmo y España* (Mexico City: Fondo de Cultura Económica, 1966), pp. 792-5.
⁵⁴ Márquez Villanueva, 169.
⁵⁵ Márquez Villanueva, 186.
⁵⁶ See B 481. The role(s) animals play in the story and their motifs deserve a separate 'structuralist' study; dogs are noticeably absent.
⁵⁷ On ballet versions, *ATC*, 31, 180; Víctor Espinós, *El* Quijote *en la música* (Barcelona, 1947).
⁵⁸ See the article by Avalle-Arce and Riley in *SC*, 47 ff. Critical commentary on the cave episode is of course extensive, B 483.
⁵⁹ See the study by W. F. Jackson Knight, *Vergil, Epic and Anthropology* (London: George Allen & Unwin, 1967), Part II, *Cumaean Gates*, originally published in 1936 (Oxford: Basil Blackwell).
⁶⁰ On Cervantes' sources in Spanish epic poetry see my article, "Don Quixote as Renaissance epic," *CR*, 51-70, 65. The initiation theme has been studied by Augustin Redondo but without reference to the epic tradition of the cave and underworld, "El proceso iniciático en el episodio de la cueva de Montesinos del *Quijote*," *COM*, 749-766; *Iberoromania*, 13 (1981): 47-61.
⁶¹ *Sergas de Esplandian*, B. A. E., v. 40 (Madrid, 1963), chs 48 & 49. The similarity was first noted by Clemencin, ed. *Don Quijote*, IV, (1835), Commentary to ch 23, note 4. The similarity to *Espejo de Príncipes* (*El Caballero del Febo*) was first noted to my knowledge by Maxime Chevalier, *L'Arioste en Espagne* (Bordeaux, 1960), 458-9.
⁶² See my article, "Don Quijote as Renaissance epic," *CR*, p. 67.
⁶³ "*Paciencia y barajar*" (literally "Patience and shuffle the cards") and "*Cepos quedo*" ("Go slow") are expressions of card playing with a special sense in the underworld. "Cards and dice have a natural connection with themes of descent into a world of fatality . . .", Northrop Frye, *The Secular Scripture*, p. 156.
⁶⁴ George Haley, "The narrator in *DQ*: Maese Pedro's puppet show," *Modern Language Notes*, 80 (1965): 145-165; in Spanish, *QC*, 269-87.
⁶⁵ *The Golden Dial*, p. 148.
⁶⁶ The mythical and ritualistic sense of the beatings was enlarged on by Thomas Mann, *CEN*, p. 61.
⁶⁷ See Monique Joly, *La Bourle et son interpretation. Recherches sur le passage de la facetie au roman; Espagne, XVIe-XVIIe siècles* (Toulouse: Ibérie Recherche, U de Toulouse, 1982), pp. 53 ff, 523 ff; "Casuística y novela: de las malas burlas a las burlas buenas," *Criticón*, 16 (1981): 7-45.
⁶⁸ See Conchita Herdman Marianella, "*Dueñas*" and "*Doncellas*": *A Study of the "Doña Rodriguez Episode. . .*", U of North Carolina Studies in the Romance Languages and Literatures, n. 209 (Chapel Hill, 1979), on whose findings I elaborate.
⁶⁹ See Augustin Redondo, "La 'Mesnie Hellequin' et la 'Estantigua' [*hueste antigua*]: Les traditions hispaniques de la 'Chasse Sauvage' et leur resurgence dans le *DQ*" *Traditions populaires et diffusion de la culture en Espagne* (XVIe-XVIIe siècles), Publications de L'Institut d'Etudes Ibériques, Vol. I, U de Bordeaux III (Bordeaux: Presses Universitaires, 1983), 1-27.
⁷⁰ On the connection between the abduction motif and the underworld in Celtic myth see T. P. Cross and Wm. A. Nitze, *Lancelot and Guenevere* (U of Chicago P, 1930), pp. 52-3.
⁷¹ Herdman Marianella, 40-41.
⁷² Herdman Marianella, ch 3.
⁷³ See items listed under B 489 on literary sources of/and the magical horse in legend and chivalric romance.
⁷⁴ The question has come up not surprisingly in the conclusions of both 'soft' critics and the 'hardline'. See the statements by John J. Allen in the article cited above (Note

35) and of Anthony Close, who says in part ". . . it is still a puzzle why this novel which is after all a satiric burlesque, should have become the object of a Romantic style of interpretation—serious, sentimental, philosophical—and Spain's national bible. Was it all an accident? Does not the nature of the book in some way justify modern criticism's interpretation of it? The answer is Yes to both questions, despite their apparent mutual exclusiveness," *The Romantic Approach*, p. 245.

[75] On folk motifs see John J. Guilbeau, "Some folk-motifs in DQ," *Studies in Comparative Literature*, ed. Waldo F. McNeir (Louisiana State UP, 1962), 69–83, 287–91; Mac E. Barrick, "The form and function of folktales in *DQ*," *Journal of Medieval and Renaissance Studies*, 6 (1976): 101–38.

[76] Augustin Redondo, "Tradición carnavalesca y creación literaria, del personaje de Sancho Panza al episodio de la ínsula Barataria," *Bulletin Hispanique*, 80 (1978): 39–70. Also: Michael Bell, "Sancho's governorship and the 'vanitas' theme in *DQ II*," *Modern Language Review*, 77 (1982):325–38.

[77] See Anson C. Piper, "A possible source of the clawing-cat episode in *DQ II*," *Revista de Estudios Hispánicos*, 14 (1980): 3–11.

[78] See the in-depth analysis by Márquez Villanueva, *Personajes y temas*, 229 ff; 283.

[79] See B 288, 299. ". . . y no hay acaso en toda la tristísima epopeya de su vida pasaje que nos labre más honda pesadumbre en el corazón," *Vida de Don Quijote y Sancho, Obras completas* (Madrid: Escelicer, 1968) III, 205. There is a standard English trans., Princeton UP, 1967 (B 288).

[80] Luis G. Manegat, *La Barcelona de Cervantes* (Bacelona: Plaza y Janes, 1964) gives a good though popularized account of Roque and an evocation of the Barcelona of Cervantes' time.

[81] On Cervantes' last work see Alban K. Forcione, *Cervantes' Christian Romance, A Study of* Persiles y Sigismunda (Princeton UP, 1972); Kenneth P. Allen, "Aspects of time in *Los Trabajos de Persiles y Sigismunda*," *Revista Hispánica Moderna*, 36 (1970–71 [1975]): 77–107; and Jennifer Lowe "Themes and structure in Cervantes' *P y S*," *Forum for Modern Language Studies*, 3 (1967): 334–51.

[82] Marasso, 210–11.

[83] "The Christ of Fiction," to my knowledge, was first applied to Don Quixote by G. E. Morrison in the preface to his play *Alonso Quixano, Otherwise Don Quixote* (London: Elkin Matthews [1895?], p. 15.

[84] Jorge Luis Borges, "Análisis del último capítulo del *Quijote*," *Revista Universidad de Buenos Aires*, 5a época, 1 (1956): 28–36.

www.ingramcontent.com/pod-product-compliance
Lightning Source LLC
Chambersburg PA
CBHW070241230426
43664CB00014B/2376